WILL THE REAL

NORMAN MAILER

PLEASE STAND UP

Kennikat Press
National University Publications
Series in Literary Criticism

General Editor
Eugene Goodheart
Professor of Literature, Massachusetts Institute of Technology

WILL THE REAL

NORMAN MAILER

PLEASE STAND UP

Edited by LAURA ADAMS

1974
KENNIKAT PRESS • PORT WASHINGTON, N.Y. • LONDON

Library of Congress Catalog No. 73-83259
ISBN: 0-8046-9066-9

Manufactured in the United States of America

Published by
Kennikat Press, Inc.
Port Washington, N.Y./London

From *Miami and the Siege of Chicago* by Norman Mailer. Copyright © 1968 by Norman Mailer; From *Armies of the Night* by Norman Mailer. Copyright © 1968 by Norman Mailer. Reprinted by arrangement with The New American Library, New York, New York; *Modern Fiction Studies*, © 1971, by Purdue Research Foundation, West Lafayette, Indiana. Reprinted with permission; From *Running Against the Machine* by Norman Mailer, Jimmy Breslin and edited by Peter Manso. Copyright © 1969 by Norman Mailer. Reprinted by permission of Doubleday & Company, Inc.; Reprinted by permission of New York University Press from *The Structured Vision of Norman Mailer* by Barry H. Leeds. Copyright © by New York University; *Out of the Machine* by Joyce Carol Oates reprinted by permission of the author and Blanch C. Gregory, Inc. Copyright © 1971 by Joyce Carol Oates; "Mailer: Good Form and Bad" by Richard Poirier. Copyright © 1972 by Saturday Review, Inc. First appeared in *Saturday Review*, April 22, 1972. Used with permission; "Norman Mailer at the End of the Decade" by Matthew Grace. *Etudes Anglaises*, January-March, 1971. Reprinted with permission; "When Sam and Sergius Meet" by Richard M. Levine reprinted with permission from *New Leader*, July 8, 1968. Copyright © The American Labor Conference on International Affairs, Inc.; "Mailer and His Gods" by Raymond Schroth reprinted with permission from *Commonweal*, May 9, 1969. Copyright © Commonweal Publishing Co., Inc.; From *Radical Sophistication* by Max Schultz, Ohio University Press, 1969. Reprinted by permission; "The Americanness of Norman Mailer" by Michael Cowan in Leo Braudy, ed. *Norman Mailer*, Prentice-Hall, 1972. Reprinted by permission of the author; "On the Parapet" (Norman Mailer) in *City of Words: American Fiction 1950-1970* by Tony Tanner. Copyright © 1971 by Tony Tanner. Reprinted by permission of Harper & Row, Publishers, Inc.; "The Park in the Playhouse" by Gerald Weales, *Reporter*, April 6, 1967, reprinted with permission of the author; "Maidstone: A Mystery" by Leo Braudy, *New York Times*, December 19, 1971. Copyright © 1971 by The New York Times Company. Reprinted by permission; From *The New Journalism* by Michael L. Johnson, University Press of Kansas, 1971. Reprinted by permission of The University Press of Kansas; "Aquarius Rex" by Bruce Cook, November 4, 1972, *The National Observer*. Copyright © 1972, The National Observer, Dow Jones & Co., Inc. Reprinted by permission.

To my reality factors, Bob and Tom

CONTENTS

Grateful acknowledgment is made to the Liberal Arts Research Committee of Wright State University for its research grant in aid of this collection.

WILL THE REAL

NORMAN MAILER

PLEASE STAND UP

INTRODUCTION

Laura Adams

Some years ago the BBC produced a film entitled *Will the Real Norman Mailer Please Stand Up?* The question raised in the film's title is one which many commentators and critics have wished to have answered as they have observed the career and public personality of Norman Mailer over the past quarter-century. Through the years Mailer has acquired notoriety through incidents ranging from the stabbing of his second wife to his New York mayoralty campaign, and his facility for antagonizing his audiences is well known. Whatever the circumstances of his exposure to the public, Mailer rarely fails to be "good copy" and consequently has been fair game for the media newsmakers. Because of the difficulty of reconciling this notorious Mailer with the much-admired author of *The Naked and the Dead* and *The Armies of the Night*, critics have commonly, at their most charitable, dismissed Mailer's public acts as irrelevant to his written work, or, at their least, considered them damaging to his reputation as a writer.

Fortunately, the time for justifying Mailer's written work is past. The literary merit of his controversial novels, *An American Dream* and *Why Are We in Vietnam?* is now acknowledged, and although some consider it more lucrative but lesser work than the fiction so is the interpretive journalism of the years since 1968. However, Mailer's nonliterary performances are still suspect. It would appear that his only consistency has been in deviating from commonly accepted literary manners and the means by which a serious writer may display his talents if he expects to be taken seriously. Ironically, with the awarding of the 1968 Pulitzer Prize and National Book Award to *The Armies of the Night,* Mailer was admitted to the American literary establishment despite his continued violations of its decorum, which, indeed, since that time are more often received as the eccentricities of a literary genius than as the self-indulgences of a publicity-seeking minor novelist.

Far from being antipathetic to his writing, however, as *The Armies of the Night* demonstrates, Mailer's public acts are the tests of the efficacy of his theories without which he could grow neither as a man nor as a writer. To attempt to separate Mailer's art from his life is to invite the question, "What is his art if not the creation of himself?" Part of the problem we have had in accepting this relationship in Mailer (although not in his Romantic predecessors) stems from his huge ambition and his usurpation of the critic's role with respect to his own work. At a time when he had only one popular and critical success to his name, his fine 1948 war novel, *The Naked and the Dead,* and three comparative failures, his ambitions seemed presumptuous. He was "imprisoned with a perception which will settle for nothing less than a revolution in the consciousness of our time," he announced at the beginning of *Advertisements for Myself,* and he planned to outdo all other American writers, past and present, by trying to hit "the longest ball ever to go up into the accelerated hurricane air of our American letters." Were these not presumptions enough, the book itself was a rejection of conventional criticism, conventional themes, conventional forms. While Mailer freed himself in *Advertisements* from customary practices, as our best writers have always done, he committed himself to closing the gap between his accomplishments and his ambitions in full view of his critics.

Committed also to altering the contemporary consciousness, Mailer continually changed and refined his methods in
his search for the most effective means to this end. The years
between *Advertisements for Myself* (1959) and *The Armies
of the Night* (1968) were rich in explorations into both subject matter and style, always aimed at pushing back their
existing limits. Much of the difficulty readers had with *An
American Dream* and *Why Are We in Vietnam?*, for example,
was caused by the unconventional subject matter of the former
and the difficult style of the latter. Out of this period of
fermentation came, in addition to these, his best novels, a book
of poems, a monthly column in *Esquire,* two collections of
wide-ranging essays, a Broadway play, a "photographic narrative" of bullfighting, a collection of short fiction and one of
political writings, and his first film, as well as uncollected bits
and pieces. While of uneven quality, the quantity of work produced during this period is prodigious.

Mailer resolved his thematic and stylistic concerns in the
work which may be considered the end product of this ex-
perimental period, *The Armies of the Night.* That *Armies* is
further the culmination of twenty years of writing may be seen
through the perspective I have termed Mailer's aesthetics of
growth. Since the late 1950's Mailer has had a vision of forces
at war for possession of the universe, metaphors for our moral
directions which he calls God and the Devil, whose victories
or defeats are seen as ultimately productive either of life or
death for the human race. The forces of evil, or totalitarians,
have been winning for too long, he believes, so that "God is
in danger of dying." The machine technology and those who
would extend its power have characteristically been Mailer's
villains and the human spirit their victim. In order for man's
consciousness to grow once more toward the vitality and
creativity it had enjoyed during the Renaissance and in frontier
America, when the limits of human possibility were explored,
each individual must wage his own war against the totalitarian
systems which would control and segment him. The battle-

ground is anywhere, the opponent anyone or anything that would prevent human growth, the moment of battle "existential," for in summoning the courage to confront an adversary one pushes himself out onto the end of a limb where "he does not go necessarily to his death, but he must dare it." The reward for victory is growth through renewed courage and self-confidence and the remission of old sins.

To be defeated, on the other hand, is to permit the life-sapping forces to take hold in oneself (cancer is Mailer's metaphor), making future victories more difficult. Our only defenses are our knowledge of the danger and our capacity for courageous action against the enemy. The progress of a human life, then, in Mailer's design, is charted as a series of moments of synthesis resulting from the interaction of opposing forces and aimed ultimately at embracing all contradictions.

To seek victory over what one considers evil and productive of death is to strive toward the heroic condition. Convinced of the need for a heroic leader, a man capable of embodying the ambiguities and contradictions of this discordant age, Mailer began to develop him through the contours of style. That style has always been heavily metaphorical, and attempts to take him literally have often obscured his meaning. The initial reception of *An American Dream* is a case in point. Read as realism, the book seems to justify murder and sexual perversion.* However, as a metaphor for America's need to rid itself of its corruption and to seek a new and better self truer to the old American Dream, the novel is one of the finest contemporary visions of America's possibility through a courageous and radical heroism.

Over the years Mailer moved through a series of possible heroes including the amoral hipster of the "The White Negro" and President John F. Kennedy, as well as Stephen Rojack of *An American Dream,* before concluding that the viable hero for our time must be a man in whom the schizophrenic halves

---

*Interpretations by two respected literary critics, Elizabeth Hardwick and Philip Rahv, cited in the bibliography, are illustrative.

of the American psyche, the dream of the extraordinary and the mundane reality, can come together. And so Mailer settled upon a man whom he created as much as discovered for the role: himself.

It is in the combination of the actual and the metaphorical functions of the hero known as "Mailer" in *The Armies of the Night* that Mailer's life and art grow together most significantly. Because we live in an anti-heroic, deflating age, the hero for our time must be comic, capable of ludicrous self-debasement on the one hand and courageous action on the other. Such is Mailer's portrayal of himself. His mock-heroics are described at the book's beginning: Mailer is to act as master of ceremonies at an anti-Vietnam rally sponsored by such liberal and literary dignitaries as Dwight Macdonald, Paul Goodman, and Robert Lowell. Arriving at the theater, he wanders off in search of the men's room and we are treated to a lengthy account of the significance of his missing the urinal, after which he appears late at the rally, drunk and obnoxious and highly offended that it has begun without him. It is against this episode that we are to measure his later action, his arrest and overnight incarceration for transgressing a line of police guarding the Pentagon in a gesture of protest against the Vietnam War. Clearly the Mailer hero is no Superman but a very human being who on occasion summons up the courage to rise above the beast in himself, to outweigh and redeem his failures, although because he is human he will fail again. This knowledge is what makes him a whole man and can make America a whole nation.

Having established himself as the representative American hero, Mailer is obliged to confront those events which are capable of influencing our national destiny, as his works since *The Armies of the Night* demonstrate. The significances of manned spaceflight (*Of a Fire on the Moon*), Women's Liberation (*The Prisoner of Sex*), and the 1968 and 1972 political conventions *(Miami and the Siege of Chicago* and *St. George and the Godfather)* have all been expanded through his consciousness. The method used in these books is similar, that of the "detached ego," the persona generally known as "Aquarius" whose confrontations with and experiences of current events provide Mailer the writer with material. The use of himself as an objective observer in these books, rather than as a literary character, represents a shift in emphasis since *The Armies of the Night* from the method to the material. Mailer has overcome the historian's traditional difficulty, determining the reliability of his sources of information, through his own presence at and participation in the making of history. His resulting interpretations, which combine certain functions of the journalist, the historian, the novelist, and the autobiographer, are products of his long search for effective means to alter the human consciousness for the better. Significant too is the insight Mailer has gained through this writing into the positive role technology may play in the development of the human spirit. When technology becomes creative, when our astronauts can communicate the wonders of the universe in the language of the poet, the synthesis toward which Mailer has tried to move us will be reached.

The progress from the Norman Mailer who wrote a fine war novel in the best American tradition a quarter-century ago to the Norman Mailer of *The Armies of the Night* who created a new literary form to encompass his expanding vision of American life is the result of Mailer's uncompromising adherence to his goals. While it may surely be argued that much of Mailer's work has been ineffective for his purpose, it must also be granted that the nonliterary portions of the work, which have seemed so various, so ill-conceived, so egocentric to some are part of a progressive whole. After all, it is the process itself and the aesthetics that move it rather than his separate performances which constitute Mailer's greatest contribution to his age.

Consequently, in choosing the articles for this collection, I have had in mind something like the Compleat Mailer and have selected articles which illustrate and illuminate the variety of Mailer's work. I have not included unsound criticism in order to be representative. With this collection I offer a supplement to Mailer's self-commentary, and it is my hope that the sum of these perspectives, including their contradictions of one another, will approximate the phenomenon which is Norman Mailer. Finally, the reader is directed to the full bibliography to seek for himself further perspectives on Mailer.

OVERVIEWS—1

Matthew Grace

Norman Mailer at the End of the Decade

Critics have often described Norman Mailer as a parasite on current moods and events. Norman Podhoretz observes Mailer's "capacity for seeing himself as a battle ground of history."[1] And Jack Richardson has commented that "Mailer himself admits, in the swaggering boxing metaphors he occasionally uses, to being a counter-puncher and it appears that only when he is struck by something on the scale of a social movement is he moved to hit back, to draw on the literary energy he apparently keeps ready for all occasions he considers to be in his weight class."[2]

Norman Mailer's historical perspective is essentially private. The war in the Pacific, the communist witch hunts, and the apocalyptic history of America in the 1960's, have inspired Mailer to write about himself as a witness to events. He sees the political arena as a vast metaphor for the psychic conflicts, within the man and the artist. His final three volumes of the 1960's, *Why Are We in Vietnam? Armies of the Night,* and *Miami and the Siege of Chicago,* show him coming to terms with his own personality.

"What a mysterious country it was. The older he became the more interesting he found her," exclaims Mailer in *Armies of the Night.*[3] The language reveals America as both a woman

Mailer is in love with and a mysterious, hidden extension of his own psyche. A passionate man, Mailer has discovered that involvement in another's life leads to insights into his own moral existence. His recent political writings are really about America, literature, and the recesses of the novelist's soul. The violent love and hate which Mailer feels for his country is a refinement of the tortured sexual relations in his earlier novels. But as a historian, Mailer does not merely indulge in psychotherapy. The complexity and intellectual honesty of a really interesting mind saves Mailer's works from being maudlin self-dramatizations. Mailer emerges as an engaging figure who has learned from the sex-haunted early works how to forge his mature style.

This transformation was nearly achieved in *An American Dream* (1965). Mailer exorcized his personal demons by identifying neurotic fantasies with the social and political mood of the early sixties. The hero of this novel, Stephen Rojack, is a facet of the American Dream. He is the creation of the novelist who loves to appear in public, cannot tolerate being known as a nice Jewish boy from Brooklyn, and who is torn between the life of the mind and a life of action. Combining the best of Jew and Christian, Rojack is a philosophy professor and television personality. He succeeds in murdering his wife (a bitch goddess who resembles the former Jacqueline Kennedy), avenging Nazi atrocities, fulfilling a blonde Southerner, castrating a black man, destroying the Mafia, deceiving the police, and overpowering the corrupt forces of wealth. Although Mailer himself attempted to murder his second wife, subsequently married a blonde girl from the South, and had other experiences parallel to this American Dream, the novel is really a bizarre synthesis of Mailer's life, fantasies, and political attitudes. This novelistic catharsis allowed him to write the less private but still personal historical works: *Armies of the Night* and *Miami and the Siege of Chicago*.

Armies of the Night is a description of the October 1967 anti-war march on the Pentagon. It is divided into two parts: "History as a Novel," and "The Novel as History." In Book

One the author is the protagonist of a third-person narrative. Historical events are seen in relation to his own private thoughts and fears. In Book Two of the volume, "The Novel as History," a concise account of the origins of the march and its most important events is delivered in a straightforward, factual manner. If, as Mailer contends, a novel is "the personification of a vision which will enable one to comprehend other visions better," history is, ideally, an impersonal rendering of events.[4] By first describing the Pentagon march in the form of a novel with a protagonist and a carefully controlled point of view, Mailer has revealed the human aspect of an almost incomprehensible public event. This section of the book is four times as long as the objective account, illustrating Mailer's conviction that the process of history is illuminated by private experience.

In fact the word *process* is a key to Mailer's political ideas. He describes himself as a Left Conservative: "that lonely flag—there was no one in America who had a position even remotely like his own."[5] This paradoxical terminology identifies thought which is essentially Hegelian. Mailer says that, "He tried to think in the style of Marx in order to attain certain values suggested by Edmund Burke."[6] Rational and intellectual, Mailer despises the kind of historical determinism favored by classical Marxists and believes in the preservation of the good things in society, unless the ultimate nightmare of totalitarianism occurs. He comments:

> The terror to a man so conservative as Mailer, was that nihilism might be the only answer to totalitarianism. The machine would work, grinding out mass man and his surrealistic wars until the machine was broken down. It would take a nihilist for that. But on the other hand, nothing was worse than a nihilism which failed to succeed—for totalitarianism would then be accelerated.[7]

This intellectual cul-de-sac is unavoidable for Mailer the Existentialist, who posits that uncertainty, flux, violence, mystery and sin are the most vital forces in human experience.

If history is movement toward an unknown destination,

then a mysterious event with uncertain outcome is the arche-typal situation which man must seek. Communists and fascists are detestable because they claim to understand human events: the one through the application of dialectical ma-terialism and the other with computers, the tools of electronics land and corporation land, Mailer's epithets for a pre-totali-tarian America which wages war with advanced technologies.

But Mailer cannot be pigeonholed, for he distrusts the hippies and the new generation as much as he despises the liberal middle class and the new black supremacists. Hippies have destroyed their minds with drugs and electronic music, two manifestations of a synthetic culture. Sons and daughters of the upper middle class, they have revolted against technol-ogy by fleeing into it and have lost their sense of history. The hippies' apparel indicates profound psychic dislocation and disorientation. They march towards the Pentagon wearing American Indian costumes and the uniforms of the Foreign Legion, Wehrmacht, the Confederate and Union Armies. Masquerading as a millenium of history, they have divested their minds of the symbolic and historical perspective their clothing represents.

Without a sense of history, intelligence, reason, and progress are impossible. This Marxist axiom provokes Mailer's abhorrence of the drug and electronic assault upon the delicate fabric of mind and flesh. The ironies of history so important to Mailer's sense of life are hidden from the gaily costumed youth whose attack upon the corruption of their elders is vitiated by their own political naiveté. Those flower children are also dissociated from creative human experience because they are unaware of the sexual guilt which Mailer feels is the well-spring of moral energy and consciousness, the leavening in the bread of experience. Without sexual guilt, the possibil-ities and limitations of life become adumbrated.

The middle class academic liberal is also guilty. Like the hippies, the intelligentsia has succumbed to corporation land's brainwashing. Mailer posits:

If the republic was now managing to convert the citizenry to a

plastic mass ready to be attached to any manipulative gung-
ho, the author was ready to cast much of the blame for such
success into the undernourished lap, the over-psychological
loins of the liberal academic intelligentsia. . . . Liberal academics had no root of a real war with technology land itself,
no, in all likelihood they were the natural managers of that
future air-conditioned vault where the last of human life
would still exist.[8]

Revolted by the Vietnam War, but not by the attitudes and
technologies which have made it an historical inevitability
for America, the intelligentsia's faith in social engineering
is unshaken by such temporary aberrations as the Pacification
Program in South Vietnam. The implicit assumptions in the
program are not in question because the sexless, frightened
and selfish liberal academic is hesitant to challenge the system which has given him his role in society.

The black militants frighten Mailer, and he admits it.
As a white man, he admires their physical grace and moral
audacity. But he knows that these black racists, like the
manipulators in corporation land, the hippies, and the liberal academic intelligentsia, are programmed for a course
in history which is unrealistic. Mailer's distrust of the black
man is both visceral and intellectual, for he knows he will
be a victim of their racism and, as a former liberal, he is tired
of hearing about America's victimization of its black citizens. He is bored by the moral righteousness and enervating
guilt which white Americans are supposed to endure for the
sake of the blacks.

Of course Mailer's critique of America is not exclusively
historical, for he takes a novelist's delight in observing and
describing individuals. He knows that the small town, once
the heart and soul of the Republic, has become an extension
of corporation land, enveloped by superhighways, fed by
shopping centers, and educated by television. The variety and
perversion of life was once able to come to terms with society in the American small town. But now, Mailer declares,
the balance

between lives and ghosts, the solemn reaches of nature where insanity could learn melancholy (madness some measure of modesty) had all been lost now, lost to the American small town. It had grown out of itself again and again, its cells traveled, worked for government, found security through wars in foreign lands, and the nightmares which passed on the winds in the old small towns now traveled on the nozzle-tip of the flame thrower. . . . Technology had driven insanity out of the wind and out of the attic, and out of all the lost primitive places: one had to find it now wherever fever, force and machines could come together.[9]

Mailer contrasts the slack-faced marshals who guard the Pentagon and beat the demonstrators with the army men he knew during the Second World War. In twenty-five years virile, wily and courageous youth had aged into sunken-cheeked, empty-eyed and rabid men whose bitterness and ambition had curdled to hate. "The day of power for the small town mind was approaching—and in measure of the depth of their personal failure [it] would love Vietnam, for Vietnam was the secret hope of a bigger war. . . . "[10]

In *Miami and the Siege of Chicago,* an account of the 1968 Republican and Democratic presidential nominating conventions, Mailer observes the prosperous and respectable Midwestern counterpart of the Southern small-towner. The bland, innocent visages reflect the vacuity of men who do not know the primeval forces which tear at their psyches. They are Middle America: from Iowa to Kansas, Nebraska and Arizona. Decent, respectable and mindless, they are Nixon's great silent majority whom Mailer sees as the ulti-mate and most pathetic victims of American technology. Con-flict and consensus for them means little more than patriotic adherence to the white Anglo-Saxon Protestant ethic of Sin-clair Lewis's Babbitt, and loyal faith in what the experts, the engineers, the leaders (who all know so much more than they do) have decreed. Richard Nixon at the Republican convention in Miami is the schizophrenic incarnation of Mid-dle America: he has been a rabid and unscrupulous commu-nist baiter, a powerless vice-president to General Eisenhower for eight humiliating years, a bitter and frail political candidate, a tireless hand-shaker, speaker and political organizer, a wealthy martini-drinking Wall Street lawyer from California, and finally now, through the madness of assassination and a disastrous war, he is a man who embodies the fear, uncertainty and lack of identity of a frightened and confused people.

Two months later, during the Democratic convention in Chicago, the bland ceremonies of Miami gave way to blood-letting near the stockyards. While the steaming jungle of Miami had been paved over and decorated with grotesque, air-conditioned hotels, Chicago remained the metropolis in which the stench and blood of the abattoirs were never far away. The people of Chicago are the denizens of the last great American city. Mailer writes that they "had great faces, carnal as blood, direct, too impatient for hypocrisy, in love with honest plunder."[11]

The police riot which occurred during the Democratic Convention of 1968 was inevitable. Storm Troopers ran amuck, the police smelled the blood and entrails on the slaughterhouse floor, received the electronic messages from corporation land, and enacted the private dreams of gore which had brought America to the battlefields of Vietnam. President Johnson ran the convention from Texas and Mayor Daley ran the police from the convention floor. It was not until the mass media, Mailer's *bête noire,* fell victim to the chemicals and billy clubs of the Chicago police and proceeded to report the police riots, that American blood on American streets became a reality to the moribund delegates. The blood-letting in Chicago was a dramatic result of the forces in America which had prompted Mailer to write *Why Are We in Vietnam?* a year earlier.

In *Armies of the Night* and *Miami and the Siege of Chicago* Mailer uses the force of language to describe an external reality which may be greater than literary style itself. Jack Richardson has posited that before these volumes, "Mailer's response to the controversy in which he is so much engaged, is almost completely stylistic and one soon realizes

that his literary manner is in itself a dramatic dialectic."[12] But
if this odyssey from the purlieus of language to a style which
recognizes that life is more real than letters may be called tragic
in a novelist, *Armies of the Night* and *Miami and the Siege
of Chicago* are meant to be keys to his novels. These *expli-
cations de textes* may be unique in American letters, for
Mailer has modulated the wildly antic style of *Why Are We
in Vietnam?* into the suggestive and rich fiber of *Armies of
the Night,* and finally into the straightforward prose of *Miami
and the Siege of Chicago.* The battle between the novelist's
public and private style is nearly resolved in these volumes.

But Mailer has not abandoned the use of metaphor in
his political journalism. Salient images inform the design of
his work. Miami is the primeval jungle and swamp transformed into a concrete sheathed, air-conditioned tomb. The
savagery and fecundity of nature have been perverted by the
gargantuan and tasteless luxury hotels where politicians pan-
der to the burnt out lusts of spiritually emasculated delegates.
Only for a moment, during the pageantry and carousal which
characterize the American political shindig, does the jungle
intrude into the frozen havens of the Miami hotels. In Chicago,
the stockyards adjacent to the convention hall are the significant brooding presences. And in Washington, the endless
corridors of the Pentagon dominate the action. Columns
which decorate the loading platform of the Pentagon, "those
ultra-excremental forms of ancient Egyptian architecture,"
move the novelist to compare America and ancient Egypt.[13]
The obvious parallel between Rome and the United States is
passed over in favor of more subtle images evoking slave
built monuments of inhuman proportions, entombment, and
the monstrously egotistical celebration of death.

> The Egyptian forms, slab-like, excremental, thick walls,
> secret caverns, had come from the mud of the Nile, mud
> was the medium out of which the Egyptians built their civiliza-
> tion, abstract, ubiquitous mud equalled in modern times only
> by abstract ubiquitous money, filthy lucre. . . . And American
> civilization had moved from the existential sanction of the
> frontier to the abstract ubiquitous sanction of the dollar bill.

> Nowhere had so much of the dollar bill collected as at the
> Pentagon, giant mud pile on the banks of America's Nile, our
> Potomac![14]

But perhaps the most arresting stylistic device in Mailer's writing at the end of the decade is his devotion to obscenity. Mailer defends obscene humor as a manifestation of the American creative spirit. He realizes that "the noble common man was obscene as an old goat and his obscenity was what saved him."[15] Sanity resides in obscenity, for it restores "the hard-edge of proportion to the overblown values."[16] The ability to juxtapose the obscene and the sublime in the face of suffering and imminent death is a creative wellspring of the American spirit:

> All the gifts of the American language came out in the happy
> play of obscenity upon concept, which enabled one to go
> back to concept again. What was magnificent about the word
> shit is that it enabled you to use the word noble: a skinny
> Southern cracker with a beatific smile on his face saying in
> the dawn of a Filipino rice paddy, "Man, I just managed to
> take me a noble shit." Yeah, that was Mailer's America.[17]

Because obscene humor is a creative release, a rational tonic, and an intellectual stimulant, it is feared in technology land. American devotion to deodorant, deodorizers, plastic, Formica, synthetic and frozen foods, and antiseptic forms of entertainment on the clean electronic airwaves, shows a pathological fear of the biological processes. Not so much part of the puritanical heritage as a manifestation of the new totalitarianism, abhorrence of obscenity is a result of corporation land's attempt to sterilize the brains of the American people. It is a political technique, for obscene humor allows man to see through the sham and hypocrisy of society.

Obscenity also liberates the novelist's literary style. Mailer claims that he has captured the American idiom in *Why Are We in Vietnam?* a novel where obscenity is humorous, violent and symbolic. If American society and the war are obscene, then filthy language is the appropriate metaphor to describe it. Written a year before *Armies of the Night* and

Miami and the Siege of Chicago, Why Are We in Vietnam?
is a paradigm of Mailer's political writings, a metaphorical
statement on the American spirit.

Why Are We in Vietnam? is the first-person narrative of
an eighteen-year-old Dallas boy on the eve of his departure
for Vietnam. Speaking in aggressive and obscene language
which derives from the hipsters, William Burroughs and the
disk jockeys of mass media, D. J., who resembles both Huckleberry Finn and Holden Caulfield in his hate of sham and
his precarious innocence, describes an Alaskan bear hunt with
his father, "Rusty," and friend "Tex" Hyde. [18] The protagonist's name, D. J., stands for disk jockey, Dr. Jekyll and, with
the letters reversed, juvenile delinquent. The novel is divided
into chapters prefaced by introductory digressions, called
"intro-beeps."

After imagining an interview between his mother and
her Jewish psychiatrist, which may be among the most obscene episodes in serious literature, D. J. launches into an
attack on his father, "Rusty" Rutherford-David-Jethroe-
Jellicoe-Jethroe. "Jethrone" Jethroe is in charge of an enormous corporation which manufactures deodorant and Pure
Pores, a plastic cigarette filter, which—"the most absorptive
substance devised ever in a vat—traps all the nicotine, sucks
up every bit of your spit. Pure Pores also cause cancer of
the lip but the surveys are inconclusive, and besides, fuck
you!"[19] The bear hunt is a proof of Jethroe's prestige in the
corporation and of his superiority to D. J. Conducted with
helicopters, portable radios, and a veritable arsenal of ele-
phant guns and smaller arms, the hunt's bloodlust is subli-
mated in a welter of neurotic and technological concerns.
After several days of slaughtering caribou, mountain goats
and other assorted wild life, the party sets out to kill a
grizzly bear. D. J. and his father break from the party, track
a giant bear and shoot it. Several days later, D. J. and his
half-Indian, half-Nazi friend, "Tex" Gottfried Hyde, set off
alone into the Alaskan wilderness to escape from civilization.
They leave their guns behind and receive a cosmic message,

transmitted by "nature's Magno-Electric-Fief of the dream."[20] The message is: kill! The novel ends with the words: "Vietnam, hot damn!"[21]

D. J. is the archetypal American youth. Fed up with the shams of American corporate totalitarianism, he nonetheless depends upon the transistor to convey his freaked-out disk jockey message. His violent and obscene puns are obsessed with masturbation, oral sex, the anus, and excrement. In fact, his vision of America is within the context of the human body and its functions and electronic technology. Yet he is a product of the society he despises, and the lesson he learns during the initiation rite of the Alaskan bear-hunt comes from electro-magnetic intelligence gleaned from the region above the Arctic Circle. Lying under the stars next to the vicious and terrible "Tex" Hyde, D. J. touches his friend's genitals and realizes that there was "murder between them under all friendship, for God was a beast not a man, and God said 'Go out and kill—fulfill my will, go and kill'."[22] The benign and essentially generous D. J. (Dr. Jekyll) is confronted by his malevolent alter ego, Mr. Hyde, and with the knowledge "heard before in the telepathic vaults of their new Brooks range electrified mind, . . . the killer brothers, owned by something, prince of darkness, lord of light, they did not know," gird their loins for the slaughter in Vietnam.[23]

Mailer posits that "obscenity probably resides in the quick conversion of excitement to nausea."[24] D. J.'s youthful excitement and innocence are converted into the nausea of disenchantment. His vision of the world is scatological and violent. Lyrical awe in the presence of nature, fascination with firearms and technological hunting methods, and above all, the necessity of proving manhood through slaughter, are elements in American society which explain the war in Vietnam. Like Americans in the jungles of Asia, the hunting party descends into the wilderness equipped to destroy any foe. Mailer retells the traditional hunting story in terms of human welfare. This paradigm of American society is illuminated by his explanation of the Vietnam war in *Armies of the Night:*

> Certainly all wars were bad which took some of the bravest young men of the nation and sent them into combat with outrageous superiority and outrageous arguments: such conditions of combat had to excite a secret passion for hunting other humans.[25]

The history of the United States in the 1960's was apocalyptic. Seemingly irreconcilable forces emerged to confront each other. Norman Mailer has shown that the problem, like all history, is dialectical and therefore never-ending. As each synthesis becomes a thesis, it clashes with an antithesis. But the simultaneous operation of this principle on different levels obviates the possibility of a simple formula to explain the sickness at the center of American life. Mailer's sensitivity to this dilemma would seem to inspire despair but he bravely resists falling over the brink, although he confesses that nihilism is always a possibility. Yet his vision is constantly moving towards a tragic awareness that chaos and destruction may be the ultimate truths of human experience.

For Mailer, Christian love and charity are based upon the essential mysteries of the Son of God. But America now is at spiritual war with itself, for "the center of the corporation was a detestation of mystery, a worship of technology. Nothing was more intrinsically opposed to technology than the bleeding heart of Christ."[26] Western man's devotion to the mysteries of Christ and of the human heart are now being torn asunder not by Darwin, but by his false allegiance to the computerized world and the corporation. This schizophrenia drives man to rage and frustration. It was fitting that the title, *Armies of the Night,* should allude to Matthew Arnold's "Dover Beach," written in 1867. The poem's fatality becomes doubly ironic for Mailer, who precisely one hundred years later also laments the eclipse of Christianity in a pre-totalitarian America:

> And we are here on a darkling plain
> Swept with confused alarms of struggle and flight,
> Where ignorant armies clash by night.

NOTES

1. Norman Podhoretz, "Norman Mailer: The Embattled Vision," *Partisan Review* (Summer, 1959), p. 371.
2. Jack Richardson, "The Aesthetics of Norman Mailer," *New York Review of Books,* XII, No. 9, 3.
3. *Armies of the Night* (New York, 1968), p. 133.
4. *Ibid.,* p. 245.
5. *Ibid.,* p. 203.
6. *Ibid.,* p. 208.
7. *Ibid.,* p. 199.
8. *Ibid.,* p. 26.
9. *Ibid.,* pp. 173-174.
10. *Ibid.,* p. 175.
11. *Miami and the Siege of Chicago* (New York, 1968), p. 90.
12. Richardson, p. 3.
13. *Armies,* p. 175.
14. *Ibid.,* pp. 179-180.
15. *Ibid,* p. 61.
16. *Ibid.*
17. *Ibid.,* pp. 61-62.
18. The hunt as initiation rite is a traditional theme in American literature. In this century, Hemingway and, most successfully Faulkner, have explored its ritualistic connotations.
19. *Why Are We in Vietnam?* (New York, 1967), p. 31.
20. *Ibid.,* p. 208.
21. *Ibid.,* p. 208.
22. *Ibid.,* p. 203.
23. *Ibid.,* p. 204.
24. *Armies,* p. 62.
25. *Ibid.,* p. 208.
26. *Ibid.,* p. 211.

OVERVIEWS—2

Richard M. Levine

When Sam and Sergius Meet

In *Advertisements for Myself* Norman Mailer describes waking up one morning with an idea for a huge eight-part novel, "the prologue to be the day of a small frustrated man, a minor artist manqué. The eight novels were to be eight stages of his dream later that night, and the books would revolve around the adventures of a mythical hero, Sergius O'Shaugnessy, who would travel through many worlds, through pleasure, business, Communism, church, working class, crime, homosexuality and mysticism." This ambitious plan was eventually scrapped, but not before the prologue became Mailer's most successful short story, "The Man Who Studied Yoga" and the eight-part novel, weakened and loose-skinned from loss of weight, metamorphosed into *The Deer Park,* an interesting failure by a writer who until now has made that literary genre his own.

In the story Sam Slaboda makes a statement—repeated word for word by his counterpart in the novel, the film director Charley Eitel—that seems to me the explanation for both the interest and the ultimate failure of much of Mailer's work: "It is the actions of men and not their sentiments which make history." The idea is as true now as when Karl Marx first thought of it, but unlike Mailer, Marx could afford to remain unaware of a corollary notion: It is the sentiments of men, in addition and often in contrast to their actions, which make novels. If history is a nightmare, great novels are written on the morning after a great novelist awakens from it.

Mailer's latest work, *The Armies of the Night*—significantly subtitled "History as a Novel, The Novel as History"— is an interesting success because it is a record of that awakening. The second part of the book—"The Novel as History"— presents a detailed reconstruction of the events of the four-day anti-Vietnam protest held in Washington in October 1967. It is as objective and controlled a piece of writing as the author has ever done (partly of necessity, since he was in jail during most of the goings-on) and shows us what we already knew —that Mailer wears many hats and, were he content with a by-line in eight-point type, could remain exactly what Robert Lowell calls him, "the best journalist in America."

"Well, Cal," Mailer answered Lowell, "there are days when I think of myself as being the best writer in America." In the first and longer part of the book—"History as a Novel" —Mailer calls his own bluff and emerges the Cassius Clay of letters—a better writer and weaker puncher than we thought. In the guise of a very personal account of the March on Washington, Mailer has created—is constantly creating—his only character worthy of a great novel, Sam (the writer) and Sergius (the fighter) united in the complex personality of the author himself. For the first time in a book by Mailer it is clear that Sam is doing the dreaming; the novelist in Norman Mailer is in complete control of the hero of history.

I do not mean to imply that Mailer comes across as Sam Slaboda in *The Armies of the Night,* for Sam without his nighttime alter ego is clearly Bellow, Malamud and Roth country, and Mailer has a keen sense of literary property rights. The Sams and Sergiuses of his novels are presented as opposing pairs of characters: Hearn and Cummings in *The Naked and the Dead;* McLeod and Hollingsworth in *Barbary Shore;* Eitel and O'Shaugnessy or Marion Faye in *The Deer Park;* Tex and Rusty in *Why Are We in Vietnam?* (Stephen

Rojack in *An American Dream,* Mailer's purest Sergius, goes unopposed, but then the product is clearly labeled a dream.)*
In *The Armies of the Night* Mailer successfully joins together these fragments of himself, and the result is a self-portrait more complete and imaginative than any of his fictional characters.

Because Mailer contains these polarities in his own personality, those who view his public image merely as press agentry miss the point. After 20 years of public and private imagery, it should be clear that Mailer is in the process of working out his own salvaticn in stages that closely resemble the progress of Sam Slaboda's dream of Sergius O'Shaugnessy. His novels are devotional exercises; taken together they represent a kind of 20th century Book of Hours—again like Sam's dream. Mailer's special genius is the realization that in the age of mass and mixed media, one does not have to go to the mountaintop to save one's soul; a coast-to-coast TV hookup will do even better. One does not confess to a priest but to a national audience in books and the pages of *Esquire* and *Harper's.* This may be press agentry. The times, not Mailer, have narrowed the gap between confessions and True Confessions.

Too great a concern with salvation can be a problem for the novelist. All of Mailer's novels have been marred by a tug-of-war between the artist and the moralist, the novelist and the allegorist. It is as if the two stages of Tolstoy's career were chronologically merged, and the author of *Anna Karenina* forced to write with the restrictions and proscriptions of *What Is Art?*

The difficulty is that the minds of the allegorist and the novelist work in opposite directions. The allegorist uses characters to advance his ideas; the novelist uses ideas to delineate his characters. The allegorist portrays the Fair Maiden and the Dark Lady as fleshed out symbols of Chastity

*Rojack confronts a series of opponents, of whom Barney Oswald Kelly presents the strongest opposition. [Editor's note.]

and Lust; the novelist must be concerned more with particular women. There is plenty of sex in Mailer's novels but
very little sense of the prosaic psychological intricacies of
sexual relations. Not for Mailer the first feints of desire or
post-coital languor. Orgasm is all, and even orgasm is only a
metaphor for the apocalyptic scheme of Mailer's own Big
Bang theory of the universe. Sex is neither for pleasure nor
for babies; it is an indication of spiritual health, one's place
in that larger scheme. General Cummings' wife in *The Naked
and the Dead* sums up the impossibility of mature relations
between the sexes in Mailer's novels when she discovers that
her husband "is alone, that he fights out battles with himself
upon her body."

Children are excluded altogether from Mailer's fictional
world, where life begins at puberty (not surprisingly, two of
his chief characters, Mikey Lovett in *Barbary Shore* and
Sergius O'Shaugnessy in *The Deer Park,* are orphans who
suffer from amnesia), and women are reduced to biology's
stick-figure symbol for the female. Nor are the adult males
in his novels independent characters who live out complex
and ambiguous destinies which can help us define our own.
They are, instead, representatives of conflicting principles—
the rational and the instinctual, the contemplative and the
active, the spiritual and the physical. Here the allegory
thickens.

Sam and Sergius play out their assigned roles very
close to the center of the Jewish—and specifically the East
European Jewish—imagination. Examples of the conflict
could be taken from Freud and Kafka—the ego and the id,
K. and his assassins—but it is most explicitly presented in
the work of Isaac Babel, perhaps the most talented writer
to emerge from that artistically extraordinary decade following the Russian Revolution.

A Jew from the Odessa ghetto, Babel served as the
supply officer of a Cossack regiment during General Buden-
ny's 1920 Polish campaign and wrote about his experiences
in the autobiographical stories of *Red Cavalry.* The Cossack

was the traditional enemy of the Jew; his aimless violence and cruelty contrasted to the Jewish self-image of humaneness, pacifism and rationality. But Babel's acquaintance with Cossacks led him beyond this animosity. He recognized the animal vitality and grace of his fellow soldiers, just as he came to appreciate the spiritual strength of the Polish Jews they confronted.

In a beautiful phrase, the narrator of *Red Cavalry* describes himself as a man "with spectacles on his nose and autumn in his heart"; yet at the end of one story, when he is unable to shoot a badly wounded soldier who begs to be put out of his misery, he asks fate to "grant me the simplest of proficiencies—the ability to kill my fellow men." Although *Red Cavalry* and *The Armies of the Night* could hardly be more different stylistically—Babel's prose is taut and laconic, Mailer's sentences somersault to a full stop like enthusiastic but overweight gymnasts—their authors describe the same battle, between the Jew and the Cossack, and achieve a similar resolution by internalizing the struggle within themselves.

Of course, the change of battlefield has affected the outcome of the battle. A generation and half a world later, the Cossack has become irrelevant as an historical reality—the American white Protestant never really replaced him as the symbol of repressive Authority—and the Jew is no longer an alien element in the dominant culture. But the value of the Jew and the Cossack as indications of contrasting life styles is undiminished. Sam Slaboda, fortyish and balding, a failed husband, father, lover and novelist, is only one-quarter Jewish, "yet he is a Jew or so he feels himself . . . the Jew through accident, through state of mind." The irony is that just at the moment when this state of mind seemed universal, when American Jewish writers were pressing their claim for the Jew as the most representative American in the '50s—the only possible hero of an urbanized and mechanized society—Mailer has transformed an older historical reality into a Jewish dream, nightmare and wish fulfillment both.

This Jewish dream of the Cossack, like Sam's dream of Sergius, moves through many worlds in Mailer's novels, but these all reduce to his principal concerns—sex, history and religion. And when one considers that for Mailer sex is orgasm, history is revolution and religion is Apocalypse, Sam's dream—all of Mailer's work—becomes a succession of related metaphors of power that form a single comprehensive vision of the world.

Mailer doesn't mix his metaphors carelessly. In his most explicit version of the Jewish dream of the Cossack, a short story entitled "The Time of Her Time," Sergius O'Shaugnessy says, "When you screw too much and nothing is at stake, you begin to feel like a saint. . . . I was the messiah of the one-night stand." Marion Faye in *The Deer Park* is a pimp who "follows sex to the end, turns queer, bangs dogs and sniffs toes," yet Mailer writes that "he was religious (in a most special way to be sure)." In *Advertisements for Myself* Mailer says of himself, "Sex was the sword of history to this uncommissioned General. . . ." And in *An American Dream* Stephen Rojack thinks of his alternation between anal and vaginal intercourse with Ruta the maid as "a raid on the Devil and a trip back to the Lord."

God is certainly not dead in Norman Mailer's universe, but then He isn't His old Self either. Mailer seems literally to believe in a kind of Manichaean vision of the cosmic battle between God and the Devil, with the winner still very much in doubt. As Rojack remarks on his TV program, "God's engaged in a war with the Devil and God may lose." Sex and history become religious rites for Mailer, expressions of God's enormous destiny. In *Presidential Papers* he argues that "the form of society is not God's creation, but a result of the war between God and the Devil."

Salvation is no longer a purely private affair. Mailer may call himself an American existentialist, but he has little in common with the modern existentialist's view of man as a pitiful extra in the cosmic drama. If, as Sergius says in "The Time of Her Time," "God is like me, only more so," then man has a starring role to play, for God's ultimate victory depends on him. From *The Naked and the Dead* to *Why Are We in Vietnam?* the true heroes of Mailer's novels understand their role. Man, says General Cummings, is a being "in transit between brute and God," and his deepest urge is to "achieve God." Rusty's "secret is that he sees himself as one of the pillars of the firmament."

Salvation, for Mailer, is not the broad road of official religion; it is the mythical hero's trip through hell and the mystic's faith that "the way up is the way down." In the war between God and the Devil, great saints are great sinners, for one must learn the Devil's stratagems in order to do service for the Lord. This is the meaning of Mailer's ethic of power; violence, murder, sexual perversion and the fear of death can be religious acts for him, more life-giving than life-denying. The dialectical conception of existence that he expounded most fully in "The White Negro" abstracts ultimate alternatives from life and then connects them: ". . . incompatibles have come to bed, the inner life and the violent life, the orgy and the dream of love, the desire to murder and the desire to create . . . a dark, romantic, and yet undeniably dynamic view of existence for it sees every man and woman as moving individually through each moment of life forward into growth or backward into death."

Only the Cossack in Mailer's novels can accept these incompatibles. The Jew cannot. The Sergius of Sam Slaboda's dream is "capable of sin, large enough for good, a man immense," while Sam himself "seeks to live in such a way as to avoid pain, and succeeds merely in avoiding pleasure." Try as he might to make the Jew the hero of his novels, Mailer's sympathies are with the Cossack. In *Presidential Papers* he writes: "The characters for whom I had the most secret admiration . . . were violent people."

By emphasizing the extremes of existence and scorning the middle way, Mailer has schematized the life of his novels, melodramatized it. Few of us are Jews *or* Cossacks, most of us are Jews *and* Cossacks. There is a sense in which all novels are sentimental journeys, with the combination of internal and external experience that phrase implies. The Jew and the Cossack, contemplation and action, are false alternatives for the novelist, since he can only change the world by understanding it.

In *The Armies of the Night* Mailer for the first time rejects these alternatives. Instead of creating characters who are representatives of conflicting principles, he has let these principles represent the conflict within his own character. One no longer cares that most of Mailer's metaphysics is shoplifted from the five-and-dime store of fashionable thinking, nor that his politics—however dressed up in phrases like "Constitutional Nihilism" and "Left Conservatism"—is pretty much Founding Father liberalism at heart. An allegorist can be judged by the originality of his ideas, a novelist only by his use of them. The curious fact is that in this crucial area of the relationship between ideas and character development, Mailer's latest work of non-fiction is closer to a novel than his previous works of fiction.

Perhaps other novelists could have written equally fine self-portraits and other social critics perceived the significance behind an event which had a surreal quality, as if co-directed by Cecil B. DeMille and Walt Disney. But only Norman Mailer could have seen the connection between the two. Like those Disney characters in drag, the Hippies who tried to levitate the Pentagon, Mailer has a fine sense of history as spectacle and of politics as the exorcism of both public and private demons. "Mailer is a figure of monumental disproportions," he writes in this third-person narrative, "and so serves willy-nilly as the bridge—many will say the *pons asinorum*—into the crazy house, the crazy mansion, of that historic moment. . . ." Mailer sees America wandering lost and bewildered somewhere between Frontierland and Technologyland, and this national schizophrenia mirrors, or is mirrored by, the schizophrenic division within himself. Sergius, the Cossack in Mailer, fearlessly enters the fray, while Sam, the Jew, watches from the sidelines in terror:

For a warrior, presumptive general, ex-political candidate, embattled aging *enfant terrible* of the literary world . . . champion of obscenity, husband of four battling sweet wives, amiable bar drinker, and much exaggerated street fighter, party giver, hostess insulter—he had . . . a fatal taint, a last remaining speck of the one personality he found absolutely insupportable—the nice Jewish boy from Brooklyn. Some-things in his adenoids gave it away—he had the softness of a man early accustomed to mother-love.

At the very beginning of *The Armies of the Night*, Mailer writes of his public image in words that could as easily describe the relationship between Sam and Sergius: "Mailer had the most developed sense of image. . . . He had in fact learned to live in the sarcophagus of his image—at night, in his sleep, he might dart out, and paint improvements on the sarcophagus."

A few pages further on he accepts Sergius not as image or dream but as one aspect of his personality: "But as Mailer had come to recognize over the years, the modest everyday fellow of his daily round was a servant to a wild man in himself: the gent did not appear so very often, sometimes so rarely as once a month, sometimes not even twice a year, and he sometimes came when Mailer was frightened and furious at the fear, sometimes he came just to get a breath of air." At a party he attends on his first night in Washington, where most of the guests are liberal academics—Sams to the core—Mailer explains his hostility to them in personal terms: "His deepest detestation was often reserved for the nicest of liberal academics, as if their lives were his own life but a step escaped."

Once the action begins, Mailer wrings some wonderful comedy—pie-in-the-face comedy as opposed to the wit often found in his novels—from his "monumental dispropor-tions." And yet we laugh off Norman Mailer at our peril; like the ambiguous event he is reporting, the moment we judge this Don Quixote tilting at the Pentagon a fool, he shows us his heroic side. As Mailer rhetorically asks the reader, "Is he finally comic, a ludicrous figure with mock heroic associ-

ations; or is he not unheroic, and therefore embedded somewhat tragically in the comic?"

He gets drunk at the liberal academic party, and later
at a rally in the Ambassador Hotel shocks the other "notables" on the platform by delivering an outrageously obscene
speech—replete with fake Irish, fake LBJ and fake Norman
Mailer accents. Hung over the next morning, he finds that
his bravery has evaporated with the liquor: "Revolution-
aries-for-a-weekend should never get hangovers. Mailer
detected that he was secretly comforted by the thought there
would probably be no violence today; even worse, he was
comforted by the conclusion that the best police in Washington would be at the Department of Justice to maintain order."

As he watches students and faculty turn in their draft
cards that afternoon, "a deep gloom began to work on
Mailer, because a deep modesty was on its way to him, he
could feel himself becoming more and more of a modest man
as he stood there in the cold with his hangover, and he hated
this because modesty was an old family relative, he had been
born to a modest family, had been a modest boy, a modest
young man, and he hated that, he loved the pride and the
arrogance and the confidence and the egocentricity he had
acquired over the years . . . he was a figurehead, and therefore
was expendable, said the new modesty—not a future leader,
but a future victim: *there* would be his real value."

Saturday afternoon at the Pentagon wears on and neither
Mailer nor his companions, Robert Lowell and Dwight Macdonald, succeed in getting arrested ("He had a picture again
of three notables, silly to themselves, walking about with a
candle, looking to be copped"). The first violent encounter
between the demonstrators and the MPs throws Mailer into
a state of panic: "He didn't want Mace. He sprinted a few
steps, looked over his shoulder, stepped in a drainage trough
where the parking lot concrete was hollowed, almost fell with
a nasty wrench of his back and abruptly stopped running,
sheepishly, recognizing that some large fund of fear . . . lived

in him like an abscess quick to burst now at the first mean threat."

Furious at his reaction, Mailer decides to get busted as soon as possible. Looking like a "banker gone ape" in a dark pinstripe suit, regimental tie, and a vest that strains to cover his middle-aged paunch, he steps gingerly over a rope separating the parking lot from the lawn in front of the Pentagon, skirts one startled MP at a jog and weaves between the troops until finally stopped and led away by two burly marshals. This is the book's climactic scene. Once Mailer has been carted off to the detention center, he no longer has the comic irony —the tension between action and reflection—going for him to sustain the narrative. Sergius blusters and Sam whimpers in a vacuum. But this extraordinary honest self-portrait of "a simple of a hero and a marvel of a fool" is already well past the point where much damage can be done to it.

In an early chapter of *The Armies of the Night*, Mailer confesses that "he had been suffering more and more in the past few years from the private conviction that he was getting a little soft, a hint curdled, perhaps an almost invisible rim of corruption was growing around the edges. His career . . . his idea of himself—were they stale?" He needn't worry. They have never been fresher.

OVERVIEWS—3

Raymond A. Schroth

Mailer and His Gods

Norman Mailer arrived in Chicago for the [1968] Democratic Convention smelling blood. In the "last great American city," where "life was in the flesh and the massacre of flesh," he rightly feared that the plague he had written about for years was coming in. The antithetical forces of our society were marshaling for violent confrontation; and something ugly in the American heart was about to be revealed. Mailer sensed too, that, if the revolution was about to begin, he—because he had helped expose the cancer in our system—would share in the responsibility.

He was there as "the reporter" to write *Miami and the Siege of Chicago* for *Harper's*. But he was there also as the new Hemingway, exposing sham, testing his manhood. Masculinity, he had written, was not given but gained by winning small battles with honor in a cosmic war. His art could be no better than his character, and his character had to be forged living on the edge of violence, balancing and curbing the socially destructive and self-destructive urges within himself.

The great experience in any generation is its war. War puts the microscope to the generation, exposes its nerve, its roots, its holiest and unholiest ambitions. Beginning with

The Naked and the Dead (Rinehart, 1948) and carrying
through to Vietnam, Mailer has interpreted his generation's
wars and warriors as manifestations of deeper tensions in
civilian life. Since, for Mailer, man is most himself in crisis
—skirting death, teetering on the brink of a ledge, dodging
federal marshals in a dash for the Pentagon—conflict is the
condition in which his nature can best be explored. In his
Manichean vision of the universe, Mailer's paradoxically
gentle, religious hero's freely plunging into violence is most
likely to bring him into contact with God.

In *Advertisements for Myself* (Putnam's, 1959) Mailer
described the "burning point of Hip" as the notion that God
was in danger of dying. Man's fate is tied up with God's. God
is not all-powerful but a warring element in a divided universe, and we are part of his destiny. This, he is convinced,
is the only explanation of the problem of evil—"that God
himself is engaged in a destiny so extraordinary, so demanding, that he too can suffer from moral corruption, that he can
make demands on us that are unfair, that he can abuse our
beings in order to achieve his means, even as we abuse the
very cells of our body." Mailer sees himself as one of God's
explorers, his "seed-carrier," the embodiment of God's enormous embattled vision. Like Walt Whitman, he is part of God;
he sums up the experience of distant men and past generations in himself. For him, as for Whitman in "Years of the
Modern," "The earth, restive, confronts a new era, perhaps a
general divine war,/No one knows what will happen next,
such portents fill the days and nights. . . ."

Mailer becomes America. For him, as for the Transcen-
dentalists, the structure of the universe duplicates the structure of the individual self, all knowledge begins with self-
knowledge. He has so steeped himself in contemporary
culture, drawing together so much of our literary history,
political conflicts, pop art, and religious heritage, that in his
work we experience both a writer and a nation becoming,
struggling, splitting, groping for a new form.

His method, of course, is artistically dangerous. As Richard Gilman has pointed out, Mailer has blurred the distinction between life and art, thought and action. He has disregarded the traditional meanings of philosophical and theological terms and has defined his own brand of existentialism entirely in terms of doing. He has abandoned the artist's traditional role of transcending politics at least to some degree, staking his whole career on the conviction that he is his art, and that he is legitimately his own most appropriate subject matter. For him, existentialism is the "feel of the human condition." For each book he reshuffles the cards of his sometimes unorthodox political, sexual and quasi-suicidal experiences—four marriages, arrests, a stabbing, socialism, bouts with alcohol, marijuana and mescaline—translating his ego into a literary portrayal of American life. Interpreting himself as the contemporary version of the Renaissance man, growing as he charges from activity to activity, he conjures up a vision of God remarkably like himself—an imperfect being at war with other gods, fighting the Devil (God's waste) and worthy of love because he is growing and because he is weak.

Mailer most successfully synthesized his life, literature and theology in *The Armies of the Night* (New American Library, 1968). Here he found his voice in a new impressionistic, almost Joycean journalism, giving contemporary history the existential historian's subjective sympathy without sacrificing the novelist-journalist's detachment. Here he gave his most mature and perceptive presentation of the central political theme he introduced in *The Naked and the Dead:* a diabolic totalitarian strain co-exists and interacts with the dominant American Christian democratic culture.

Mailer's achievement in *The Armies of the Night* is the perfection of a method with which he has been experimenting since his first books. Even as a novelist he has always been a journalist and a social critic, more interested in the social forces his characters represent than in the characters themselves, more anxious to convince the reader than to lead him through the imaginative experience of literature. Few of his fictional characters—soldiers, actors or congressmen—are memorable as persons. We remember rather the author, who seems to have parceled out his personality traits and beliefs— his Marxism, his sexual athleticism or ambivalence, his nostalgic religious zeal—to various one-dimensional creations.

His heroes are Hemingway romantics with danger-filled pasts, but inhibited by physical or psychological weakness, war wounds, amnesia or half-memories of violent events in their early years. We explore their lives through flashbacks or long-winded narrations embellished with political rhetoric. Often they are engaged in some enterprise that is worthless or destructive but which has been rationalized according to some higher ideal. They climb mountains that do not need to be climbed, produce movies that are artistic trash, pursue grizzly bears in a hunt that corrupts the hunters. They risk their lives in morally ambivalent symbolic acts: they violently storm the Pentagon on a "peace" march or invade Chicago in a protest which is morally right but (here I must disagree with him) symbolically empty. Each enterprise is in its own way a barbarous endeavor, taking its toll in moral integrity or human lives, revealing the best within man.

In *The Naked and the Dead* Lieutenant Robert Hearn, who dies leading his reconnaissance patrol to a mountain top on a Pacific island, and Sergeant Sam Croft, who pursues the summit as passionately as Ahab pursued Moby Dick, represent two strains in American politics: the Harvard boy "Christian" bourgeois idealist, infatuated with Marxism and Melville; and the "Cannibal" war-lover, the white Texan Protestant who has renounced God and put his own thirst for power in God's place. Like Stephen Rojack in *An American Dream* (Dial, 1965), whom he foreshadows, Croft makes a religion of power and a ritual of courage.

Like the Pentagon in *The Armies of the Night,* Hearn's commander, General Cummings, personifies order, technology, the latent fascism—tinged with homosexuality—that will claim America for its own in the aftermath of World War II. For

Cummings, the only morality is power morality. "There's one thing about power," Cummings tells Hearn. "It can flow only from the top down. When there are little surges of resistance at the middle levels, it merely calls for more power to be directed downward to burn it out." Cummings, of course, will return in later books. He is the diabolic millionaire Kelly in *An American Dream* and the mythical unseen power in Chicago who lifts the phone and orders the police to wade into the young and destroy them on the awful Wagnerian Wednesday night in front of the Hilton Hotel.

Hearn returns as Sergius O'Shaugnessy in *The Deer Park* (Putnam's, 1955). In postwar Hollywood the combined forces of fascism and lust have triumphed. Art, which should be a symbol of liberation, has been commercialized into a symbol of perversion. The resort Desert D'Or is part hell, part Sodom and Gomorrah. Just as the lives of a generation were offered on the altar of totalitarian power in the Pacific war, the creative talent of O'Shaugnessy, who is trying to free himself from the memories of his orphaned boyhood and his napalm bombing raids by writing a novel, is squandered in a trashy "religious" film. Commercialism has usurped the role of religion and would-be artists are terrorized by McCarthyism.

But in *The Deer Park* Mailer's vision and his imagery have begun to move to a larger subject—the warning of universal apocalyptic destruction that will be brought about by uncontrolled technology and sexual failures that are symptoms of failures in society. In what might be *The Deer Park's* most significant scene, the bisexual pimp, Marion Faye, drives out alone in the night to a hill overlooking the New Mexico desert. Faye looks to the east and remembers the night in the great gambling city of the Southwest when he had gambled around the clock, "not even pausing at dawn when a great white light, no more than a shadow of the original blast somewhere further in the desert, had dazzled the gaming room and lit, with an illumination colder than the neon tube above the green roulette cloth, the harsh faces of the gamblers who had worked their way through the night." The citizens of America play on like the citizens of Sodom, while technological society feeds its new God, its nuclear furnace, preparing its own holocaust.

In *An American Dream*, Mailer united Croft and O'Shaugnessy in Stephen Rojack, the composite American "success"—a wounded war hero obsessed with brutal battle memories, ex-congressman, professor, commentator and wife-murderer. The plot concerns Rojack's battle of wits with an inquisitor detective, but Mailer's purpose is to diagram a whole set of political and personal relationships representing various aspects of the "American Dream" society rotten on every level.

An American Dream is also, in a bizarre way, Mailer's epitaph for the man on whom he would have liked to model himself—John Kennedy. In *Cannibals and Christians* (Dial, 1966) he depicts Kennedy as the Kierkegaardian hero, the man who *was* his own idea—half political opportunist, half Faustian adventurer—combining two halves of his personality to become the "movie star come to life as President." With the Kennedy face as the face of America, Mailer believed the old frontier America would once again risk its future—not knowing whether the face would, in its continual recreation, turn out to be Abraham Lincoln or Dorian Gray. It was as if the prisoners of *The Deer Park* had a chance to redeem themselves in this new millennial age. The President's murder made *An American Dream* a portrait of America as Dorian Gray; the death of the dream man, in Mailer's judgment, had thrown the nation back into its original chaos of which the dream man himself had been too intimate a part.

In the epilogue, Rojack drives west to Las Vegas. He stops in Missouri where he happens to view an autopsy of an old man who had died of cancer. The man is America. The stench of the cadaver follows him across the blazing sands to the gambling tables where, like Marion Faye, he plays and plays, and walks out into the desert night. He is given a vision not of an atomic blast but of a "jeweled city on the horizon"; but the jewels are not the amethysts and sapphires of the New Jerusalem, but the neon diadems of the new technology.

In *Why Are We in Vietnam?* (Putnam's, 1967) Mailer raises *Dream* to the nth degree. Technological America has exported itself, spread its galloping cancer to another land in the allegory of a grizzly hunt in Alaska. Armed with helicopters, high-powered rifles and credit cards, a party of rich barbarian Texans devastates the primitive Alaskan landscape in an orgy of egomaniacal self-assertion. The hunt, which in earlier American literature could have symbolized the American Adam's struggle to master his Eden, here symbolizes the last stages of degradation. And, as Eliot Fremont-Smith pointed out, Mailer's distressing emphasis on the uninterrupted rhetoric of anality in this beautiful repulsive work, reflects the distortion of the American image of masculinity and exposes the unrealized self-disgust of those who lust, or think they should lust, to verify virility in violence.

By *The Armies of the Night,* the story of the October 1967 peace march against the Pentagon, Mailer frankly calls his hero Mailer and makes him a Jewish-Christian, God's millennial warrior against the schizophrenia in his own person. In this quasi-theological account of a key weekend in American history, the antithetical forces in our culture came face to face. The urban-bred college boys and flower children squared off against the town-bred paratroopers of their own generation. The marchers are "primitive" Christians, who interpreted Christianity in terms of "mystery" and peace, lining up in defiance of the "militant" Christians who have fallen into the corrupting embrace of the corporation. Mailer, Robert Lowell and Dwight Macdonald are cast in the roles of literary apostles proclaiming the gospel of dissent and inspiring a modern children's crusade against the military industrial high priests of Order. Here were the two Americas: the pure, old America, the Puritan conscience symbolized by Robert Lowell exuding as "unwilling saintliness," pitted against the new technological America, summed up in Lyndon Johnson and the American corporation executive, who does not mind burning unseen women and children in Vietnamese jungles, but who winces at dirty words.

In *Armies,* Mailer brings together the two main theological interpretations of American history: America as the new Eden, the primitive paradise that must keep itself innocent, and, at the same time, set an example for the world; and the new Israel, the land of Joshua rather than the land of Adam, God's kingdom destined to be his Empire. The sober tone, maturity and detachment suggest that Mailer has begun to recover from the death of JFK. Redemption, through suffering, is still possible. After giving free range to his scatology and morbid pessimism in two apocalypses of doom, he has made this novel-as-history a muted apocalypse of hope. The march on the Pentagon is Eden's attempt to prove Cummings wrong. The children of Adam sense that either the Vietnam war will bring on the final conflagration of the world or that this strange pilgrimage of theirs, their ritual pot-smoking, their offering of their bodies for arrest, their burning draft cards, their obscene placards, their exorcism of the great gray tome-like Pentagon, will usher in a new age, an Edward Hicks' "Peaceable Kingdom" where the wolf can lie down with the lamb.

Mailer's own grand moment comes following his arrest in his rush on the Pentagon. Given a chance to speak in court, he realizes he must deliver the best of himself to the microphones and reporters. It is Sunday, so he gives a Christian sermon: "You see, my fellow Americans, it is Sunday, and we are burning the body and blood of Christ in Vietnam. Yes, we are burning him there, and as we do, we destroy the foundation of this Republic, which is love and trust in Christ." And the author adds, "Wow."

A novelist who reaches too quickly for theological imagery to add substance to what otherwise might be flimsy material runs the risk of exposing his shallowness if the imagery is misapplied. If Christ is suffering through American actions in Vietnam, this could be Mailer's grand moment, if not, it is a cheap trick. The speech is consistent with the rest of Mailer's work. He does not merely toy with theological notions. Thoroughly absorbed as he is with almost every aspect of American culture, he interprets and challenges that culture just as the prophets challenged the ancient Jews. And for this modern hip prophet, the main sin is still infidelity to a religious heritage. His final paragraphs draw together the first and last books of the Bible. It is a romantic—almost embarrassingly nostalgic—plea to return to the American Eden juxtaposed against a vision of America heavy with child, groaning in labor. It is an obvious reference to the Woman of the Apocalypse (12:1); America is Israel struggling to give birth to a messianic savior.

The question now is whether the post-election mellowed Mailer, resigned to the return of the WASP to the center of American history and willing to explore what is alive in the conservative dream, will use the years of Nixon normalcy to retire to work on his "big" novel or whether he will continue to grow as what he essentially is—a moralist. It may be that as a nation we do not need a big novel as much as we need a brutal and fearless chronicle of what is happening to our life, interpretive records of our glorious and shameful moments—our conflicts and conventions—where we either honor or betray our belief in the immanence of God and the sanctity of life.

PHILOSOPHER-METAPHYSICIAN—1

Max F. Schulz

Norman Mailer's Divine Comedy

Advertisements for Myself and *The Presidential Papers:*
TESTAMENTS I

In his idealistic desire to reform society Norman Mailer has
moved steadily away from his early agitation for a political
solution toward the call for an erotic, quasi-religious redefini-
tion of the modern consciousness. In the process the unorthodox methods he advocates have obscured the traditional
character of the values espoused in his fiction. Only George
A. Schrader,[1] to my knowledge, has hinted his recognition, in
passing, that Mailer's ideas fit into a tradition;* but Schrader
is narrowly concerned with Mailer's divergence from European
existentialism and does little with his insight. Essentially
Mailer is in the tradition of eighteenth- and early nineteenth-
century English and American primitivism. He believes man
to be essentially good, or as he puts it, "man is . . . roughly
more good than evil, that beneath his violence there is finally
love and the nuances of justice."[2] Visions of human goodness inevitably acquire either rational or theological overtones. In Mailer's writing the latter appears to dominate. With
a diction weighted as heavily with religious as with erotic
terms, he speaks out like a moralist, thundering anathemas not

---

*See the essays of Finholt and Cowan in this volume for additional contexts
of tradition for Mailer's thought. [Editor's note.]

at the licentious of heart but at the insensible of spirit. Nor, as Diana Trilling notes in her excellent analysis of Mailer's intellectual position,[3] is his invitation-to-sin-so-that-we-may-find-grace an unfamiliar heresy.

Where Mailer departs most from his early political activist position is in the configurations he makes of personal being and economic theory. Man's puny or *bad* orgasm, as contrasted with his apocalyptic or *good* orgasm (to use Mailer's Hemingway manner with the hipster's *graffiti*), Mailer defines in "Reflections on Hip" and in "Hip, Hell, and the Navigator" as manifestation of a dying which is evil. For, "as one dies a little more, one enters a most dangerous moral condition for oneself because one starts making other people die a little more in order to stay alive oneself [*Adv,* p. 385]." The Mephistopheles in this drama of human diminuendo is vaguely our capitalistic economy. "Built on property and such inhuman abstractions of human energy as money, credit, and surplus value," Western society has congealed the texture of being, the "productive, purposive, creative, and sexual energies," into an ice age of "cancerous ambivalences and frustrations [*Adv,* pp. 362–363]." Clearly the case is no longer the simple nineteenth-century one of mercantilistic haves and proletarian have-nots. Hence, in part, Mailer's loss of enthusiasm for the cause of Marxism is explained. The emergent affluent society, however, as he sees it, poses new dangers to the human spirit. At "the center of the problem," which he defines in "Heroes and Leaders," is the paradox that "life in America becomes more economically prosperous and more psychically impoverished each year."[4] To combat these doldrums of the flesh and the spirit, Mailer prescribes strong existential medicine. Man, he advocates in "The White Negro," is to "find his courage [his sense of life, of being,] at the moment of violence, or realize it in the act of love [*Adv,* p. 351]."

If Mailer seems to occupy the incongruous philosophical position of advocating change of the politico-economic structure of society by a revolution in its habits of coition and achievement of utopia through the apotheosis of murder, his worship of the power that devolves from sex and murder would seem to be even more perverse. Power is a key concept for him. In this respect he is a legitimate heir of the reformers of the last century. Yet careful distinctions must be made here, or one errs like Diana Trilling and others in mistaking Mailer's ambivalent fascination for a Croft or a Faye as an admiration for the courage and willed power drive of the fascist. It is true that Mailer is interested in the uses and abuses of power, and that he sees clearly that sex and killing are the ultimate forms of human power. Yet power per se is peripheral, not central (as Edmond L. Volpe[5] contends), to most of the novels. The use of sex and killing to gain control over another appears to be as evil to Mailer as it does to others. Whereas *The Naked and the Dead* is conceived in terms of political and military authority, the subsequent novels increasingly define power in terms of religious and psychological growth. A conventional release of spirit, a going out of self with its resultant joy—an existential control over self, not a totalitarian authority over others—is what ulimately fascinates Mailer in the mystique of sex and death. Is not this the belief that informs his remarkable Carlylean analysis in "Heroes and Leaders" of John Fitzgerald Kennedy's failure as a leader and a man? In this respect Mailer is not unlike the eighteenth-century antinomian Blake, who started out a political revolutionary, became disillusioned by the excesses of the French Revolution, and turned increasingly to advocacy of a Gestalt revolution in the concept of self as a means of man's gaining psychic and spiritual health. Like Blake, Mailer calls repeatedly for man to restore his vitality "by an exceptional demonstration of love"[6]—to work a second revolution in this century that moves "not forward to the collectivity which was totalitarian in the proof but backward to the nihilism of creative adventures . . . backward towards being and the secrets of human energy [*Adv*, p. 363]."

As for his offensive pitch in "The White Negro" for the hipster's "incandescent consciousness" based on a knowledge of the "possibilities within death [*Adv*, p. 342]," Mailer's essay on "The Existential Hero" makes clear that his faith in the frontier myth of Edenic America and primal purity has supplied his rationale as much as has the raffish camaraderie of his Greenwich Village escapades. Echoing the corollary disillusionment of the Adamic fall, which accommodates to this myth the contrary reality of industrial America, Mailer acknowledges a fall "from individual man to mass man [*Pres*, p. 39]." Yet the old myth "that each of us was born to be free, to wander, to have adventure and to grow on the waves of the violent, the perfumed, and the unexpected" survives, leading a subconscious existence in our psychic lives. Hence a split personality afflicts the American character, which Mailer formulates thus:

> Since the First World War Americans have been leading a double life, and our history has moved on two rivers, one visible, the other underground; there has been the history of politics which is concrete, factual, practical, and unbelievably dull if not for the consequences of the actions of some of these men; and there is a subterranean river of untapped, ferocious, lonely and romantic desires, that concentration of ecstasy and violence which is the dream life of the nation. [*Pres*, pp. 38–39]

Schrader has observed that Mailer is a romantic who "would undo the Fall of mankind" and "carry the human race back to the Garden of Eden on his own shoulders."[7] The novels since *The Naked and the Dead*—*Barbary Shore, The Deer Park*, and *An American Dream*[8]—are attempts to construct fictional worlds that tell how the lost American can gather together the scattered parts of his being and find his way back to a Gestalt existence, a unified emotional life. A reminder of Mailer's intentions with *The Deer Park* is instructive in grasping their overall design. Mailer told Richard Stern in 1958 in reference to the play version that he thought of the characters as existing in Hell and not knowing it. Thinking of the Prologue in Hell, which Mailer had written to introduce the play, Stern asked ironically, "How about a Prologue in Heaven?" Mailer answered, "Oh, it would be more interesting. . . . But it would be more difficult. That was beyond my grasp."[9] By 1964 his ambition and skill were sufficient to turn the trick with *An American Dream*. Whether he is fully aware of his frame of conceptual reference is problematic, but in these three novels Mailer has written a divine comedy of modern love. *Barbary Shore* depicts the purgatory of disordered love in contemporary life. *The Deer Park* describes the hellish "depths of the dead" into which commercial onanistic man descends when he turns inward and in the dark terror of his soul worships what Mailer (in "The Existential Heroine") has called "the voice of . . . pinup magazines, dreamy, narcissistic, visions of sex on the moon."[10] *An American Dream* presents the heavenly city of ecstasy glimpsed phoenix-like by those who dare to leave the "antechamber of Hell," mounting "fire stairs . . . through locks and ambushes" (as Rojack conceives fantastically of the route of his ascent to Kelly in the Waldorf Towers) "up through vales of anathema . . . fear and fever [*AD*, ch. 7]," until they emerge, scalded clean of middle-class moral funk, in the expanding continuum of life and death.

Barbary Shore: PURGATORY

Barbary Shore comes closest of Mailer's novels to having an allegorical surface. Ostensibly, it is a political polemic in the Huxley tradition of the novel of ideas. Actually, it is a modern morality play in which is acted out the agonizing drama of contemporary man's effort to find through the dynamics of love some kind of human restoration in contemporary society.

Here politico-economic allegory coincides with existentialist ethics more firmly than in the two novels that follow it. Hell, as well as purgatory and heaven, are states of mind in Mailer's cosmology in addition to being places of abode. Mailer identifies the commercial mind (typed "Moneybags, the haunted [ch. 24]" by Lovett) with hell, the world of self-interest. In the economic sphere this selfishness reveals itself as acquisitiveness and in the psychological and social sphere as narcissism. The goal of Dante's journey in *Purgatorio* was earthly paradise, won by purging the self of the sin essentially of disordered love. "Set love in order, thou that lovest me," is the dictum on which, according to Edmund G. Gardner,[11] *Purgatorio* rests. Most twentieth-century men, Mailer contends, subsist in purgatory. With dormant hearts they long for the sweet emotion that will change for bad or good their future. The contemporary scene, as Mailer conceives of it, offers us a halfway house of penance, a wild border, a Barbary shore, between the hell of flaccid feelings and a heaven of dynamic being—a purgatory where, morally and emotionally bent by circumstances, we either retreat into solipsistic sensuality (whose hell is pictured in *The Deer Park*) or advance toward existential renewal (whose heaven is depicted in *An American Dream*). Hence, unlike Dante, Mailer begins his triptych of society with purgatory.

Purgatory in the world of *Barbary Shore* is presented as a penitentiary of cubicles in anonymous brownstone rooming houses. Here dwell the transistory and the faceless for whom time has run out. Lovett is an amnesia victim who has "no past [ch. 24]." Lannie is a mental patient who has lost the "record of [her] self [ch. 17]" during a series of shock treatments. McLeod, in fleeing both the Communist Party and the FBI, had destroyed his identity ten years earlier and has been "obliged to take up a wholly new existence [ch. 24]." Hollingsworth is an equally anonymous government agent. Their surrealistic isolation extends even to an absence of commercial ties with life. Lovett as a would-be writer has no steady job. Lannie has lost hers. McLeod has quit his. And Hollingsworth is "on vacation" from his dummy cover-up job in a broker's office.

In purgatory one's past is initially judged, one's sins contritely acknowledged, and one's progress toward moral regeneration begun. Although almost all the characters in *Barbary Shore* are engaged in such a pilgrimage, the man whose soul is most concentrated on this struggle with itself is McLeod. Pursued by the inexorable "guards" of the two rival economic powers, capitalism and communism [cf. ch. 23], his effort to save his life is presented as an allegory of a twentieth-century soul's penitential progress toward salvation. Ten years ago he had gone underground, severing his connections with both political apparatuses. Since quitting the world, so to speak, he has devoted his energies to the selfish task of saving merely his skin. To create a new identity he has married and had a child. But the marriage has been contracted out of selfish reasons. His wife, Guinevere, accurately has tagged her marriage when she accuses McLeod, "I'm your bloody salvation, that's all [ch. 26]."

Mailer's language, here, and throughout the novel, performs on two levels, the political-economic and the psychological-moral—one literal and the other usually ironic. Guinevere has been McLeod's savior for an unspecified number of years in that his pursuers, the agents of America and Russia, have mistakenly sought an unmarried man. This mask, however, does not protect McLeod indefinitely. After ten years of running he has been tracked to his attic hideaway in his wife's rooming house by Hollingsworth, an American agent. If ultimately she does not save his life (body), she does in the end prove ironically to be the savior of his soul, in a sacramental sense instrumental to his salvation.

To document the means of this salvation—*agapé*—*is to* define a central tenet of Mailer's ethics. McLeod's marriage had been one of expedience. Out of selfish concern for his own safety he had taken a woman with rich resources of love, who was in his own words "ready to share" herself "with somebody." It was "the only period of your life," he admits to her, "when you could have been in love. And I betrayed that potentiality. You needed a man who would give you a great deal, and I gave you very little [ch. 26]." He is guilty of warping a second being into the inward bent of the purely private life that tortures his own heart. His living apart from his wife and daughter in a barren room separated by three floors from their apartment, with none of the other roomers aware of his identity, skillfully dramatizes his isolation and emotional sterility. Similarly, Guinevere's promiscuity and responsiveness to Lannie's homosexual advances presents in vivid allegory the extent to which McLeod's selfishness has pushed her into narcissism. Thus, Guinevere is a witness to the "wrongful love" that is denounced by Dante in the tenth canto of *Purgatorio*. She is witness to the involuted excesses into which another's refusal of love can mislead the heart.

Mailer underscores this role of Guinevere in the comic charade of her first meeting with Lovett. "I'm a Witness [meaning Jehovah's Witness]," she lies to him outrageously. But she speaks with poignant truthfulness in terms of the sacramental level of the story. "We're going to Gethsemane, that's the truth. We're going to be destroyed [ch. 4]," she harangues Lovett. Again the words refer both to the political theme that the two capitalistic systems are driving the world to the brink of barbarism and to the ethical theme that commercial emotionalism—acquisitiveness of the heart—is damning mankind to narcissism and sterility. "The world is so full of sin. Nobody loves his neighbor any more [ch. 4]," she laments in pointed allusion to the latter theme.

Denial of love has been McLeod's sin (and political crime, since an additional irony is that he has dedicated himself to the socially ameliorative task of guiding man "from hell to Arcady [ch. 29]," paradoxically by performing the professional revolutionary role of the notorious "Hangman of the Left Opposition [ch. 20]." Conversely, an avowal of love marks his moral reintegration. For ten years McLeod concentrated with single-minded devotion on saving his skin. His bitter summary of those misspent years is, "I devoted myself to nothing [ch. 24]." He has in mind his cessation of political activity; but he also recognizes that his life has been empty. "Petrified in my bones," he confesses to Lovett, "I was already dead so I must call on [Guinevere] to thaw me out, and I've never given her the time of day [ch. 25]." To "force a revolution into [his] life," he seeks out his daughter in play. "I'd give an arm to have the child love me," he avows to

Lovett [ch. 19]. He also confesses to Lovett his discovery that he could now "feel the most intense love" for his wife [ch. 25].

The first step in moral regeneration is to admit one's guilt with a contrite heart. McLeod's confession of his frozen heart prefigures its thaw. And the narrative underpinnings support this renewed flow of his feeling for Guinevere. There is his obsession with cleanliness—especially his regular scrubbing of the bathroom—which symbolizes a state of mind desirous of purification. A similar longing for the grace of illumination is indicated when he turns the lamp bulb, in sardonic parody of the third degree Hollingsworth is about to resume, "so the light glared into his eyes [ch. 20]." Following his long audience with Hollingsworth, McLeod admits to being the mysterious "Balkan gentleman" high up in the Bolshevist apparatus and to having stolen a "little object" from the American organization [ch. 24]. He then exposes to his own eyes and to Lovett's through one night and most of another "the last festering cocci of the sore" of his life, in a lacerating search "deeper and deeper into the mesh of motive," in an effort to bring the "moralist and the criminal . . . to dock" together [ch. 25].

The ultimate disposition of McLeod's fate depends on the outcome of his duel of nerves with Hollingsworth. Hence Hollingsworth could be mistaken for the angel of divine judgment, particularly since the informal hearings he holds in effect trigger McLeod's final reformation. A sardonic irony, however—key to the *Weltanschauung* of *Barbary Shore*—is involved in the actual details of Hollingsworth's background. On the surface he passes as quite orthodox. Hailing from a small town in the Midwest, he is presentable, polite, a freckled, blue-eyed boy with a corn-colored cowlick. Lovett imagines "the places in which [Hollingsworth] had slept through his boyhood: a bed, a Bible, and in the corner a baseball bat perhaps [ch. 5]." God's emissary as the boy next door! Disturbing contradictions, however, qualify our response to these marks of respectability. He is brutal toward women, lecherous, hard-drinking, a lowbrow, with a mind (according to McLeod) "like a garbage pail." His mirth is indistinguishable from "the mechanical laughter in a canned radio program, the fans whirring." His eyes are "Two circles of blue, identical daubs of pigment . . . opaque and lifeless [ch. 5]." Like Faulkner's detestable emblems of twentieth-century civilization, Popeye and Flem Snopes, Hollingsworth has something mass-produced, stamped, and labeled about him.

Hollingsworth's intention is to double-cross his superiors by making a private deal with McLeod in a power drive to gain the unidentified object he has been sent to get back. As recompense Hollingsworth promises to "save" McLeod. The situation has strong overtones of the classic contest of bartering for one's soul with the Devil. But McLeod's developing conscience prevents his succumbing to the temptation of "playing upon [Hollingsworth's and his own] cupidity." He recognizes that he would leave the house "alive and better off dead." In a cryptic formula, reminiscent of the ancient mariner's encounter with Nightmare-Death-in-Life in Coleridge's *The Rime of the Ancient Mariner,* McLeod reduces his choice to "alive it's dead, and dead I'm alive [ch. 25]." The phrasing is charged with Christian overtones. To save his soul ("the little object") McLeod must risk losing his life.

The purgatorial investigation of McLeod which Hollingsworth has been unofficially conducting is then a black parody of Saint Peter's justice. Hollingsworth represents not Christ's mandate but Antichrist's. His organization is the identical twin of the enemy organization. The Gods of both are "collective [ch. 21]," dedicated to "standardization," and "abdication of the best in human potentiality." Both preach "exploitative systems [ch. 29]"; and, appropriately, Hollingsworth in his cover-up job is associated with a Wall Street firm. To deal with him then is to sell one's soul to the Devil. Neither capitalistic power, McLeod comes to see, is interested in him personally; both want only "the little object" he possesses, his integrity, his soul. "If possession of the little object by neither power is a disadvantage to both," McLeod postulates, then "to deprive them is a moral act [ch. 24]."

To act upon this insight, however, he must progress beyond his narrow claim of love for Guinevere to the Socialist ideal of love he has proselytized for so many years. This selfless love of mankind McLeod rises to when he relinquishes Guinevere and his daughter to Hollingsworth as the price of salvaging "the little object" (that is, the human soul) for all men. As he prepares to face Hollingsworth for the last time with his final answer of "no," McLeod bequeaths the "object" to Lovett (surely a pun is intended), who despairingly had "lived like the hermit in the desert who sweats his penance and waits for a sign [ch. 1]," and who had been "at the crossroads [ch. 2]" of his life when he met and accepted McLeod's legacy of "the rudiments of selfless friendship [ch. 33]." McLeod's "exceptional demonstration of love [*Pres,* p. 51]" not only restores Lovett's faith in man but also Lannie's. As Dante climbs upward to the sixth terrace of Purgatory [Canto 22], he is instructed by Virgil that "Love, / Kindled by virtue, always has inflamed / Another, if its flame were but displayed." When McLeod takes leave of the emotionally exhausted Lannie, he asks Lovett to treat her with "a little mercy." His overflowing heart touches Lannie's and inflames her love for man and rekindles her hope for the coming of a new Jerusalem [ch. 30]. Here the political-economic and existential-ethical levels of the narrative unite in one vision of brotherly love. As an ex-Trotskyite Lannie alludes, of course, to the true (as opposed to Bolshevist) inauguration of Socialist justice on earth. Also, under the pressure of the story of regeneration and salvation of McLeod's soul, she alludes to the institution of that earthly paradise (which Dante portrays all penitent souls toiling upward toward) atop the mountain of purgatory.

One hesitates to call Mailer a Christian apologist; yet in *Barbary Shore* he has written a modern morality play that seems to advocate traditional Christian values. Everyman McLeod (the politico-economic creature in this century of passionate ideologies) saves his soul through apparently orthodox means. Surely his death at the end is a sacrificial slaying, not the suicide that all the critics claim. Unless he is lying, he indicates to Lovett every intention of joining up with him after the final unpleasant interview with Hollingsworth. At the moment of McLeod's death, Lovett overhears Hollingsworth say, "You've hurt a fellow's feelings . . . and that is why I am forced to punish you"; then Lovett imagines "the slow rapt movement of each man about the other" and finally hears "some sound of attack [ch. 31]." This hardly sounds like suicide! In an existential act of will McLeod elects to withdraw his allegiance from the two great commercial systems of the world in favor of an utopian faith in the human heart. In that decision he confronts "the possibilities within death" which Mailer claims in "The White Negro" provide "the curious community of feeling in the world of the hipster [*Adv*, p. 342]." The result is McLeod's death but also, in the legacy of "the little object" consecrated with his life that he passes on to Lovett, a confirmation is made of the inexhaustible power of the heart's "love for every man our brother." Here, Mailer seems to say, is the choice open to contemporary man: to be a prosperous cannibalistic digit in the calculating machine of bureaucracy or to be an enriched psyche at the "limits of [its] growth [*Pres*, p. 21]" in a full emotional life.

The Deer Park: HELL

The Deer Park extends Mailer's exploration of political-economic and psychological-moral patterns of conduct, centering on the American tendency to identify man's acquisitive and erotic instincts and on the debilitating effect of this confusion of values for a whole society. Eros is the totem of Hollywood; its directors, producers, actors, and hangers-on buy and sell love as readily as they contract to make a movie. Under the tyranny of such contempt for life, the buried nature of man—"the noble savage" Eitel calls it—is "changed and whipped and trained by everything in life until it [is] almost dead [ch. 11]." The chief eunuch of this "deer park" is the film mogul Herman Teppis, who connives, for example, to marry his top sex goddess Lulu Meyers to his leading matinee idol—but notorious homosexual—Teddy Pope, because the marriage would give Supreme Pictures "a royal couple, the Number One married lovers of America [ch. 20]," and hence be good for business. A widower, he derives sexual satisfaction from demeaning young girls, Hollywood hopefuls supplied regularly from the stock room by his son-in-law and producer Collie Munshin. Motherhood, sex, compound interest, religion, and patriotism are hypocritically jumbled in his thought and speech until they lose all identifiable value.

In the contrapuntal structure of the novel, the apparent opposite of Teppis's sentiment is Marion Faye's hard-boiled existential idealism that has only scorn for the "self-swindles" of Hollywood. A "religious man turned inside out [ch. 13]" by his distaste for the human race, he sees himself as a Baudelairean "saint in Hell," bent on purifying his soul through "some black heroic safari" of complete submission to sin [ch. 25]. His motto is that "There is no pleasure greater than that obtained from a conquered repugnance [ch. 13]." Since he most detests people, he systematically occupies himself with love—of all varieties and degrees of perversion—until, guided by his misanthropy, he drifts into the role of professional procurer. Thus, in his pursuit of nobility, he succumbs to the same vice of commercialized love that Teppis does, and in his private life becomes an ironic confirmation of his belief that nobility and vice are "the same thing" viewed from different directions [ch. 13].

Between sentimental submission to commercial conformism and perverse assertion of individual integrity, Charles Eitel and Sergius O'Shaugnessy act out the compromises of their lives. In the story of Eitel, Mailer most fully develops the political-economic and psychological-moral structures of meaning of his novel. An idealistic film director, Eitel had refused to testify before a congressional investigating committee and had been blacklisted by the movie industry. To that extent he had striven to dissociate himself from Hollywood commercialism; but he moves only as far as Desert D'Or, a satellite of the film capital two hundred miles away, where his sentimental faith in love and his reputation as a proficient man in bed become his major occupation. Inevitably, sex stales. To sweeten his soured life, he eventually cooperates with the investigating committee so that he can return to Hollywood—and the confusion of economic, sexual, and ethical motive is significant—to make profitable movies whose dishonest excellence his professionalism "lusted for [ch. 15]." He is last seen manipulating a press release for Lulu Meyers, an ex-wife, with whom he is conducting a postmarital affair.

The Deer Park, then, depicts the failure in human spirit of the Horatio Alger dream. In one way or another the transients of Desert D'Or find themselves permanent occupants of the treadmill of a self-indulgence—whether economic power as with Teppis or erotic power as with Eitel—that is infernally sanctioned as the goal of their society. Only O'Shaugnessy resists the twin temptations of love and money, rejecting an offer to star in the filming of his life story and losing Lulu Meyers as a result. In the aftermath of this decision, he inhabits the literal hell of a restaurant kitchen where he attends a steam-heated dishwasher, burning himself week after week on the hot dishes, "mortifying my energy," as he puts it, "whipping my spirit, preparing myself for that other work I looked on with religious awe [ch. 21]." Bent on making himself into a writer he escapes Desert D'Or; but whether he escapes the hell of the spirit, which is the real meaning of Desert D'Or, is problematic, since in the second half of the story he is a shadowy undeveloped figure. With the possible exception of O'Shaugnessy, the moral experience of the novel is directed toward the dismal round of life that has submitted to mass commercial values. Love is treated in this context as an expedient way of cashing in on people, of using them for one's own ends. The movie industry exploits love as a commodity, idealizing it, ironically, into the ultimate expression of individual sincerity and morality. The circularity of the cash-sex nexus portrayed here is only too apparent.

In the symbolism of place and time as well as in the narrative of events, this tautology of existence is emphasized. Unlike the transient world of *Barbary Shore*, the ethos of *The Deer Park* is without hope, fixed in the windless lee of stopped time. Parched for nine months of the year, Desert D'Or burns without surcease from a sulfurous sky that blasts every living thing and from the lusts of the flesh that enthrall every inhabitant. It is an analogue of "that second circle of sad Hell," where, Keats tells us,

> . . . in the gust, the whirlwind, and the flow
> Of rain and hailstones, lovers need not tell
> Their sorrows.[12]

Like those living in the Valley of Ashes in *The Great Gatsby*, the sojourners of this desert community are indistinguishable in appearance and spirit from the landscape. They are exiles, renegades, ex-movie stars, has-beens, temporary and permanent refugees from the film capital, drifters—the damned and the defeated—all reminiscent of the lost souls of Sartre's *The Flies* and of the Paris expatriates of Hemingway's *The Sun Also Rises*. Self-loathing is only second to hatred of others as the principal emotion. Eitel sums up the response to life in words that sardonically reverse those of Brett Ashley at the end of *The Sun Also Rises:* "In the end that's the only kind of self-respect you have. To be able to say to yourself that you're disgusting [ch. 22]."

In such a context of hatred, ironically, the preoccupation of the denizens of Desert D'Or is love. But their pursuit of adulation and orgasmic gyrations as panaceas merely confirms their self-disgust and moribund sensibilities. They begin each affair "with the notion that life [has finally] found its flavor, and end with the familiar distaste of no adventure and no novelty [ch. 16]." What could conceivably be more hopeless than this new version of the myth of Sisyphus? Each is interred within his loathed self, doomed to a tautological titillation of his own sensations, unable to communicate with another even through love-making. Instead of being productive of life, sex has become a deathtrap. Thus, Eitel makes love to a prostitute, all the while having "never felt so lonely in his life." An hour later, crying "I love you, I love you," in the monotone of an acolyte chanting the dead form of a once meaningful rite, he makes love to his stale mistress, whose body has become "a cove where he could bury himself." Then he takes a sleeping pill in order to drift into unconsciousness. Despairingly, he considers himself "locked in Elena's love [ch. 16]."

In an essay in the February 1963 issue of *Commentary*, Mailer defines hell as "a pantomime of small empty activities."[13] So it is with these lost souls, for whom love remains an enervating round of solipsistic movements across the bleak terrain of oneself.

> "And who do you love now?" Eitel asks Elena in the first rank bloom of their love.
> "You," she said, and then looked away. "No. I don't. I don't love anybody at all."
> "You feel on your own?"
> "Yes."
> "It's a good way to feel." [ch. 10]

Such solo love, advocated here by Elena and Eitel in dialogue that makes them a parody of the Hemingway hero and heroine, is a charade, a "closed rehearsal of the comic and the entertaining [ch. 10]," condemning each actor to the treadmill of inventing endless new games of sex to make it palatable. Hence Lulu and Sergius play at being model and photographer, movie star and bellhop, queen and slave. "She was never so happy," Sergius recalls, as when she played "the bobby-soxer who sat with a date in the living room and was finally convinced, always for the first time naturally enough [ch. 12]." Understandably, these profane souls, condemned to such mummery, fail even through ordinary discourse to communicate with each other.

In handling this theme of incommunicability, Mailer makes the most of a defect in the structural pattern of the novel. In both *Barbary Shore* and *The Deer Park* he appears to have conceived of his narrative as a dialogue between two men, an experienced mentor and a neophyte writer who puts himself to school under the older man's somewhat tarnished but still idealistic tutelage. Neither story, however, is as successful as its prototype *The Great Gatsby* [cf. *Adv,* pp. 235, 242–243] in coping with its dual assignment of two centers of consciousness, particularly since in each instance the first-person narrator (Lovett, O'Shaugnessy) never seems certain which story, his or the older man's (McLeod, Eitel), should occupy center stage. The problem is brought into the open when O'Shaugnessy recalls the night that Eitel related his theory about human nature. "Although I do not want to go into theory," O'Shaugnessy hastens to say, "maybe it is a part of character. I could write it today as he said it, and I think in all modesty I could even add a complexity or two, but this is partly a novel of how I felt at the time, and so I paraphrase as I heard it then, for it would take too long the other way [ch. 11]."

Although the characterization of Eitel suffers, as in this instance, from the indirection of the first-person narrative and from the divided emphasis on two heroes, the characterization of O'Shaugnessy suffers even more from this general lack of dramatic development. For *The Deer Park* is essentially the story of Eitel (as the pun on his name, "I tell" would suggest), not of O'Shaugnessy who was, as Mailer admits in *Advertisements for Myself,* "the frozen germ of some new theme [p. 236; cf. pp. 237, 242–243]." Mailer also implies as much in his subsequent attempt to write the story of Sergius O'Shaugnessy in an as yet unpublished novel [cf. *Adv,* pp. 248, 478–503, 512–532]. Still, sketchiness in *The Deer Park* regarding O'Shaugnessy serves a thematic function. Since it leaves his connection with Eitel shadowy and lacking in dramatic development, it underscores the irresolvable gap of time and space that separates the cynical commercialism of the older man from the existential *Angst* of the younger. And at the end of the novel O'Shaugnessy imagines Eitel, years later and a continent away, remembering with a pang "the knowledge he wanted to give me, suffering the sad frustration of his new middle age, since experience when it is not told to another must wither within and be worse than lost [ch. 28]."

Considering the cul-de-sac into which the denizens of Desert D'Or have relegated love and life, the novel ends on an additional irony when Sergius asks in a fancied dialogue with God,

> "Would You agree that sex is where philosophy begins?" But God, who is the oldest of philosophers, answers in His weary, cryptic way, "Rather think of Sex as Time, and Time as the connection of new circuits." [ch. 28]

The infernal reference to life in Desert D'Or is only too self-evident. For like hell, the desert metropolis exists in a state of suspended time. The horror of unending sameness of existence has been vividly evoked by poets from Greek myth onward. The Struldbrugs of *Gulliver's Travels* and the Tithonus of Tennyson convey with considerable pathos this dilemma of man's experience with time. Blake renders the paradox eloquently in *Milton* when he writes:

> Time is the mercy of Eternity: without Time's swiftness Which is the swiftest of all things: all were eternal torment. [I, xxiv, 72–73]

Life in Desert D'Or consists of moribund activities performed without hope of surcease by way of what Blake elsewhere calls the "production of time." Its inhabitants—the "middle-aged desperadoes of the corporation and the suburb"—have lost their past, living in an "airless no-man's-land of the perpetual present."[14] Its inferno-like environs merge day and night into a sequence of endless sameness. In his opening description of the place, Mailer is at considerable pains to make this clear. "Everything," Sergius tells us, "is in the present tense." "Built since the Second World War," he adds, "it is the only place I know which is all new." Drinking in the "air-cooled midnight of the bar," he remarks,

> I never knew whether it was night or day . . . afternoon was always passing into night, and drunken nights into the dawn of a desert morning. One seemed to leave the theatrical darkness of afternoon for the illumination of night, and the sun of Desert D'Or became like the stranger who the drunk imagines to be following him. [ch. 1]

Thus, Mailer works brilliantly to efface the boundaries of time, consigning Desert D'Or to an Alice-in-Wonderland where seconds and minutes, days and nights, consume each other into faceless limbo. And this horror of arrested time carries over as a leitmotif in the published fragments of an unfinished novel that presumes to continue the life and times of O'Shaugnessy. The title of one section, "The Time of Her Times," oracularly calls attention to this self-conscious obsession with duration. In the other fragment, a Joycean "Advertisement for Myself on the Way Out," time—or more accurately not-time—figures as a narrative strategy for limning the paradox of modern consciousness.

Writers are fond of imagining love as an experience capsuling time (and space) into momentary experiences of eternity (and infinity). Contrariwise, love is naturally associated with the temporal rhythms of life: with the sequences of fertility and the periods of gestation. Through its generative connection with life, love links man to past and future. In this sense God's fancied answer to Sergius that sex is time, and time the connection of new circuits, is meaningful. But when the Delphic assertion is used as a lens through which to see and measure Desert D'Or and the "life" of its people, it becomes an acrid summary of what has transpired in the story. Trapped by the stifling commerce of their egos, their lives endlessly the same, Eitel, Elena, Lulu, Dorothea O'Faye, Marion Faye, and the others seek to escape into the outer world of sentience. Sex offers them the semblance of life, but even with it they know only the dry salvages of lust.

The receptacle for all the human refuse of Hollywood, that gaudy symbol of American civilization, Desert D'Or represents rather precisely (given Mailer's special Messianic views) the deadened nerve ends of a commercial society which has lost the secret of feeling and thinking morally but continues to sleepwalk through the dead forms of an old dispensation. Thus, in *The Deer Park* Mailer explores the nightmare of emotional totalitarianism, when bereft of all but "the scurry beneath the stone [ch. 10]." In the third of this trilogy, *An American Dream,* he attempts through the fictional parable of "Raw-Jock" Rojack to teach modern man, a twentieth-century Pilgrim afflicted with "anxiety of the anxieties [ch. 7]," how to renew his "exhausted spasm of the heart [ch. 8]."

An American Dream: PARADISE

At the conclusion of *The Deer Park* Eitel in imagined dialogue with O'Shaugnessy declaims dejectedly, "One cannot look for a good time . . . for pleasure must end as love or cruelty . . . or obligation." Sergius objects to this sermon of the commercially respectable and the ideologically cynical with the inspired fervor of an incipient hipster:

> I would have told him that one must invariably look for a good time since a good time is what gives us the strength to try again. For do we not gamble our way to the heart of the mystery against all the power of good manners, good morals, the fear of germs, and the sense of sin? Not to mention the prisons of pain, the wading pools of pleasure, and the public and professional voices of our sentimental land. If there is a God, and sometimes I believe there is one, I'm sure He says, "Go on, my boy. I don't know that I can help you, but we wouldn't want all *those* people to tell you what to do."
> . . . Then for a moment in that cold Irish soul of mine, a glimmer of the joy of the flesh came toward me, rare as the eye of the rarest tear of compassion, and we laughed together after all, because to have heard that sex was time and time the connection of new circuits was a part of the poor odd dialogues which give hope to us noble humans for more than one night. [ch. 28]

Before selling out to Hollywood and big business Eitel had tried to serve this "joy of the flesh," theorizing that love fed the happy blossoming of one's blood. The core of his faith was that people had a buried nature—"the noble savage" he called it—which was changed and whipped and trained by everything in life until it was almost dead. Yet if people were lucky and if they were brave, sometimes they would find a mate with the same buried nature and that could make them happy and strong. At least relatively so. There were so many things in the way, and if everybody had a buried nature, well everybody also had a snob, and the snob was usually stronger. The snob could be a tyrant to buried nature. [ch. 11]

The Deer Park is about Eitel's defeat by the "public and professional voices" of emotional totalitarianism. *An American Dream* is an audacious romantic assertion that the embattled "noble savage" in man, given the courage and strength and luck, can prevail against the establishment of the tyrannical snob.

Put simply, *An American Dream* narrates Stephen Richards Rojack's recovery from "a private kaleidoscope of death [ch. 1]," engendered by his killing of four German soldiers during World War II and by his barren love for his wife Deborah Kelly. His recovery with its "new grace [ch. 1]" of life is triggered by equally strong medicine: the purgative murder of his carnivorous wife and the avowal (with the consequent underworld threat to his personal safety) of love for the nightclub singer, Cherry. Stated thus blatantly in terms of its bare story line, the novel becomes a travesty of human action and religious values. As polemic it advocates something just short of running amok, replete with the metallic distaste of lust and murder. To deal with the book on its own terms, however, one needs also to consider its dialectical conception and rich texture of language.

A few years ago, in a brilliant article on Faulkner, Jean-Paul Sartre argued that to know an artist's metaphysics is to know his form.[15] This is true no less for Mailer than for Faulkner. A Manichaeism with its "lights and darks, and all the other mysterious dualities of our mysterious universe"[16] provides a substratum to much of Mailer's analysis of man and society. His social revolutionist's faith in a dialectic that reduces the world to stark blacks and whites is at odds, however, with his artist's sensibility, which finds complex patterns of parallels and contrasts in otherwise simple designs. Such fracturing of a neat dualism into a dynamic continuum of human reactions appears in his definition in "The White Negro" of the "curious community of feeling" to be found in the world of the hipster. It is, he says,

> a muted cool religious revival to be sure, but the element which is exciting, disturbing, nightmarish perhaps, is that incompatibles have come to bed, the inner life and the violent life, the orgy and the dream of love, the desire to murder and the desire to create, a dialectical conception of existence with a lust for power, a dark, romantic, and yet undeniably dynamic view of existence for it sees every man and woman as moving individually through each moment of life forward into growth or backward into death. [*Adv*, pp. 342–343]

In Mailer the American faith in the efficacious event is united uneasily with an older European allegiance to the conceptual and the ideological. This unstable syndrome of contraries can serve as a gloss to *An American Dream.*

The near alliance of the "desire to murder and the desire to create"—"eternal Eros" and "his equally immortal adversary," as Freud called the two "heavenly forces" in *Civilization and its Discontents*[17]—particularly fascinates Mailer. The narrative design of the novel takes its shape from the yoking of these incompatibles: Rojack's love for Deborah that contains in it also a yen to kill her; his rapid movement in less than twenty-four hours from the murder of Deborah to the love of Cherry, as if the two disparate acts were links in a chain of cause and effect; his eagerness to test his new love by challenging death in the persons of Shago and Kelly, and by walking the parapet of Kelly's penthouse balcony. But equally significant is the way these incompatibles mold the texture of the language, giving the surface statement some of the metaphysical substance that Donne's puns on death have. Thus, Deborah's love "always offered its intimation of the grave." Rare was the instance of making love to her that Rojack did not feel "a high pinch of pain as if fangs had sunk into" him, his "mouth on hers, not sobbing but groping for air [ch. 2]." After their separation, his telephone talks with her were moments when he felt he was committing hara-kiri, with the remains of his love for her "drawing from the wound [ch. 1]."

One could cite many more examples of this marriage of love and hate, of life and death; but it is the corollary heaven-hell antithesis which more narrowly defines the symbolic action of the novel—that is, the central struggle of Rojack, somewhat intuitively, to find his way between the opposing claims of what one might call old-fashioned good and evil. As he quipped on his TV program, "God's engaged in a war with the Devil and God may lose [ch. 8]."

Arrayed on the side of Satan are Barney Oswald Kelly and his daughter Deborah, who is the Devil's own child. Kelly describes her conception as occurring under Lucifer's aegis. "I took a dive deep down into a vow," he discloses to Rojack, and "said in my mind, 'Satan, if it takes your pitchfork up my gut, let me blast a child into this bitch!' [Deborah's mother]. And something happened, no sulphur, no brimstone, but Leonora and I met way down there in some bog, some place awful, and I felt something take hold in her. Some sick breath came right back out of her pious little mouth. 'What the *hell* have you done?' she screamed at me, which was the only time Leonora ever swore. That was it. Deborah was conceived [ch. 8]." Married to her, Rojack finds himself to his bewilderment and eventual horror in the constant presence of the Devil. The "afterbreath" of making love to her leaves him in hell: "floated on a current of low heavy fire, a sullen poisonous fire, an oil on flame which went out of her and took me in [ch. 2]." Hers is a subtle Satanism. She "did not wish to tear the body, she was out to spoil the light." She appears to him ironically and dualistically as "ministering angel (ministering devil) [ch. 1]," whose "grace always offered its intimation of the grave [ch. 2]."

Through his murder of Deborah, then, Rojack rids himself of the haunting presence of Satan and begins his return to paradise. At the moment of her death, his "flesh seemed new," he "had not felt so nice since [he] was twelve [puberty?]." He felt that he had acquired a "new grace [ch. 1]," but he still has a far road of soul rebuilding to travel. And the distance is measured by the love he makes to two women, Ruta (root, of the earth, dark) and Cherry Melanie (virginal in the sense that none of her lovers until Rojack has succeeded in bringing her to an orgasm), both former mistresses of Barney Kelly.

With these two women Rojack enacts the existentialist's progress from mass conformity to individual choice. Thus, their narrative function further defines the Manichaean frame of conceptual reference of the novel. Ruta continues in the service of Kelly, ostensibly as a maid to his daughter but actually as a spy for him. Cherry has courageously cut free of him and the Mafia at the risk of her life. Rojack encounters Ruta twice: minutes after killing his wife in her apartment and twenty-four hours later in Kelly's Waldorf Towers suite. In his first encounter with Ruta, the life-death antithesis predominates. To him paradoxically her flesh seems alive, her skin dead. "Cold gases" exhale from her womb; her vagina is a "storehouse of disappointments." He breaks into her bedroom immediately after killing Deborah to find her masturbating. In subsequently making love to her he alternates between sodomy and fornication—between what, through a perverse reversion in her, is identified as her "bank of pleasures" and her deserted warehouse, "that empty tomb." This quickly becomes a contest in Rojack's mind between "a raid on the Devil and a trip back to the Lord." At the moment of orgasm he has a choice. At first he selects the "deserted warehouse . . . a chapel now, a modest decent place"; but he can still "feel the Devil's meal beneath, its fires . . . lifting through the floors." At the last minute he switches to the Devil and "felt low sullen waters wash about a dead tree on a midnight pond." He is not yet ready to pay his "respects to God," he concludes [ch. 2]. Evil, lust, and sterility are the keynotes of this love-making.

The contrast between Ruta and Cherry is nowhere better illustrated than in this sterility-fertility motif. At first (as with Rojack and Ruta), Rojack and Cherry meet each other with locked wills. There is a "casing of iron about [his] heart, and . . . her will [is] anchored like a girdle of steel about her womb. . . . Nothing was loving in her; no love in me; we paid our devotions in some church no larger than ourselves." When he removes her diaphragm, however ("that corporate rubbery obstruction" to the realization of life), their wills "begin at last in the force of equality to water and to loose tears, to soften into some light which is shut away again by the will to force tears back, steel to steel, until steel shimmers in a mist of dew," and Rojack hears "a voice like a child's whisper on the breeze" and glimpses "that heavenly city which had appeared as Deborah was expiring in the lock of my arm." They both happily believe that they have conceived. Symbolic of a new dawn and renewed life, this hoped-for conception occurs the morning after Deborah's murder [ch. 5]. Later that night Rojack and Cherry meet a second time and find that the iron in their wills has fully dissolved, replaced with "one cornucopia of flesh." "God," Rojack in effect prays, "let me love that girl and become a father, and try to be a good man [ch. 5]."

The antitheses are self-evident. In the course of twenty-four hours Rojack progresses from lust to love, from sodomy to fruitful coition, from selfish willfulness to willed selflessness, from the stench of stale gases to the aroma of honeysuckle [ch. 5], from the neighborhood of hell to the environs of heaven.

Not without Hemingway aplomb and manner, Mailer develops Rojack's intuitions of the flesh into a code of bravery that Jake Barnes and Brett Ashley would happily assent to. As he unites with Cherry, Rojack senses in the room a "sweet presence" of wings, which "spoke of the meaning of love": "I think we have to be good," he says to Cherry, "by which I meant we would have to be brave [ch. 5]." Rojack is no antinomian of the flesh. The penance of courage must precede the sacrament of love. He "believed God was not love but courage. Love came only as a reward [ch. 8]." The reason is that evil can also masquerade as love. This is the lesson he learns from his love bouts with Deborah, Ruta, and Cherry. When love is a sensation which belongs to one alone (as Mailer shows in *The Deer Park*), it is the "art of the Devil [ch. 6]." Only when it includes transcendence of self in willing "journey of knowledge . . . from the depth of one being to the heart of another [ch. 1]," does it become the gift of God. The latter demands courage. And Rojack, who has lived for years in cowardly capitulation to the Daddy Warbucks milieu of the Kellys, has to practice bravery if he is to deny power and to affirm love. This is the significance of the opening references to a wartime experience that has continued to haunt him. As a "stiff, overburdened, nervous young Second Lieutenant," he had found himself trapped in World War II by four German machine gunners, with "the full moon giving a fine stain to the salient of our mood (which was fear and funk and a sniff of the grave) [ch. 1]." His marriage to Deborah and submission to her world of the *New York Times* only confirmed the "sickness and dung" that filled "the sack of [his] torso [ch. 1]." He discovered that swimming in the well of her evil intuitions brought him nearer to his memory of the four Germans than anything encountered before or since. Not until the barren and hence occultly sinister ninth year of their marriage is he finally goaded by Deborah into a fury sufficient to push him to strangle her. An outgrowth of this act is the will to face the tests of courage, which the love of Cherry demands. Hence the vomiting by his "burned-up lungs" of all "the rot and gas of compromise, the stink of old fears, mildew of discipline, all the biles of habit and the horrors of pretense," when he goes to the nightclub where Cherry sings [ch. 4]; and hence his set-tos after this prelude of ritual cleansing, involving repeated threats to his life, with Ike "Romeo" Romalozzo, Shago Martin, and Barney Kelly— all contenders for her love.

This is Hemingway brought up to date—the not unnatural ethic of Rojack, a man who is a university "professor of existential psychology with the not inconsiderable thesis that magic, dread, and the perception of death were the roots of motivation," who "had one popular book published, *The Psychology of the Hangman* [ch. 1]," and who taught as a corrective an anti-Freudian metaphysic that "the root of neurosis is cowardice rather than brave old Oedipus [ch. 8]." Although a distortion of reality, when viewed according to traditional morality, this philosophy of eros/*agapé* is not Priapus run riot, but an honest effort to wrench experience into a shape answerable to the needs of the times. Following its exercises, Rojack realizes the power and the glory of the golden age of sexuality. This is not the power which so many of the characters in *An American Dream* (Deborah, Ruta, Kelly) exercise. This is not Satanic power with its totalitarian drive to gain ascendancy over another, which "is only power for the sake of power, and . . . is cowardly power for it masquerades in coy and winsome forms."[18] This is rather the Godly power of the uninhibited innocent sexuality that controls human actions from womb to tomb. It is regained by commercially and culturally brutalized man's purging from himself "the lead and concrete and kapok and leather of . . . ego [ch. 1]" and thereby winning mastery over the circumstances of his life.

Mailer can assert this Godwinian-Rousseauistic faith in human goodness, because he holds an essentially monistic view of being. That is, he believes man to be intrinsically good but affected physiologically, and hence physically, by external substances and stimuli. In the dialogue on "The Metaphysics of the Belly," written in July 1962, he defines *being* as a wedding of matter and soul: "*Being* is first the body we see before us. That body we see before us is that moment of the present for a soul, a soul which must inevitably be altered for better, for worse, or for better and worse by its presence in a body [*Pres,* p. 295]." And the body he argues, using the conceit of eating, is engaged in a constant digestion of the external world of experience, with "the possibility of illness every time opposites do not meet or meet poorly, just as there is the air to gain life every time opposites meet each other nicely [*Pres*, p. 290]." In this respect Mailer would appear to look upon love as not unlike the impulse that leads primitive man to eat his enemy's heart to gain its courage. Significantly, after he kills Deborah, Rojack imagines himself and her maid supping on Deborah's flesh for days while "the deepest poisons in us would be released from our cells [ch. 2]." Mailer then sees the choices of evil or good as physiological gratifications from which man realizes either adulterated fragmentation or healthy unity of self.

Brom Weber has rightly called our attention to the ambiguous meaning of the title.[19] It is an ironic comment on the tenuousness of the official American dream, "that hyperconglomerate of success, salesmanship, health, and wealth,"[20] so perfectly epitomized in the life story of Barney Kelly. At the same time it is a straightforward assertion of the frontier dream that still obsesses the American below the surface of his respectability. That is, the dream of "ferocious, lonely and romantic desires, that concentration of ecstasy and violence which is the dream life of the nation [*Pres*, p. 38]." *An American Dream* is, ultimately, an audacious effort to show Americans how to shuck off old habits and return to the primal innocence that "the fresh, green breast" of this continent has for hundreds of years beguiled man into believing was possible in the New World (so Nick Carroway epitomizes it at the end of *The Great Gatsby*). The novel thus simultaneously restates one of the most persistent of American illusions and attempts to blaze another Northwest Passage to its elusive Cathay.

Cannibals and Christians: TESTAMENTS II

Barbary Shore, The Deer Park, and *An American Dream* are honest statements of an original, independent mind. They argue stubbornly that the Northwest Passage of violence will lead not only the deadened soul of Rojack but the "electronic nihilism" of all men to similar renewed joy at the "core of life [*Adv*, p. 385]." In this respect the three novels accurately reflect Mailer's nonfictional polemics against "modern man's ability to swallow nausea."[21] Mailer's Socratic dialogue, "The Political Economy of Time," stands at the end of *Cannibals and Christians* as a summation to date of his fears and hopes. Here he reiterates his insistence that the only "true and passionate lovers are those who love each other because they give life to one another," and that "There are souls which can be expressed—that is, *un*deadened—only by violence [*CC*, p. 342]."

Despite the coherence of a unified view that the novels and testaments alike present, there is reason to suspect that Mailer is ambiguous in feeling, if not outright doubtful, of the rightness and certainty of this faith that the individual can prevail against the pressures toward conformity of mass culture. Hence, doubtless, his gradual shift from advocacy of social action to enthusiasm for spiritual nodes becomes clear. The ending of each novel doggedly hints as much. With collapsed hopes, McLeod goes not unwillingly to his death. Lovett becomes a fugitive, fleeing "down the alley which led from that rooming house . . . only to enter another, and then another . . . obliged to live waiting for the signs which tell me I must move again [ch. 32]." Eitel succumbs to the blandishments of a congressional investigating committee, testifies in open hearing, is reinstated in the good graces of Hollywood, and deteriorates into making commercial movies and carrying on an affair with his ex-wife Lulu Meyers. O'Shaugnessy flees to a university in Mexico where he subsists on the G. I. Bill of Rights. Shago and Cherry meet violent deaths. And while Rojack wins out over the police and the Mafia in his revolt against society, with the resultant reassertion of his individuality, he does not in the end seem to have succeeded wholly in realizing his desires. With Cherry dead, he drifts off to Yucatan, a finesse that ends his confrontation with society.

The uncertainty and even masochism of such gestures is

self-evident. Despite his noisy claims for the hipster as existentialist man, Mailer still remains essentially a disgruntled intellectual in search of something to believe in. Both McLeod and Eitel, who most nearly represent the idealists Mailer has created, exist in a state of existential doubt. Bereft of ideational belief and stuffed with frustrated fervor, each is left with only his frantic assertion of self, which ironically seems to win for him only physical death or spiritual torpor. Hence, Mailer desperately resorts, in F. J. Hoffman's words, to "passion without a context." Analyzing Mailer's opening statement in *Advertisements for Myself*, Hoffman concludes,

> It is all here: the rage at the state of "The Republic," the retreat from the shock of annihilation, the recourse to "nihilism," the dependence upon minimal physical verities, which are not attached to a cause or a principle since these seem to have become inoperative. Courage, sex, consciousness, the beauty of the body, the search for love: these are minimal necessities of a passionate life, but they are not identified with any specific form of justification or objective. They are simply, nakedly there, to be rescued from annihilation, to be revalued without recourse to ideological strategy. . . . Mailer is reduced to the task of describing passion without a context, or at best within a context that is entirely misunderstood.
>
> When Mailer becomes "philosophical," as he must, it is in terms of an unphilosophical situation: nondidactic, self-defensive, expansively hopeful, and frustratingly, repetitiously sentimental, or passionate. The dynamics of "courage, sex, consciousness, the beauty of the body" are all a part of a self-consuming passion; vigor seems to contain its own philosophical reward. The self is preserved through its relocation at "the center of the Universe."[22]

Consequently, Mailer in all honesty finds great difficulty in imagining either Lovett or O'Shaugnessy as very successful in "the reconstitution of the self"[23] through sex and violence; nor is his selection of their mentors, for whom both ideas and passion have staled, guaranteed to lead them out of the wilderness. O'Shaugnessy breaks free of the false world of

Hollywood; but ends up playacting at violence and love by operating a matador's school for frustrated girls in a Greenwich School warehouse loft. Rojack fares more successfully; but he too at the end lights out for Yucatan.

So far Mailer has been standing on dead center ideationally. Expressive of this fact is that the fictional worlds he has created exhibit unresolved tension that eventually goes slack and is allowed to leak away. Whether Mailer will ultimately resolve his own doubts is, of course, problematic. Should he bring it off, he may yet realize his ambition, audaciously confessed in *Advertisements for Myself* [p. 477], to "hit the longest ball ever to go up in the accelerated hurricane air of our American letters."

There is no doubt of Mailer's ambition for the novel in general—and for his own in particular. He admires the work of realism done for the nineteenth century by Balzac and Zola and chides his contemporaries that someone has not yet done it for the mid-twentieth century. In an address to the American Studies Association of the Modern Language Association in 1965, he defined the two dominant impulses in the American novel as realism and manners. Both, he believes, have deteriorated from the range of achievement of Dreiser and Henry James to the restricted localism of a Steinbeck and the camp of a Terry Southern.[24] At other times, with more clear-cut antithesis, he has characterized American fiction as devoted to either a social or psychological point of view. The serious novel, he says, begins today from "a fixed philosophical point—the desire to discover reality—and it goes to search for that reality in society, or else must embark on a trip up the upper Amazon of the inner eye [*CC,* p. 128]."

Some of Mailer's problems as a novelist stem from his effort to write both kinds of novel at once. The schizophrenia of *Barbary Shore* and *The Deer Park* derives in part from his dualistic conception of Eitel and O'Shaugnessy, McLeod and Lovett, as twin routes into the unexplored world and into the unknown self. Undoubtedly, disjunction between the social and the psychological accounts for some of the surrealistic focus of these two novels. In *An American Dream* Mailer most successfully combines the two aims in one of the few courageous attempts in this century at a novel of manners embracing a comprehensive picture of American society, which is also a psychological novel traveling "unguided into the mysteries of the Self [*CC*, p. 129]." Unlike the eight heroines of Mary McCarthy's *The Group,* whom Mailer flagellates in *Cannibals and Christians* for remaining classbound, Rojack comes "from one class" and makes "heroic journeys to other classes [*CC*, p. 136]." And the novel's violent style, while underscoring the unreality of the "postwar" era, aims at breaking through the routine of fixed and minimal standards. Not since Scott Fitzgerald has a writer come directly and so close to the reality of the modern American experience.

To date, however, one cannot say in all honesty that Mailer has succeeded in rendering fictionally the plan I have described at great length in this essay. The language and narrative of his novels outline his views, but the characterization is flawed. Eitel, O'Shaugnessy, and Rojack never convince us of the larger spiritual reference of their sexual lives. Not love but lust with its rancid smell haunts their sexual acts in spite of the nervous pitch of the language claiming otherwise. Perhaps this reaction derives in part from our ingrained moral resistence to sexual license and lawless violence. We dissent to the possibility (as Mailer claims for all besieged souls in his essay "The Metaphysics of the Belly") that Rojack is sweetened and softened to love by way of the violent murder of his wife. We dissent to his capability of leaving "the bitter sores" of his soul behind and ascending by way of his fetid flesh into the jeweled light of spiritual bliss, even as the rhetoric convinces us of his emotional regeneration. This failure would suggest that Mailer's style has risen to the demands he has increasingly placed on it, but his novelistic skills have not matured comparably.

Indeed, Mailer's language is clearly an achievement. A prose style is difficult at any time to realize—and hence rare in the history of English literature. Mailer bids fair to pull off this feat. Furthermore his style rarely bores. It does not, like Salinger's with increasing frequency, impose on the reader; nor, like Philip Roth's, sap one's interest and strength with arid wastes to traverse; nor, like Bellow's move unevenly between precision tooling and mass production; nor, like Wouk's, blunder past the target. At its best, it is feisty, yet virile, at once personal and universal.

Even more praiseworthy, Mailer's style at its best is expressive of his ideas. Most commentators agree about the controlled rhetoric of *The Presidential Papers,* but boggle at the baroque excesses of *An American Dream.* Stanley Edgar Hyman in a review of that novel has considerable fun at Mailer's expense decrying what he calls "Mailer's immortal longing, to be a *big* fancy writer like Thomas Wolfe."[25] He deplores Mailer's poetic inversions, unidiomatic tenses, syntaxless sentences, tritely romantic and deranged similes, and mystique-of-spirit odors, quoting at great length instances of these faults—a practice reminiscent of the early nineteenth-century critiques of such offenders against the aesthetic decorum of that day as Wordsworth and Keats. Hyman seems to have set himself up as an unofficial watchdog over the purity of the language. Witness his title *Standards* for the selected edition of his reviews in *The New Leader,* and his quotation on the title page of the definition of the word from Webster's Second (not Third!) International Dictionary. As with Croker and Lockhart in their day, so with Hyman in ours, long quoted lists of blemishes torn from their context fail to grapple with the aesthetic problem of the work of art as a conceptual unity of theme and form. Surely Brom Weber is more to the point when he suggests that *An American Dream* depicts Rojack's psychic growth, hence the importance of the style, with its intense psychological and sensory perception, which shows the extent to which Rojack has "escaped the banal and become aware of himself."[26] In a review of Victor Lasky's *John Fitzgerald Kennedy: The Man and the Myth,* Mailer asserted that Kennedy "was without principles or political passions except for one. He knew the only way he could re-create the impoverished circuits which lay between himself and the depths of his emotions was to become President [CC, p. 170]." With a few changes these words equally describe the efforts of Rojack to revive his deadened nerve ends on a nourishment of murder and sex, with the violent imagery of the book nervously underscoring this trauma of growth. The mystique-of-spirit odors, which so offends Hyman, is in fact then a superbly functioning vehicle for the dramatization of character and development of the central thesis of the novel.

Similarly the extensive cave and dungeon imagery in *The Deer Park,* descriptive of the solipsistic hell in which its protagonists exist, conveys, as in Blake's poems, a metaphysical undercurrent of meaning heavily charged with emotional connotations. One example of the rich resources of language at Mailer's disposal will suffice. After she leaves Eitel, Elena goes to live with Marion Faye. Bent upon an existential resistance to his fear of death and to his revulsion from nauseating sensory experiences, he welcomes Elena as a further mortification of his flesh. But his defenses are insufficient to withstand the seductive temptation of answering Elena's human cry for help to stave off loneliness. To his chagrin he finds himself "jailed in the keep of his bed with Elena beside him, enduring the venial mortification of having his skin itch near her presence, his nostrils repelled by the odor of her body which Eitel had savored so much [ch. 25]." The ironic union of contrary situations in the metaphor of the fortress-become-jail reverberates to the multiple strands of the tale. It echoes in its primary sense the embattled isolated existence of the denizens of Desert D'Or. It defines Faye's retreat from love, illustrated also by his engaging "in the trade" of prostitution. It characterizes his (as well as the other Desert D'Orites') belief that sex is a divisive strategy for gaining power over another instead of a unitive expression of procreative love for another. Furthermore, it comments on his failure to keep himself emotionally uninvolved and condemns him as the criminal in his sacrifice of humankind to his existential needs. He fails in his repellent effort to drive Elena to commit suicide, hence also in his desire to confront death vicariously. He is compromised by a feeling of pity for her. In desperation, while taking her to the airplane which will return her to Los Angeles, he steers his car into the path of an oncoming truck. Thus he is forced irrationally as a result of his failure with Elena to court the suicide himself.

Not since the nineteenth century and the heyday of the Darwinian hypothesis has a writer used images of war, march and countermarch, as compulsively as Mailer. Given his view of twentieth-century man as locked in a struggle for the survival of his integral self, a combatant against the forces of a world which believes in *The New York Times,* Mailer exhibits in his use of this battle metaphor a cohesive, synthesizing imagination that works with powerful directness to organize experience into meaningful order. If he shows weakness in creation of characters, he reveals on the other hand an attraction to ideas and great inventiveness in finding objective correlatives for these ideas. Most importantly, he has an imagination that deploys language and the larger structural units of the novel with the ruthless deft hand of a sergeant-major. And like a gung-ho marine he will take chances, risk defeat, to win large objectives. The faults of exuberance of such a mind are the faults not of a minor, but of a potentially major, artist.

With the publication of *An American Dream,* Mailer appears to have reached the end of one line of development as a thinker and as an artist. The three novels *Barbary Shore, The Deer Park,* and *An American Dream* present a fully articulated view of life. And in *Cannibals and Christians* [p. 248] he indicates that he has grown tired of the word *orgasm.* He can now do one of two things: (1) continue to explore the territory whose boundaries these novels have surveyed, or (2) make a fresh start, as he did after *The Naked and the Dead.* Which route he will pursue remains to be seen.[27]

NOTES

1. George A. Schrader, "Norman Mailer and the Despair of Defiance," *Yale Review*, LI (1961-62), 267–280.

2. Part of Mailer's reply to Jean Malaquais' reflections on "The White Negro" (Part 4, "Reflections on Hip"), included in *Advertisements for Myself* (New York: G. P. Putnam's Sons, 1959), p. 363; henceforth referred to as *Adv*.

3. Diana Trilling, "Norman Mailer," *Encounter*, XIX (1962), 45-56; reprinted as "The Radical Moralism of Norman Mailer," *The Creative Present*, eds. Nona Balakian and Charles Simmons (Garden City, N.Y.: Doubleday and Company, 1963), pp. 145–171.

4. Norman Mailer, *The Presidential Papers* (New York: G. P. Putnam's Sons, 1963), p. 4; henceforth referred to as *Pres*.

5. Edmond L. Volpe, "James Jones–Norman Mailer," *Contemporary American Novelists*, ed. Harry T. Moore (Carbondale, Ill.: Southern Illinois University Press, 1964), pp. 106-119.

6. "Superman Comes to the Supermarket," *The Third Presidential Paper —The Existentialist Hero* [*Pres*, p. 51]. The specific referent of this phrase is the hope that the Democratic party had for John F. Kennedy as President.

7. George A. Schrader, "Norman Mailer and the Despair of Defiance," *Yale Review*, LI (1961–62), 278.

8. All references are to the following editions: *Barbary Shore* (New York: Holt, Rinehart and Winston, Inc., 1951), *The Deer Park* (New York: G. P. Putnam's Sons, 1955) *An American Dream* (New York: The Dial Press, 1965); henceforth referred to as *BS*, *DP*, and *AD*.

9. "Hip, Hell, and the Navigator, an Interview with Norman Mailer by Richard G. Stern," *Adv*, pp. 383–385.

10. "An Evening with Jackie Kennedy, or, The Wild West of the East," *The Fifth Presidential Paper—The Existential Heroine* [*Pres*, p. 94].

11. Edmund G. Gardner, *Dante* (New York: E. P. Dutton's Sons, 1923), p. 176.

12. John Keats, "On a Dream," 11. 9–12.

13. Reprinted as "Responses and Reactions II," *Pres*, p. 154.

14. So Mailer characterizes America in "She Thought the Russians Was Coming," *The Second Presidential Paper—Juvenile Delinquency* [*Pres*, p. 21]; and in "An Evening with Jackie Kennedy, or, The Wild West of the East," *The Fifth Presidential Paper—The Existential Heroine* [*Pres*, pp. 95–96]. Cf. Mailer's remark in "The Metaphysics of the Belly," *The Twelfth Presidential Paper—On Waste*: "I write often of the enormous present, of psychopathy, of how mass man has no sense of past or future, just now [*Pres*, p. 279]."

15. Jean-Paul Sartre, "Time in Faulkner: *The Sound and the Fury*," *Faulkner: Three Decades of Criticism*, eds. Olga W. Vickery and Frederick J. Hoffman (East Lansing, Mich.: Michigan State University Press, 1960), pp. 225–232.

16. So Mailer wrote in *The Village Voice* in a note on obscenity, reprinted in *Adv*, p. 288.

17. Sigmund Freud, *Civilization and Its Discontents*, trans. Joan Riviere (Garden City, N.Y.: Doubleday and Company, Inc., 1958), p. 105.

18. Norman Mailer, "Power," *Fifth Advertisement for Myself* [*Adv*, p. 287].

19. Brom Weber, "A Fear of Dying: Norman Mailer's *An American Dream," The Hollins Critic,* II (1965), 1–6.
20. *Ibid.,* p. 2.
21. Norman Mailer, *Cannibals and Christians* (New York: The Dial Press, 1966), p. 247.
22. Frederick J. Hoffman, *The Mortal No: Death and the Modern Imagination* (Princeton, N.J.: Princeton University Press, 1964), p. 478-479.
23. *Ibid.,* p. 483.
24. Norman Mailer, "Modes and Mutations: Quick Comments on the Modern Novel," *Commentary,* XLI, (1966), 37–40.
25. Stanley Edgar Hyman, *Standards* (New York: Horizon Press, 1966), p. 278.
26. Brom Weber, "A Fear of Dying: Norman Mailer's *An American Dream," The Hollins Critic,* II (1965), 4.
27. Since I wrote this chapter, Mailer has published two books. *Armies of the Night* (New York: New American Library, 1968) continues the nonfictional ambience of personal confession and social-political journalism of *Advertisements for Myself, The Presidential Papers,* and *Cannibals and Christians.* Devoted to an odd combination of dispassionate analysis and provoking narration of the Washington peace march and riots of several years ago (in which history and fiction are curiously blurred), it need not concern us here. *Why Are We In Vietnam?* (New York: G. P. Putnam's Sons, 1967) is a novel of considerable power, wit, and ultimately the source of much exasperation. That it promises a new fictional direction, however, is not clearly enough presaged.

Both old and new Mailer leave their imprint on the novel. The preoccupation with the Hemingway cult of physical bravery shows no sign of dimming. Nor has Mailer rid himself as yet of the naughty boy syndrome that delights in shocking the stuffy respectability of one's elders with dirty words. A case can be made for his stress on the scatological and the obsessively sexual, given the narrative point of view of a wiseacre Texan adolescent, with a family background of more money than breeding; but the exuberant excesses of Mailer's language inevitably end up pummeling the reader into stunned insensibility. In this respect, a concern for America's psychic and sexual health continues to exercise Mailer and to betray him into extravagances.

Yet *Why Are We In Vietnam?* is by no means the instance of stunted powers, of solipsistic infantilism, that so many of the reviewers would have us believe. Indeed, the novel shows Mailer still ready to take chances, still determinedly striking up the Amazon River of the American psyche. And the indication is that he has grown in literary power and sophistication, in his ability to work within a literary tradition, drawing strength from it without being overpowered by it. His updating of Faulkner's *The Bear,* by placing that Mississippian tale of initiation and Southern guilt into the contemporary frame of national guilt and Texan sanctimony and bumptiousness, contributes startlingly to the continuing discovery of America. His control of narration, point of view, character, and particularly dialogue, is firmer than in the past. There is also heard the saving grace of humor, a new note of willing suspension of judgment that augurs well for the future. Whether this growth adds up to a new departure is a moot point; but it does indicate that Mailer cannot yet be written off as a writer who never realized his initial promise.

PHILOSOPHER-METAPHYSICIAN—2

Richard D. Finholt

Otherwise How Explain? Norman Mailer's New Cosmology

Norman Mailer began his career writing safely within the American naturalistic tradition. *The Naked And The Dead,* according to M. H. Abrams, is characteristic of novels written within this tradition that takes as its premise the "post-Darwinian" notion that "man belongs entirely in the order of nature and does not have a soul or any other connection with a religious or spiritual world beyond nature; that man is therefore merely a higher-order animal whose character and fortunes are determined by two kinds of natural forces, heredity and environment. He inherits his personal traits and his compulsive instincts, especially hunger and sex, and he is subject to the social and economic forces in the family, the class and the milieu into which he is born."[1] Such an understanding of human motivation seems sufficient for many modern writers to explain the human actions they wish to picture. And few, especially since the rise of existentialism, seem to have needed to fall back on the older conceptions of various spiritual forces transcending and controlling human motivation and behavior. In his two novels of the 1960's, however, Mailer seems to have transformed modern naturalistic and existential insights into a new vision of the supernatural forces determining man's "heredity and environment." The first and better of these novels, *An American Dream,* attempts an answer to a question the detective Leznicki asks, "Why'd you kill her, Rojack?" (*AD,* p. 72.)[2] Had Rojack been ready or able to confess, probably the most valid reply he could make would be another question, *Why Are We in Vietnam?* the title of the second novel. Both questions have the same answer, but that answer cannot be found in the various naturalistic and behavioristic formulas with which modern man likes to characterize the absurdity and despair of his new found existential condition. It cannot be found there, that is, unless modern man looks into them for the supernatural implications of the fantastic and inexplicable mysteries behind man's natural "compulsive instincts." As Mailer puts it: "We are all after all agents of Satan and the Lord, cause otherwise how explain the phenomenological extremities of hot shit and hurricane?" (*WV,* p. 27-28). The gist of Mailer's intellectual challenge seems clear: there are more things in your "milieu," post-Darwinians, than are dreamt of in your determinism.

Mailer seems to have built a complete cosmology around his resurrection of the notion that man acts as the agent of external, eternal, and omnipotent cosmic forces. They are not "Satan and the Lord" exactly, this identification being more metaphorical than anything else. But Mailer's system does appear to be analogous to the conception of the "Great Chain of Being" that dominated traditional Christian cosmology well past the Elizabethan age. Mailer appears to be aware of the psychological principles underlying the Elizabethan's attraction to such a concept. E. M. W. Tillyard suggests that the old-time cosmology proceeded from man's fear and his longing for a benevolent "order" to a world he could not hope to control: "If the Elizabethans believed in an ideal order animating earthly order, they were terrified lest it should be upset, and appalled by the visible tokens of disorder that suggested its upsetting. They were obsessed by the fear of chaos and the fact of mutability; and the obsession was powerful in proportion as their faith in the cosmic order was strong."[3] As a consequence of this fear, the conception of a "fixed system" that the Middle Ages and Renaissance developed from Plato and Christianity became not altogether separable from what Tillyard calls "the terrors of primitive superstition": "At the time when Christianity was young and growing, there was general terror of the stars and a wide practice of astrology. The terror was mainly superstitious, and the only way of mitigating the stars' enmity was through magic" (*EWP*, p. 53). But the important point, Tillyard goes on to add, is that "the Elizabethan believed in the pervasive operation of an external fate in the world." The ultimate source of this fate was to be found in God or the *Primum Mobile*, but Elizabethan man, harkening back to his primitive origins, tended to locate its controlling power in the moon. In fact, the moon became the borderline between the frightening mutability that sin had subjected man to (sublunary) and the eternal immutability of the spiritual spheres. And, because Elizabethan man could see the "correspondences" between human events and natural phenomena, he could believe in his own involuntary participation in the cosmic "dance" just as his science could comprehend "the seas dancing in obedience to the moon" (*EWP*, p. 103).

Mailer's superstition is just as primitive, but Mailer would say it is necessarily so. The truth he seeks is beyond the intellect, tamed by "sublimation" of civilized man; what he needs to recapture, he declares, "is sophistication of the wise primitive in a giant jungle."[4] Consequently, "magic," which modern man had discarded, takes its place in Mailer's scheme alongside the modern notions of "dread and the perception of death" as "the roots of motivation" (*AD*, p. 15). Appropriately, Mailer's vestigial hero Rojack talks to the moon, his master; and the moon, of course, talks back (*AD*, p. 18).

But, besides the power of magic, Elizabethan man could use his science to assure himself of not only the benevolence of the cosmic order but his own place in it. He conceived of the physical universe, including man's body, as composed of only four elements. This insured not only the harmony of the cosmic "dance" but the necessity of human participation. As

Mr. Tillyard puts it: "References to the elements in Elizabethan literature are very many and their imaginative function
is to link the doings of men with the business of the cosmos,
to show events not merely happening but happening in con-
junction with so much else" (*EWP*, p. 64).

The naturalistic idea that "man belongs entirely in the
order of nature" is not far removed from the Elizabethan idea
that man is subject, like the other animals, to a universal, di-
vinely-ordained "law of nature." What differentiates the old
conception and naturalistic ones is the Elizabethan's ability to
invest what Mr. Tillyard calls a "soul" (*EWP*, p. 46) in the
processes of nature. This belief allowed him, moreover, to
maintain a belief in his own free will even while insisting on
the determinism of natural law. The "soul" of the universe was
a benevolent God. Further, men believe that they too possessed
souls, created in the image of God, participating in the nature
of God; and, to the extent that God had free will while still
obeying his own laws, man, to the limit of his imperfections,
did too. They could go so far as to see man as the "microcosm" of the "macrocosm," and, as such, he was thought to
contain not only the pattern of physical creation, but the
"purely rational or spiritual" essence of the *Primum Mobile*
as well (*EWP*, p. 28). But modern man has no conception of
a "dual" nature in men. He does not ascribe to himself an
immutable essence that transcends his mutable physical existence. Consequently, the fatality in his outlook can be
explained by the fact that he has been forced to abdicate his
deity, that he has been forced to see himself just as rigidly
controlled by natural instincts and the laws of mutability as
any other animal.

Mailer shares this fatalism and even surpasses it, because
he grants the instincts supernatural as well as natural power.
Likewise, his only intellectual complaint with existentialists is
their ignoring the mysterious and religious in their emphasis
upon the process of this sublunary physical world:

> To be a real existentialist (Sartre admittedly to the contrary)
> one must be religious, one must have one's sense of the "pur-

pose"—whatever the purpose may be—but a life which is directed by one's faith in the necessity of action is life committed to the notion that the substratum of existence is the search, the end meaningful but mysterious; it is impossible to live such a life unless one's emotions provide their profound conviction. Only the French, alienated beyond alienation from their unconscious, could welcome an existential philosophy without ever feeling it at all. . . .[5]

Medieval man may not have been able (or may not have wanted) to ascribe the roots of his cosmology to his unconscious as Mailer does, but he was wise in his time. He knew that those unseen inner forces that motivated man *must* be assigned to a cosmic sphere, "cause otherwise how explain . . .?"

Norman Mailer, courageous enough to confront his unconscious, is now ready to admit to another idea of the nature of the universe and man's place in it. Because he knows that medieval and Elizabethan thinkers were looking into their own unconscious and not out at the stars when they saw man as the microcosm, he knows that they could not be far from wrong. And because he knows that the naturalistic thinkers were looking into their own unconscious and not out at the animals when they saw man in the grip of the natural instincts, he knows they could not be far wrong either. A synthesis of these different notions has profound implications. If God is dead, man is an animal. Take man's immutable soul away from man, and he loses his free will, becoming absolute slave to the laws of mutability, just another beast. The thinkers of the old cosmology knew this; Tillyard states that Raleigh, for example, acknowledged, "The stars . . . had absolute sway over plants and beasts" (*EWP*, p. 60). This is old wisdom. However, if one admits of man's animal nature and still insists on man as the microcosm, he puts the old wisdom into new bottles. Man, the microcosm, contains within his nature the transcending link between the process and the power, between physical reality and the laws that transcend and control it. Mailer knows that the old-time thinkers, because of the desperation of their wishful thinking, looked for the mirror image of this transcendent power within their *minds*. But he also knows that when spirit and free will are denied to man they must be denied to the "soul" and the universe also. Now when modern man looks into his unconscious for the power that transcends it, he will see the mirror image of his animal *body:* "The lights were saying that there was something up here, and it was really here, yeah God was here, and He was real and no man was He, but a beast, some beast of a giant jaw and cavernous mouth with a full cave's breath and fangs, and secret call: come to me" (*WV,* p. 217). Man is like the salmon returning to spawn; he has no free will in the teeth of the all-powerful homing instinct that transcends his unconscious and guides him to destruction. But the irony beyond irony that Mailer is suggesting is that, since God is a beast, He can have no free will either. He is as rigidly mechanistic, as rigidly non-rational, as the salmon's homing instinct, which, in turn, has no free will in the teeth of the law of mutability (the birth-death cycle) that its intricate psychological machinery serves. Thus, God has no choice but to call "come to me" to man, just as a beast has no choice but to proceed to eat the beast that it has chased and killed: it is all an integral part of the cycle. The homing instinct does not reason with the salmon; it compels the salmon. Similarly, the Beast bludgeons with the natural instincts, and man is forced to come. This is what Mailer means when he has D.J. say, "If the center of things is insane, it is insane with force" (*WV,* p. 151).

Insanity is the ultimate nature of the universe because the machinery is in control, unreasoning, forcing forward, machinery as the *raison d'être* of machinery, a macrocosmic-crazed fanatic for whom zeal is the object of zeal. The old-time thinkers, looking deep within their unconscious, sensed this fact, and with the analogical light of astrology they were able to project a vision of it into the heavens. Because they were able to feel the machinery in motion, they were able to conceive of the universe as an harmonious "dance" (*EWP,* pp. 101-106); and, because they could feel their own movement in the dance, they knew that the dancing partner of the stars must be Fate. What is fascinating to a modern thinker like Mailer is that the old conception of the universe as a "dance" is almost perfectly parallel to the picture that Einstein's Unified Field Theory provides. The more fascinating question this elicits is: if the Elizabethans were right about the *dance* of the stars, could they also have been right about their dancing *partner?*

Einstein pondered the apparent division of the universe into matter and energy, and he decided that they are one, dissimilar only in temporary state.[6] Thus, the elemental building blocks of nature are more inseparable than any Elizabethan, with his emphasis on only four elements, could have hoped. Further, Einstein decided that the motion of electricity and magnetism cannot be differentiated, that neither can gravity and inertia, that neither can uniform and non-uniform motion; that motion, indeed, is the underlying fact of the universe. Thus, according to modern theory, the bodies of the universe *do* move in a "dance," one more unified and harmonious than any Elizabethan could have imagined. The old science located the cause of the motion in the force each body exerted on other bodies. But now Einstein discovers that force does not cause motion; motion causes what had been called force. As Lincoln Barnett explains it: "Einstein's Law of Gravitation contains nothing about force. It describes the behavior of objects in a gravitational field—the planets, for example—not in terms of 'attraction' but simply in terms of the paths they follow. To Einstein, gravitation is simply part of inertia; the movements of the stars and the planets stem from their inherent inertia."[7] Every body, big and little, moves in concert with other bodies, and as they move gravitational and electromagnetic fields develop that define the tempo and direction of any given body. "And, underlying all the harmonious movement of the universe, there is a deeper reality"—in Mr. Barnett's words, "a basic universal field within which gravitational and electromagnetic fields are merely particular ephemeral forms or conditions of state."[8] Motion, the machination of the universe, is in control. Insane, but in this conception, Mr. Barnett suggests, rests the hope of ultimate explanation that the old Chain of Being promised:

> Whether the whole grand objective of a Unified Theory will be realized only many more . . . years of mathematical and experimental work can determine. But in its vast cosmic picture, when fully revealed, the abyss between macrocosmic and microcosmic—the very big and the very little—will surely be bridged, and the whole complex of the universe will resolve into a homogeneous fabric in which matter from the slow wheeling of the galaxies to the wild flight of electrons become simply changes in the structure and concentrations of the primordial field.[9]

Just as the thinkers of the old cosmology used their science to explain man's link to the nature of the universe, Mailer uses modern science to examine the nature of the "deeper reality" as it operates in man. Modern mathematics cannot say *why* its laws work; it cannot even suggest *how* they work; it can only describe *what* happens *when* they work. Similarly, Mailer does not try to explain the why or the how of that Force that the old thinkers identified as "Satan and the Lord." He only attempts to describe the *what* of that Force. It seems, and I will so assume for the sake of simplicity, that the "God" he is describing is somehow the manifestation of the primordial field, and that this universal law of motion is what the microcosm, any particular human being, participates in when he transcends his physical environment to experience the essence of God's power. In "The White Negro," Mailer goes so far as to suggest that maybe, just maybe, man, by tuning into motion, can capture a little of that deifying free will that the old cosmology promised at "the center of things": "In motion a man has a chance, his body is warm, his instincts are quick, and when the crisis comes, whether of love or violence, he can make it, he can win, he can release a little more energy for himself. . . ."[10]

Rojack can only receive his vision of "heaven" on the other side of the "door" at the climax of the periods of the purest, least reflective, most self-perpetuating, most godlike, motion: when he murders Deborah (*AD,* p. 35) and when he creates an embryo with Cherry (*AD,* p. 122). Mailer must be thinking of that sensation we all have, in a moment of intense crisis or danger, that time is suspended in a slow, graceful, terrifying dance when in reality our body rate has speeded up and events are clashing upon one another in the rapid succession of the moment. Perhaps there is a psychic analogue to Einstein's theory that as an object approaches the speed of light its relative time slows down till, at the ultimate speed, time stops altogether. Perhaps, if there is such an analogue, man could still achieve some kind of salvation or immortality. At any rate, Rojack in the end loses his courage to move, and hence he loses his godlike momentum. Facing Kelly's challenge to walk the parapet, Rojack knows from where he will have to draw his power: "I had to keep moving, everything was getting worse the longer I stayed still, but my feet were bad again" (*AD,* p. 242). He walks the parapet once for himself, the voice of God tells him he will have to walk it a second time for Cherry; but he loses his courage, and Cherry dies. He had a chance to win her on the parapet, in the deifying movement of the present, but his mind drifts to the past and then to the future, and nothing can ever move in either the past or the future.

Mailer probably intended Rojack to be a tragic hero of the new cosmological order, just as Lear and Hamlet were tragic heroes caught in the process of the old order. But it takes a certain degree of romanticism to take tragedy seriously, and Mailer in his new book *Of a Fire on the Moon* suggests that ever since the death of Hemingway he has been willing to grant man less and less of a fighting chance against the cosmos: "Hemingway had given the power to believe you could still shout down the corridor of the hospital, live next to the breath of the beast, accept your portion of dread every day. Now the greatest living romantic was dead. Dread was loose. The giant had paid his dues, and something awful was in the air. Technology would fill the pause. Into the silences static would enter. It was conceivable that man was no longer ready to share the dread of the Lord."[11] Hence, there are no Rojack-like tragic heroes in *Why Are We in Vietnam;* the narrator D.J., rather than being absorbed completely into the action, sits motionless enveloping it with his mind and memory, the static explicator of man's fate.

D.J. appears to be the adolescent counterpart of the Hipster "psychopath" that Mailer describes in "The White Negro." This is the individual whose instincts are as sharp as an animal's because his fast life of perpetual danger, drugs, and existential despair has forced him to live, as the animals must, within the unsafe "groove" or motion of the present (unlike the civilized man whose reflective existence allows him to escape into the mental world of the past and future—far from the essence and "dread of the Lord."). D.J.'s foul, scatological language can be explained as the result of the Hipster's intense experience of God in the motion of the present. He understands the underlying animal essence of our existential condition and needs a holy language adequately to express it: "It is not too difficult to believe that the language of Hip which evolved was an artful language, tested and shaped by intense experience and therefore different in kind from white slang, as different as the special obscenity of the soldier, which in its emphasis upon 'ass' as the soul and 'shit' as circumstance, was able to express the existential states of the enlisted man."[12] But, as the language of the Hipster reaches down to express the purely animal processes of man's existence, it cannot do otherwise than reach out to embrace the nature of the universe because man is the microcosm: "It is a pictorial language . . . imbued with the dialectic of small but intense change, a language for the microcosm, in this case, man, for it takes the immediate experiences of any passing man and magnifies the dynamic of his movements, not specifically but abstractly so that he is seen more as a vector in a network of forces than as a static character in a crystallized field."[13]

Get ready to experience D.J., and come ready to believe that shit is literally our circumstance and that our transcendent

essence, thanks to our godgiven participation in the primordial
field, is in our asses. The essence of the universe, like the
essence of the microcosm, is not spiritual but bestial. God
has been programed by the laws of motion to be a beast,
and God in turn programs man's instincts. Elizabethan
thinkers had been unable to find macrocosmic correspondences for man's heart and head, but they seem never to have
pondered the macrocosmic correspondence for his penis. But
D.J. knows that if God is bestial, then man's penis and not
his mind is that part that has been created in the image of
God. And he can conceptualize the Divine creative act in
terms of the sex act. The macrocosmic penis, he tells us, has
been "slipping right into us" into the "bowels of creation"
(*WV*, p. 24), our collective anus. It has conceived "DNA/
RNA," the embryo of our all-determining instincts, and mankind is off like a "vector" in a field of force.

Lear could see a correspondence between his inner
emotions and the outer phenomena of the storm because he
was sure of his own microcosmic identity and participation
in the essence of the macrocosm; D. J. holds a similar belief.
Just as God has slipped his essence into man, that "electromagnetic field called earth" is the result of the principle of
motion funneling into the earth at its North and South Pole
"orifice" (*WV*, p. 168). Thus, it is easy to contemplate how
the powers of the earth correspond to the powers within man
and why all the animals in the magnetically intense North
Pole region can be "tuned in" (*WV*, p. 57) to the powers of
motion that transcend and control them. The thinkers of the
old cosmology explained such sympathetic harmony of man
and nature in a scientific "language for the microcosm" that
compared the humor in man to the four elements that were
thought to determine the nature of natural phenomena. Mailer's parallel language turns the physics of Relativity and
Field Theory into a metaphysical vision of how the law of
motion controls human behavior just as surely and mysteriously as it does the movement of an iron filing, planet, sun,

or galaxy through whatever electromagnetic fields determine
their respective fates:

> Where you going when you sleep? Well, hole, there's only
> one place you go, and that's into the undiscovered magnetic-
> electro fief of the dream, which is opposed to the electro-
> magnetic field of the earth just as properly as the square root
> of minus one is opposed to one. Right! They never figured
> out yet whether light is wave, corpuscle, or hung up on finding
> her own identity, all they know once you get down to it is
> that light is bright, and therefore not necessarily opposed to
> being part of Universal Mind. . . . Clem—you can't get fucked
> for less—here is the sweet intimate underground poop: when
> you go into sleep, that mind of yours leaps, stirs, and sifts
> itself into the Magnetic-Electro fief of the dream, . . . you are
> a part of the spook flux of the night like an iron filing in the
> E.M. field . . . and it all flows, mind and asshole, anode and
> cathode, you sending messages and receiving all through the
> night. . . . (WV, p. 180)

And Rojack can sense this Universal Mind or primordial field
grooving the path of his intense Odyssey: "There was a
presence in the room like the command of a dead pharaoh.
. . . Even as a magnet directs every iron particle in a crowd of
filings, so a field of force was on me here. . . . That same field
of force had come on me as I left Deborah's body on the floor
and started down the stairs to the room where Ruta was
waiting" (AD, p. 220).

If man is fully to comprehend "the phenomenological
extremities" of the "hot shit" of his microcosmic self and
the "hurricane" of the natural correspondence, he must now
be ready to understand that any electromagnetic field has
within itself the capability of restructure, of reversal: "Just
no chance, know this, you are a part of the dream field, you
the square root of minus one, you off in a flux, part of a
circuit, you swinging on the inside of a deep mystery which
is whatever is electricity and who is magnetism. . . . Magnetism potential and electricity actual of the Prince himself? . . .
the electricity and magnetism of the dream field is reversed
—God or the Devil takes over in sleep—what simpler explanation you got . . . " (WV, p. 182). The essence of the

"no chance" is that, though man may swing for a time "on the inside of a deep mystery," the Universal Mind can reverse the flow of power, change the nature of its field, without notice. Whether it is the Devil or the Lord taking over the microcosm's mind depends on how the primordial field, that Beast called God, is defining itself at any given moment. Motion or God's essence appears to be "hung up on finding" its "own identity," making man's attempts at "codifying" what Mailer calls "the suppositions on which his inner universe is constructed"[14] a vain and "dangerous" pursuit.

The significance of Rojack's sexual bout with Ruta is that in alternating between her anus and her vagina, which he calls "a raid on the Devil and a trip back to the Lord" (*AD,* p. 48), he is merely acting out "the phenomenological extremities" of his microcosmic part. To say that Rojack is selling his soul to the Devil here is to think romantically (and maybe Mailer was). Rojack and his race were born sold. Rojack has no decision to make here, no existential "choice" like the one Max F. Schulz has suggested,[15] but is merely following, as he says, "a command from inside of me." Rojack knows from his first glimpse into the German soldier's eyes from whence his commands come. Riddled with superstitious fear, he may have "one toe pointing at the moon," but he knows that in reality it is " . . . instinct . . . telling" him "to die" (*AD,* p. 19).

Similarly, the sexual bout between D.J. and Tex cannot ultimately be a battle of wills since this possibility rests upon the assumption that free will exists. D.J.'s attempt to "prong" Tex is only in *his* mind an attempt to "steal the iron from Texas' ass and put it in his own" (*WV,* p. 219). On a deeper plane, it is analogous to and a microcosmic perpetuation of the pronging of mankind by the macrocosmic penis long, long ago. Man was presented then with an "asshole transistor to God" (*WV,* p. 35); and, at the moment of microcosmic repetition, it sends the message out, electricity activates the magnetic field, and God reveals the mirror image of Himself in the actions of his bestial slaves:

So they breathed hard with all of this, lying next to each other like two rods getting charged with magnetism in electric coils. . . . They could almost have got up and walked across the pond and into the north without their boots, going up to disappear and die and join that great beast. In the field of all such desire D.J. raised his hand to put it square on Tex's cock and squeeze and just before he did the Northern lights shifted on that moment and a coil of sound went off in the night like a blowout in some circuit fuse of the structure of the dark . . . now it was there, murder between them under all friendship, for God was a beast, not a man, and God said, "Go out and kill—fulfill my will, go and kill, and they hung there on the knife of the divide in all conflict of lust to own the other . . . and they were twins, never to be as near as lovers again, but killer brothers, owned by something, prince of darkness, lord of light, they did not know; they just knew telepathy was on them. . . . (*WV*, pp. 216, 217–18, 219)

Man has always known subliminally and has always been ready to deny that he is "owned by something." The thinkers of the old cosmology were willing to admit of the possibility but only so long as their rationalism and science would allow them to assume the benevolence of their owner. But modern thinkers, having been robbed by their rationalism and science century by century of the security of the old assumption, cannot afford to admit the full possibilities in being so owned. Mailer seems to understand that precisely because the old-time thinkers felt secure they could afford to take a fairly accurate analogical picture of their inner nature and its seemingly undeniable connection with the essence of the cosmos. Likewise, Mailer seems suspicious of the modern thinker's haste to explain away or ignore the mysterious and the seemingly supernatural forces operating within him. Existential man, in his quest for self-determination and self-exaltation, can afford to admit the power of the degrading but still manageable natural instincts but cannot afford to admit that the power of these instincts is supernatural and absolute.

Norman Mailer, in wedding the old vision to the new science, has broken those lingering last vestiges of romantic wishful thinking that distort the otherwise penetrating insights of "post-Darwinian" determinism. And his new cosmology provides not merely evocative metaphors but metaphors, like those of the old order, that are grounded in the truth at the "center of things"—at the center of man.

NOTES

1. *A Glossary of Literary Terms,* 3rd ed. (New York: Holt, Rinehart and Winston, 1971), p. 142.

2. Parenthetical pagination refers to the 1966 Dell edition of *An American Dream (AD)* and the 1968 G. P. Putnam's Berkley Medallion edition of *Why Are We in Vietnam? (WV)*.

3. *The Elizabethan World Picture* (New York: Random House, n.d.), p. 16. Further references to this work *(EWP)* are included in parentheses in the text.

4. "The White Negro," *Advertisements for Myself* (New York: G. P. Putnam's Sons, 1966), p. 317.

5. "The White Negro," p. 315.

6. Lincoln Barnett, *The Universe and Dr. Einstein,* rev. ed. (New York: Bantam, 1968), p. 63.

7. Barnett, p. 82.

8. Barnett, p. 111.

9. Barnett, p. 14.

10. "The White Negro," p. 323.

11. *Of a Fire on the Moon* (Boston, Toronto: Little, Brown and Company, 1970), p. 14.

12. "The White Negro," p. 322.

13. "The White Negro," p. 322.

14. "The White Negro," p. 316.

15. "Mailer's Divine Comedy," *Contemporary Literature,* 9 (Winter 1968), 53-54. In this overly complex but helpful article, Mr. Schulz traces Mailer's philosophical roots back through Western theological tradition. He analyzes the moral vision that motivates Mailer's essentially romantic heroes; however, he neglects the dark overtones of Mailer's equally traditional cosmological vision. The full implication of the new cosmology is that "dread" *is* "loose" and romantic or existential "medicine" nothing but a placebo.

IN THE AMERICAN TRADITION

Michael Cowan

The Americanness of Norman Mailer

One of the most revealing critical debates surrounding Norman Mailer's writings has had to do with his Americanness —the extent to which he has been a hapless reflector or even victim of America's prevailing middle-class mores, and the extent to which he has been a successful and self-conscious critic of, conscience for, and even prophet to his country and times. One of the most recent expressions of the first view is Kate Millett's suggestion, in *Sexual Politics,* that "Sexual congress in a Mailer novel is always a matter of strenuous endeavor, rather like mountain-climbing—a straining ever upward after achievement. In this, as in so many ways, Mailer is authentically American."[1] Alan Trachtenberg, on the other hand, has said that *The Armies of the Night* could have been written only by "a writer steeped in American life, with all his wits about him," and that Mailer's "extremities of style are directly in response to extremities and disproportions and incongruities" in the American experience.[2]

In fact, Mailer believes that one of the writer's highest goals is to "clarify a nation's vision of itself" (*CC*, p. 98).[3] As he implies at the end of *The Armies of the Night*, he has continuously judged his own career as a writer by his ability to challenge Americans to reaffirm that their nation is "the land where a new kind of man was born from the idea that God was present in every man not only as compassion but as power, and so the country belonged to the people; for the will of the people—if the locks of their life could be given the art to turn—was then the will of God" (*Arm,* p. 288).

Mailer's view of the underlying pattern of American history is not particularly original, but it places him firmly in line with many major American writers from Emerson and Melville to Faulkner: the belief that American development is the product of a confrontation with virgin nature on a vast scale; the rapid and accelerating rate of social and psychological change that results from the American attempt to fill such large natural space with a burgeoning machine technology; the heterogeneous background of the Americans—immigrants all—partly melting into a new composite American, partly exacerbating social tensions as they whirl around the white Protestant center. The "revolution of consciousness" he calls for in *Advertisements for Myself* is primarily a call for a psyche capable of confronting its own wilderness of possibilities. The American, working from a sense of large territorial possibilities, feels a vast potential for remaking himself, for becoming a "new man." But in experimenting with many possible "new selves," he begins to lose a clear sense of possessing any stable self. The goal of the American novelist, Mailer believes, is not only to dramatize this schizophrenia in the national psyche—to remain true to a vision of the essential doubleness at the heart of the American dream —but to affirm that the creative implications of this doubleness are ultimately more worthy of faith than the destructive implications. Like Faulkner in his Nobel Prize address, Mailer still clings to the hope that, although "one must balance every moment between the angel in oneself and the swine" (*MI,* p. 93), the angel still has the possibility of winning out—though only if one first faces the swine as courageously as he can. Mailer proposes that an American's best chance for salvation depends on treating the conflict at the center of the national psyche as an epic battle.

In light of such concerns, it should not be surprising that, of all nineteenth-century American writers, the one from whom Mailer most obviously draws strength and lessons is Herman Melville. No doubt one reason for his appeal to Mailer lies in the immensity of Mailer's literary ambitions. In *Advertisements for Myself,* Mailer proclaims his own ambition "to write a novel which Dostoevsky and Marx; Joyce and Freud; Stendhal, Tolstoy, Proust and Spengler; Faulkner, and even old moldering Hemingway might come to read, for it would carry what they had to tell another part of the way" (*Adv,* p. 477); and echoing Ishmael's own statement, he speaks of this novel as "a descendant of Moby Dick which will call for such time, strength, cash and patience that I do not know if I have it all to give, and so will . . . avoid the dream" (*Adv,* p. 156).

Mailer's proclamation prompted F. W. Dupee to argue that "the attraction of *Moby Dick* to Mailer . . . seem to consist largely in its bulk, profundity, and prestige. It is to him . . . an image of literary power rather than a work to be admired, learned from and then returned to its place of honor."[4] In fact, however, Mailer's response to *Moby Dick* has been more intricate and thoughtful than Dupee suggests. Another reason for Mailer's attraction to Melville is implied in his discussion of the backgrounds of modern American literature in his *Esquire* essay on "Some Children of the Goddess":

> Tolstoy and Dostoevsky divided the central terrain of the modern novel between them. Tolstoy's concern was with men-in-the-world, and indeed the panorama of his book carries to us an image of a huge landscape peopled with figures who changed that landscape, whereas the bulk of Dostoevsky's work could take place in ten closed rooms: it is not society but a series of individuals we remember, each illuminated by the terror of exploring the mystery of themselves. . . . One can point to *Moby Dick* as a perfect example of a novel in the second category—a book whose action depends upon the voyage of Ahab into his obsession. . . . [*CC,* p. 128]

Mailer's own response to the inward voyage of the self into

its own obsession is traceable in his fictional protagonists, and certainly in the self-image that he presents in *Advertisements* and other works. Whatever sense of himself that Mailer has gleaned from Hemingway or Malraux or other "artists of action," he has certainly discovered an equally powerful model in the oceanic depths of *Moby Dick.*

The decor of Mailer's Brooklyn Heights duplex apartment, as described by a *Playboy* interviewer in 1968, is perhaps one way in which Mailer has responded to this model: "Nautical items abound, from the brass ship's clock over the kitchen and the dismantled engine-room telegraph beside the big bookcases to the glass-and-wood gable forecastle, which Mailer built above the kitchen and bedrooms and which can be reached only by climbing ropes, trapezes or deck ladders." Mailer's appeal to the sense of adventurousness symbolized by a voyaging ship has often extended beyond his own residence. In an article for the *New York Times* he proposes cities reaching into the clouds whose buildings "could begin to look a little less like armored tanks and more like clipper ships" and whose airborne residents could "feel the dignity of sailors on a four-master at sea . . . returned to that mixture of awe and elation, of dignity and self-respect and a hint of dread, that sense of zest which a man must have known working his way out along a yardarm in a stiff breeze at sea" (*CC,* p. 237). It is just these sorts of complex feelings that Stephen Rojack experiences as he walks around the parapet of Barney Kelly's penthouse apartment: "as used up as a sailor who has been tied for hours in the rigging of a four-master beating through a storm" (*AD,* p. 259). Mailer's characteristic advocacy of Americans' need for adventurous voyages into the dangerous frontier world of the self seems, by Mailer's own statements, to find a strong counterpart in Melville.

We are told in *The Naked and the Dead* that Robert Hearn's senior essay, for which he "has been given a magna" at Harvard is entitled *A Study of the Cosmic Urge in Herman Melville* (*ND,* p. 345). The world that Hearn attempts unsuccessfully to come to terms with on Anopopei (perhaps this is why Mailer gives him a magna rather than a summa) is a wild landscape dominated by the mania of a commander and the presence of an unconquerable leviathan. "The biggest influence on *Naked*," Mailer remarked in 1951, "was *Moby Dick* . . . I was sure everyone would know. I had Ahab in it, and I suppose the mountain was Moby Dick."[5] It is unwise to press too hard for precise parallels between the two novels. Hearn, for example, may resemble Ishmael in his intellectual background, his speculative habits, and the ennui that drives him onto the uncharted sea of war, but in his confrontation of Cummings or Croft, he comes closer to expressing what Melville calls the "unaided virtue" of Starbuck. Cummings and Croft share the role of Ahab. And the heterogeneous backgrounds and values of Croft's patrol make it a paler version of the *Pequod's* crew. Like Melville's whalers, each soldier of the patrol finds himself on a mission that comes to involve not only a primal struggle with social authority or a non-human wilderness but a nightmarish war with the ambiguities and divisions of his own inner nature.

The central symbol of these ambiguities and dangers is Mount Anaka itself, which, like Moby Dick, casts its awesome presence over the entire novel, inspiring men to conquest but confronting them with naked ambiguities about themselves and their world. Anaka is unreachable not only physically but intellectually; like Moby Dick or the doubloon that Ahab nails to the *Pequod's* mast, the mountain is always viewed partially. And as in Melville's novel, the varying and even conflicting meanings that individual characters read into Anaka tell as much about themselves as about the mountain. To Gallagher, for example, "the mountain seemed wise and powerful, and terrifying in its size. Gallagher stared at it in absorption, caught by a sense of beauty he could not express. The idea, the vision he always held of something finer and neater and more beautiful than the moil in which he lived trembled now, pitched almost to a climax of words . . . but it passed and he was left with a troubled joy, an echo of rapture" (*ND*, p. 447). Roth fears the mountain—it seems to him "so open, so high"—and prefers even the suffocating jungle "to these naked ridges, these gaunt alien vaults of stone and sky. . . . The jungle was filled with all kinds of dangers but they did not seem so severe now. . . . But here, one misstep and it would be death. It was better to live in a cellar than to walk a tightrope" (ND, p. 638). Hearn finds that the mountain "roused his awe and then his fear. It was too immense, too powerful. He suffered a faint sharp thrill as he watched the mist eddy about the peak. He imagined the ocean actually driving against a rockbound coast, and despite himself strained his ears as though he could hear the sound of such a titanic struggle" (ND, p. 497). To Croft too "the mountain looked like a rocky coast and the murky sky seemed to be an ocean shattering its foam upon the shore." But Croft finds Anaka more compelling than does Hearn:

> The mountain and the cloud and the sky were purer, more intense, in their gelid silent struggle than any ocean and any shore he had ever seen. The rocks gathered themselves in the darkness, huddled together against the fury of the water. The context seemed an infinite distance away, and he felt a thrill of anticipation at the thought that by the following night they might be on the peak. Again, he felt a crude ecstasy. He could not have given the reason, but the mountain tormented him, held an answer to something he wanted. It was so pure, so austere. [ND, p. 497]

Whereas Hearn is more impressed with the dangers and ambiguities suggested in his mind by Anaka—"It was the kind of shore upon which huge ships would founder, smash apart, and sink in a few minutes" (ND, p. 498)—Croft is more compelled by the intensity and purity of its challenge to his own powers: "He led the platoon up the mountain without hesitation. . . . Despite all the exertion of the preceding days, he was restless and impatient now, driven forward by a demanding tension in himself. . . . He was continuously eager to press on to the next rise, anxious to see what was beyond. The sheer mass of the mountain inflamed him" (ND, p. 635). And his failure to conquer Anaka is important not for what it tells him about his physical limitations but for what it has revealed to him about his inner nature: "Deep inside himself, Croft was relieved that he had not been able to climb the mountain . . . [and] was rested by the unadmitted knowledge that he had found a limit to his hunger" (*ND*, p. 701).

As *The Naked and the Dead* suggests, Mailer mines *Moby Dick* not only for major analogues to the adventures that he has constantly stressed as an essential component of America's psychic and social health but, equally important, for a major symbol of the ambiguities and dangers that attend such excursions. Significantly, since Mailer has taken on the mantle of "historian," he has found Melville's book also a useful reference point for determining how far his countrymen have departed from their "organic" heritage. Observing the 1964 Republican convention, he is reminded of the degeneration that security-minded Americans have allowed to take place in the cultural tradition of which Melville was a part:

> The American mind had gone from Hawthorne and Emerson to the Frug, the Bounce, and Walking the Dog, from *The Flowering of New England* to the cerebrality of professional football in which a quarterback must have not only heart, courage, strength and grace but a mind like an I.B.M. computer. It marks the turn we have taken from the Renaissance. There too was the ideal of a hero with heart, courage, strength, and grace, but he was expected to possess the mind of a passionate artist. Now the best heroes were—in the sense of the Renaissance—mindless. . . . [*CC*, p. 28–29]

This "mindlessness" to which the American imagination has degenerated shows itself in the degeneration of America's major symbols of power. By the time Moby Dick has reached the rudderless world of D. J. in *Why Are We in Vietnam?* he has become merely the occasion for sophomoric wordplay: "Herman Melville go hump Moby and wash his Dick" (*WV*, p. 26). Whereas the American Renaissance's major symbol of power, Moby Dick, combined not only essential ambiguity with dignifying epic drama, contemporary America's major symbols of power, such as the Pentagon, have become not only faceless but utterly without dramatic personality, have become, in fact, "anonymous" signs of the failure of the adventurous symbolizing imagination in American public life. As Mailer treats it in *The Armies of the Night*, the Pentagon becomes almost a travesty on Melville's mighty leviathan:

> The strength of the Pentagon is subtle . . . it is doubtful if there was ever another building in the world so huge in ground plan and so without variation. . . . The Pentagon, architecturally, was as undifferentiated as a jellyfish or a cluster of barnacles. One could chip away at any part of the interior without locating a nervous center. . . . High church of the corporation, the Pentagon spoke exclusively of mass man and his civilization; every aspect of the building was anonymous, monotonous, massive, interchangeable.
>
> For [the Mobilization Committee's] revolutionary explorers, the strangeness of their situation must have been comparable to a reconnaissance of the moon. . . . It was impossible to locate the symbolic loins of the building—paradigm of the modern world indeed, they could explore every inch of their foe and know nothing about him. . . . [*Arm*, p. 226–29]

It may seem somewhat ludicrous to compare the Pentagon to the great whale's "pasteboard mask" through which Ahab wants obsessively to strike or to see in its facelessness the ultimate unknowability that Ishmael sees in the whale ("Dissect him how I may then, I but go skin deep; I know him not, and never will. But if I know not even the tail of this whale, how understand his head? much more, how comprehend his face, when face he has none"). But Mailer feels the same incongruity. The easiest way into the Pentagon, he reminds us, is through its shopping center and cafeteria, and he finds "something absurd" in this possibility. "To attack here was to lose some of one's symbolic momentum—a consideration which might be comic or unpleasant in a shooting war, but in a symbolic war was not necessarily comic at all." (*Arm*, p. 229–30). The decline in the power of the epic symbol is thus not only a reflection of a degeneration of national value but a terrifying reminder of how difficult it is for a contemporary American writer to create an image that again will move his countrymen to heroic action. Mailer is reminded again of this challenge when he visits the Vehicle Assembly Building at Cape Kennedy where Apollo 11 is being built. His first tentative attempt at surrounding the vehicle in epic hyperbole is challenged by the official language in which the vehicle is encased: "VAB—it could be the name of a drink or a deodorant, or it could be suds for the washer. But it was not a name for this warehouse of the gods. . . . Nothing fit anything any longer. The art of communication had become the function, and the machine was the work of art. What a fall for the ego of the artist. What a climb to capture the language again!" (*Fire*, p. 56).

But this imaginatively degenerated world is all that Mailer has. Loving America too much to leave it, he must dig for redemptive metaphors in his native soil. He is thus obviously pleased that, in contrast to the lack of real drama that a super-plastic Miami offers him in 1968, bloody, stockyard-smelling Chicago "gave America its last chance at straight-out drama" and thus provides potential "salvation of the schizophrenic soul." Watching the overwhelming battle at the Chicago Hilton between the protesters and the police, Mailer searches for a mighty image appropriate to the dramatic occasion and finds one in *Moby Dick:*

> It was as if the war had finally begun, and this was therefore a great and solemn moment, as if indeed even the gods of history had come together from each side to choose the very front of the Hilton Hotel before the television cameras of the world and the eyes of the campaign workers and the delegates' wives, yes, there before the eyes of half the principals at the convention was this drama played, as if the military spine of a great liberal party had finally separated itself from the skin, as if, no metaphor large enough to suffice, the Democratic Party had here broken in two before the eyes of a nation like Melville's whale charging right out of the sea. [*MI*, p. 172]

What is interesting about this passage is not merely that Mailer is searching for an epic symbol with which to give weight yet another time to the dialectic of American life, but that he has self-consciously chosen to do so by means of a traditional symbol transformed for his own purposes. Melville's Leviathan, as Mailer treats him, is no longer merely a natural force against which the American must wage his epic and perhaps tragic frontier wars. It has become a symbol of the split at the center of the American's sense of identity. Moby Dick is not merely a frontier threat, but a humanized resource from the past that the American imagination can use in its never-ending struggle to redeem the present. Without denying the existential value of remaining true to the "perpetual climax of the present," Mailer affirms also that such a present is not a break with but an outgrowth of the past, and that the frontiers of the modern consciousness require not only existential resources but in addition the creative adaptation of tools offered by a historical tradition.

In charting Mailer's implicit quest for a usable past as a literary tool, we could profitably compare him not only to Melville but to writers like Hawthorne or Faulkner. In all of these writers, an essential romantic sensibility proposes that high tragedy is more worthy of the human spirit than a divine comedy turned facile, that the individual can often show more dignity in suffering the defeat of his greatest dreams than in winning mundane victories, that guilt is as essential an ingredient as pride to the mature man's self-respect and sense of essential identity. If anything, this traditional stance has become more marked in Mailer's non-fiction since the early sixties. By the time he writes *Armies,* with his penchant for unresolvable oxymorons, he is referring to himself as a "radical conservative" and emphasizing the agony of his attempt to become "some natural aristocrat from these damned democratic states" (*Arm,* p. 41). Asserting his kinship with Robert Lowell and other *"grands conservateurs"* of America's noblest traditions, Mailer has claimed ownership of a hard-won ironic detachment from which he can approach the apocalyptic aspirations of, say, the march on the Pentagon with the sad and yet humanizing understanding that this has not been the first time—and will undoubtedly not be the last—that Americans have gone all-out for apocalypse: that the dream of revolutionary adventure is itself an essential defining characteristic of the American tradition. In fact, it is the link with the past that gives the event much of its resonance:

> As Lowell and Mailer reached the ridge and took a turn to the right to come down from Washington Monument toward the length of the long reflecting pool which led between two long groves of trees near the banks to the steps of Lincoln Memorial, out of that direction came the clear bitter-sweet excitation of a military trumpet resounding in the near distance, one peal which seemed to go all the way back through a galaxy of bugles to the cries of the Civil War and the first trumpet note to blow the attack. The ghosts of old battles were wheeling like clouds over Washington today. [*Arm,* p. 91]

The *enfant terrible* of *Advertisements,* crying for a "revolution of consciousness," has increasingly given way to the brooding "historian," "reporter," and "detective" who, in *Miami,* argues that "we will be fighting for forty years" (*MI,* p. 223).

While in Washington to participate in the march on the Pentagon, Mailer stays at the Hay-Adams hotel and, in the course of pondering his emerging mission as historian, finds himself wondering if "the Adams in the name of his hotel bore any relation to Henry" (*Arm,* p. 54). While we need not make much of his aside, it is interesting to speculate briefly on the kinship of these two historian sons of Harvard, particularly between the Mailer from *Armies* to *Of a Fire* and the Adams of *The Education.* It is in *Armies* that Mailer first dons the third-person narrative guise used by Adams in *The Education,* and for much the same reason. As Alan Trachtenberg remarks, "The implausible assault upon the Pentagon . . . becomes the perfect vehicle to bring Mailer's own inner experience into focus, and Mailer himself, 'a comic hero,' a 'figure of monumental disproportions,' becomes the perfect figure through which 'to recapture the precise feel of the ambiguity of the event and its monumental disproportions.' Much like Henry Adams in his *Education,* Mailer here discovers an aptness between his own posture in the world and the crazy disfigurations of the world itself."[6]

Like Adams, Mailer has increasingly treated his work as

the rather ironic story of an education whose value as preparation for succeeding in or at least understanding a rapidly changing modern world is at best ambiguous. Whereas Adams claims to be an eighteenth-century child trying to prepare in the nineteenth century for a twentieth-century civilization, Mailer seems a nineteenth-century romantic (with a trace of the puritan) trying to straddle the twentieth century in order to seize a twenty-first century that has arrived before its time. Like Adams, Mailer sees history as an accelerating movement from unity to multiplicity. What could be more Adams-like than Mailer's statement in *Of a Fire on the Moon* that:

> It was the first century in history which presented to sane and sober minds the fair chance that the century might not reach the end of its span. It was a world half convinced of the future death of our species yet half aroused by the apocalyptic notion that an exceptional future still lay before us. So it was a century which moved with the most magnificent display of power into directions it could not comprehend. The itch was to accelerate—the metaphysical direction unknown. [*Fire,* p. 48]

Like Adams, Mailer—if with less elegance and historical experience—probes the past for a base from which to triangulate the future. Both writers proceed primarily by manipulating the ambiguities and shifting meanings of an immense series of dualities and by couching these dualities in sweeping and even melodramatic terms. Like *The Education,* Mailer's most recent work is in important ways a poet's search for a metaphorical structure that will at least bring the illusion of order to the multiplying contradictions of modern experience.

The kinship of both writers is most strongly marked in *Of a Fire on the Moon.* Mailer's meditation on the meaning of Apollo 11 is framed usefully by Adams' comments in the last chapter of *The Education.* Approaching New York in 1905 by boat, Adams finds the view of the technologically wondrous city

> more striking than ever—wonderful—unlike anything man had ever seen—and like nothing he ever much cared to see. The outline of the city became frantic in its effort to explain

something that defied meaning. Power seemed to have out-
grown its servitude and to have asserted its freedom. The
cylinder had exploded, and thrown great masses of stone
and steam against the sky. The city had the air and movement of hysteria, and the citizens were crying, in every accent
of anger and alarm, that the new forces must at any cost be
brought under control. . . . He was beyond measure curious
to see whether the conflict of forces would produce the new
man [who could control them], since no other energies
seemed left on earth to breed. The new man could be only
a child born of contact between the new and the old energies.

It is in much the same spirit of distaste and guarded respect
that Mailer observes the "bomb" that he believes Apollo 11 to
be. And out of much the same curiosity that leads Adams to
formulate "A Dynamic Theory of History," Mailer begins to
formulate "a psychology of astronauts" to help explain the
"new men" who must guide the bomb's powers.

As preparation for this task, Mailer rather wryly takes
on the kind of role that Adams finds for himself in the latter
part of the *Education*—that of a senior American statesman
and philosopher whom the world has by-passed and who
therefore must make a virtue out of being an important if detached observer of the rapidly changing scene. If Adams "felt
nothing in common with the world as it promised to be," he
believed "he could at least act as an audience." Mailer describes himself in similar terms: "He has learned to live with
questions. Of course, as always, he has little to do with the
immediate spirit of the time. . . . He has never had less sense
of possessing the age. He feels in fact little more than a decent
spirit, somewhat shunted to the side. It is the best possible
position for detective work." This role of "somewhat disem-
bodied spirit" has an important artistic virtue for Mailer:
"He was conceivably in superb shape to study the flight of
Apollo 11 to the moon. For he was detached this season from
the imperial demands of his ego. . . . He felt like a spirit of
some just-consumed essence of the past . . ." (*Fire*, p. 6).

A philosophical but playful spirit from the past, Mailer
probes the meaning of American technology at the Manned

Spacecraft Center and at Cape Kennedy in much the way that Adams probes the implications of the dynamo at the Chicago, Paris, and St. Louis Expositions. Viewing the dynamo as "a symbol of infinity," Adams treats it as the most appropriate symbol of the age's moral values: "Before the end, one began to pray to it. . . . Among the thousand symbols of ultimate energy, the dynamo was not so human as some, but it was the most expressive." Similarly, Mailer describes the Vehicle Assembly Building as "the antechamber of a new Creation":

> He came to recognize that whatever was in store, a Leviathan was most certainly ready to ascend the heavens—whether for good or ill he might never know—but he was standing at least in the first cathedral of the age of technology, and he might as well recognize that the world would change, that the world had changed, even as he had thought to be pushing and shoving on it with *his* mighty ego. And it had changed in ways he did not recognize, had never anticipated, and could possibly not comprehend now. The change was mightier than he had counted on, the full brawn of the rocket in this cavernous womb of an immensity, this giant cathedral of a machine designed to put together another machine which would voyage through space. Yes, this emergence of a ship to travel the ether was no event he could measure by any philosophy he had been able to put together in his brain. [*Fire,* p. 55]

Facing the force of the dynamo and its problematic relationship to the force of the Virgin, Adams argues that he can search for a means of measurement only by becoming "a pilgrim of power." Mailer adopts the same strategy: "The first step in comprehension was to absorb. . . . He would be, perforce, an acolyte to technology."

As a reluctant acolyte, Mailer forces himself to treat the Apollo 11 not merely as a dynamo but as the moral equivalent to the Virgin of Mont St. Michel and Chartres. Describing the spotlighted rocket on the night before the launch, he wryly suggests that "she looked like a shrine with the lights upon her. In the distance she glowed for all the world like some white stone Madonna in the mountains, welcoming footsore travelers at dusk" (*Fire,* p. 59). He sees white Protestant

America, long deprived of a Madonna, as hopefully investing the rocket with all the powers of comfort and cure for their alienation: "All over the South . . . they would be praying for America tonight—thoughts of America served to replace the tender sense of the Virgin in Protestant hearts."

American technology, then, has attempted to harness the forces of nature which Melville had symbolized by Moby Dick, and Mailer is willing as detached observer to leave ambiguous the question of whether the launching of Apollo 11 shows man taming nature or nature's revenge on man— further, whether the rocket is a "Sainted Leviathan"—Moby Dick canonized by the American dream—or "a Medusa's head" whose only powers are those of death (*Fire,* p. 84). The rocket launch is thus the latest and one of the most dramatic of America's frontier encounters with the wilderness, and Mailer, as grimacing "acolyte to technology," identifies himself with all Americans who feel compelled to continually search for their identity by means of such ambiguous confrontations: "A tiny part of him was like a penitent who had prayed in the wilderness for sixteen days, and was now expecting a sign. Would the sign reveal much or little?" (*Fire,* p. 98).

The response to Mailer's question is appropriately less an answer than an image. As the rocket rises, the worlds of the Dynamo, the Virgin, and Moby Dick—of technology, imagination, and nature—merge into a new, powerful, but intensely ambiguous symbol of the American dream. The launch is immensely "more dramatic" than he has anticipated:

> For the flames were enormous. No one could be prepared for that. . . . Two mighty torches of flame like the wings of a yellow bird of fire flew over a field, covered a field with brilliant yellow bloomings of flame, and in the midst of it, white as a ghost, white as the white of Melville's Moby Dick, white as the shrine of the Madonna in half the churches of the world, this slim angelic mysterious ship of stages rose without sound out of its incarnation of flame and began to ascend slowly into the sky, slow as Melville's Leviathan might swim, slowly as we might swim upward in a dream looking for the air. And still no sound.

Then it came . . . an apocalyptic fury of sound equal to some conception of the sound of your death in the road of a drowning hour, a nightmare of sound, and he heard himself saying, 'Oh, my God! oh, my God! oh, my God! oh, my God! oh, my God! oh, my God! . . . and [had] a poor moment of vertigo at the thought that man now had something with which to speak to God. . . . [*Fire,* p. 99–100]

If the flight of Apollo 11 has renewed once again a feeling for the cosmic implications of the American enterprise, it has once again pointed to the overwhelming nightmares that the enterprise inevitably carries with it, and Mailer can even suggest that the God who directs this modern *Pequod* may be a colossal Ahab gone monomaniacal: "the Power guiding us . . . was looking to the day when all of mankind would yet be part of one machine . . . an instrument of divine endeavor put together by a Father to whom one might no longer be able to pray since the ardors of His embattled voyage could have driven Him mad" (*Fire,* p. 152). But the terror of such a possibility seems ultimately less important to Mailer than the sheer drama it creates. For the feeling of high drama reassures him that he is once again in an epic arena where the divided halves of the American psyche can meet in potentially creative combat: "It was somehow superior to see the astronauts and the flight of Apollo 11 as the instrument of . . . celestial or satanic endeavors, than as . . . a sublimation of aggressive and intolerably inhuman desires. . . . Aquarius preferred the . . . assumption that we were the indispensable instruments of a monumental vision with whom we had begun a trip" (*Fire,* p. 151–52).

As a Brooklyn-born "Nijinsky of ambivalence," Mailer, like Whitman, has been exasperatingly eager to contradict himself in order to keep open a multitude of possible approaches to modern American experience. His major works are hymns to incompletion and openness and rarely conclude so much as continually begin: Mikey Lovett flees with his "little secret," Sergius O'Shaugnessy begins a search for "new circuits," *Advertisements* catches the narrator on "the way out," Stephen Rojack heads for Guatemala, D. J. lights out for

Vietnam, and *Armies* and *Miami* seem calls to arms rather than final battles. Characteristically, the return of Apollo 11's astronauts to earth suggests to Mailer less the completion of a mission than the birth of a new line of thought, one embodying his desire along with that of Emerson's scholar to "see every trifle bristling with the polarity that ranges it instantly on an eternal law." At the conclusion of *Of a Fire on the Moon,* the polarity embodies itself in the small fragment of moon rock brought back by the astronauts from the lunar wilderness. Though Mailer has typically treated the moon as the symbolic home of cancer. madness, and the sickness unto death, and though the fragment is separated from him by a sterile technological casing, he finds the rock giving off to his imagination, like a blade of Whitman's grass, the smell of innocent new life:

> He liked the moon rock, and thought—his vanity finally unquenchable—that she liked him . . . there was something young about her, tender as the smell of the cleanest hay, it was like the subtle lift of love which comes up from the cradle of the newborn . . . and so he had his sign, sentimental beyond measure, his poor dull sense had something he could trust. [*Fire,* p. 472]

Many critics have found such analogical leaps unconvincing. Such opinions, however, have not dampened Mailer's zealous and constant search among the common as well as spectacular materials of his nation for new launching pads. No matter how impressive or awkward Mailer's soaring through the painful but stimulating ambiguities of contemporary American life and thought, the irrepressibility of his flight is itself a demonstration of the Americanness of his dream.

NOTES

1. *Sexual Politics,* Kate Millett (Garden City, New York: Doubleday, 1970), p. 14.

2. "Mailer on the Steps of the Pentagon," *Nation,* vol. 206, no. 22 (May 27, 1968), 701–2.

3. Abbreviations and pagination refer to the following works: *Adv— Advertisements for Myself; AD—An American Dream; Arm—The Armies of the Night; BS—Barbary Shore; CC—Cannibals and Christians; DP—The Deer Park; Fire—Of a Fire on the Moon; MI—Miami and the Siege of Chicago; ND—The Naked and the Dead; Pres.—The Presidential Papers; WV—Why Are We in Vietnam?*

4. See above, pp. 96–103.

5. Harvey Breit, *The Writer's Art* (Cleveland and New York: World, 1956), p. 200.

6. "Mailer on the Steps of the Pentagon," p. 701.

CONTEMPORARY NOVELIST

Tony Tanner

On the Parapet

> Every hundred yards Cummings steps up on the parapet,
> and peers cautiously into the gloom of No Man's Land.
> *(The Naked and the Dead)*
>
> . . . and I was up, up on that parapet one foot wide, and
> almost broke in both directions, for a desire to dive right
> on over swayed me out over the drop, and I nearly fell
> back to the terrace from the panic of that.
> *(An American Dream)*

In this chapter I will consider some aspects of the work of
Norman Mailer, and suggest why the image of a man standing
on a parapet which appeared fleetingly in his first novel should
become the crucial situation in a novel he wrote seventeen
years later. But before looking at Mailer, it is relevant to bring
into focus the fact that in considering the fiction written in
America during the last twenty years, we have had few occasions to refer to realism or naturalism—fictional genres in
which American writers of the past have secured some of their
most honorable achievements. Rather than simply attempting to transcribe the state of affairs which obtains in what
Burroughs called the cycle of conditioned action, the majority
of contemporary American writers try to offset or challenge
the realm of conditioned action with gestures of verbal auton-
omy of one kind or another. This is not to say that aspects of

contemporary American society are not admitted into contemporary fiction; of course they are. But even while recognizing these aspects the style of the writer seems to make clear its right to break free from them, or transmute them into something more amenable to their lexical organizings.

However, it would be wrong to suggest that attempts at a more direct kind of transparent, or neutral, realism are no longer made. What I want to do briefly is to cite three works from the last decade which in their differing ways attempt to convey fairly directly something of the actual horror of some contemporary American conditions, the violence, the misery, the squalor and the pathos of the innumerable incomplete and degraded human beings who live and die beneath the level of most people's attention. Hubert Selby, Jr.'s *Last Exit to Brooklyn* (1964) attempts to convey to us the quality of life in certain parts of Brooklyn in a style which has an anti-elegant harsh-edged directness about it. Selby says that his stories are about "loss of control," and inevitably he has to transcribe a good deal of brutality and all sorts of lapses from what we like to think of as human modes of conduct. It would not be fair to say that his work itself loses control, though it deliberately excludes some of the customary methods of organization open to fiction writers—perhaps because he feels that too much formal satisfaction would distract attention away from the plight of his hapless characters.

A good way to describe what Selby is doing is to say that he is trying to depict a human version of what the ecologist John Calhoun called a "behavioral sink." In a "behavioral sink" all normal patterns of behavior are disrupted, and the unusual stress leads to all forms of perversion, violence, and breakdown. This is what happens when too many animals are crowded into too little territory. On the human level that is exactly what is happening in many American cities, and one recognizes the impassioned honesty with which Selby draws our attention to what it can be like in a particularly extreme example of a human behavioral sink. But the comparative absence of any stylistic resistance to such hellish conditions makes Selby's book rather demoralizing. Of course he could argue that it is salutary to be thus demoralized. The countering proposition to that would be, I imagine, that there is enough dire evidence and information coming at us from a whole range of media and, under the circumstances, we want the fiction-maker to assert the independent power of his form. We would like to see the magic in the web of it.

Another and more famous attempt to present some of the horror of contemporary American life in a spirit of pure neutrality was Truman Capote's *In Cold Blood* (1966). On November 15th, 1959, Richard Hickock and Perry Smith shot the four members of the respectable Midwestern Clutter family for no apparent motive, purpose or profit. Brute fact. Starting from the meaningless horror of that night, Capote gathered together groups and clusters of related facts so that the sudden bout of blood-spilling was retrieved from its status as an isolated fact, and provided with a wider context in which it becomes the focal point of converging narratives. Capote worked on the valid assumption that a fact is simply a moment in an ongoing sequence, that it ramifies in all directions, and that to appreciate the full import of any incident you must see as much of the sequence and as many of the ramifications as possible. By juxtaposing and dovetailing the lives and values of the Clutters with those of the killers, Capote produced a schematic picture of the doubleness in American life.

There is no doubt that Capote brought together some very revealing facts, but his technique merits a little consideration. He claimed to have written a "non-fiction novel," to have presented only facts derived from observation, official records and interviews. He does not comment, he presents; he does not analyze, he arranges. This means, for one thing, that he cannot approach the profound inquiring psychological insights into the psychopath and his victims attained by Musil (in his study of Moosbrugger) or Dostoevsky. As a result, despite some telling details about the lives of the people involved in the case, the respectable citizens tend to be caricatured, and the forlorn, dangerous criminals sentimentalized (particularly

Perry Smith). The way Capote juxtaposes his "facts" reveals his subjective feelings about the world he presents, and this begins to press on our attention. I am not saying that Capote has twisted the facts to make life appear as a Capote novel. But he has manipulated them to produce a particular kind of *frisson*. In the past great novels have been written about criminal acts which were initally provoked by actual reported crimes (e.g., by Stendhal, Dostoevsky). But by making their works frankly fictions, the novelists recognized that to explore the latent significance of such acts the most valuable aid is the human imagination. By pretending not to avail himself of this aid, Capote produces the impression of factitiousness rather than fact. In the absence of a witnessing and controlling ego, the status of the facts is called into doubt. Oddly enough, there is finally something unreal about this true documentary which seems to have been disavowed by its author and assembler.

The Hell's Angels are another violent fact, actually existing in contemporary America. The journalist Hunter Thompson wrote a book[1] about them which the young American novelist Stephen Schneck reviewed very sympathetically.[2] He noted that Thompson's account was "punctuated with the dreadful unmelodious thud of authenticity," and commended him for writing a sort of stiff, undistinguished reportage which did not sensationalize or romanticize the Hell's Angels. Schneck drew a conclusion: "In these overwritten times, we cannot expect our authors to waste effort on such affectations as literary style. It is enough to write the facts in a clear hand: it is a mistake to attempt to embellish or improve upon the fantastic actuality." This would certainly seem to justify both Selby's and Capote's ways of writing. But Schneck went on to derive another consideration from Thompson's book—the problematical nature of just what is "actuality." "Where does the nightmare end, and where does the decent reality, the sanity of daylight, begin? The Hell's Angels, along with everyone else in America, are included in the dreadful confusion. Much of the Angels' difficulties seem to stem from their inability to distinguish between an act of somnambulism and a dream of sleepwalking." Access to the reality of people's lives is not perhaps so easy as Selby and Capote implicitly propose.

Schneck certainly seems to suggest as much in his novel, *The Nightclerk* (1966). "At 3:33 in the morning, there's only people lying wide-eyed in bed, wrongdoers creeping close to the walls, and nightclerks, sitting in haunted lobbies. Why devise elaborate narrations? Why tell everything but the truth?" We note straight away that traditional narrative techniques are equated with a falsification of reality. The feeling is that the old ways of constructing a novel cannot get at the real horrors and actual menaces of modern American life. Schneck's nightclerk is a fat, soiled monster of a man who works in a seedy hotel in downtown San Francisco. (Perhaps there is a debt to O'Neill's *Hughie*.) But Spencer Blight, the nightclerk, is no ordinary man and his role on the twilight edges of society is no ordinary role. For Blight is the obscene dreamer of the modern city; in his grossness he is the repository and expediter of the forbidden vices of society. On him all private perverted yearnings and dirty secrets converge; from him strange and horrific sexual acts mysteriously emanate. When there is a series of ugly sexual assaults (every Wednesday "something new and savage, with no satisfactory explanations"), Blight is vaguely connected with it all, not so much as a doer of the deeds, but rather as a dreamer of the deeds, a "fat spider who sat spinning the night away in the rotten core of the haunted hotel." The book is surrealistic, blackly humorous; but it puts forward the important consideration that in dreams begin realities.

For most of the novel the nightclerk sits in his chair, reading pornography, musing, remembering, his capacious mind permeable to past and present foulness, and generative of more. But, says Schneck, this state is not to be "mistaken for sleep, but must be respected as a state of magick: a trance into which Blight did withdraw at will, to hold converse with the dark and fearful Wonders whose Wednesday celebrations seemed somehow connected with a Nightclerk, wrapped in silence." "Magick" is the key word: it recurs throughout the book. Whatever happens, happens mysteriously, through occult powers which cannot be seen or plotted. This determines the dissolving shape of Schneck's book. It could be said that traditionally a lot of the energy of the novel has been directed against magic. The omniscient author may pose a mystery or uncertainty only to clarify and explain it; his work asserts and explores a universe of cause and effect, even though it may reveal that causes and effects are related to each other in stranger and subtler ways than we usually assume. Obviously one of the reasons why the novel has suffered so many mutations in this century is simply that the old shared assumptions about the nature of reality —the way of things, the why of things—have broken down. In particular this seems to be true in American fiction since the last world war. Book after book gives evidence of people simply bewildered at the workings of the world around them and one result of this is that there is a growing tendency among American novelists to refer to ghosts, demons, occult powers, and all sorts of magic when it comes to offering some account of the forces at work in the real dream, or dreamed reality, of modern life (cf. the extraordinary upsurge of interest in astrology in America during recent years).

The feeling of a world dominated by demons and magic is at work in Schneck's novel. He does not explain the city at night; he makes it vivid. There is no conventional narrative because there are no ordinary doings. There is instead an atmosphere—the city turning in its troubled sleep, and at the center Spencer Bilght in his hotel. This hotel exists "outside the laws of nature as well as most municipal ordinances." Sometimes it is the many-roomed home of all the banished perversions of the city. Sometimes something more symbolic: "The lobby is a world of trinkets, but the floors overhead are the *vacua horribilia*. Suspended over the lobby, over the vast accumulations of trash, are six flights of the void." In every sense it is a place where reality gives way to fantasy and unreality, the customary world separating out, as in so many recent American novels, into trash and void. Everything is running down and by the end the lobby is empty, the furniture is dead, and the nightclerk is "like a man all used up."

Objections may be brought against the three books I have mentioned. Selby's makes reality too crude, Schneck's makes it too grotesque, while Capote's illusory objectivity seems to falsify its evidence by seeking to hide all reportorial bias and disposition. Looking at these books one might speculate that a writer seeking to get at American reality might do well to combine the documentary and the demonic modes, to develop a sense of magic without losing the empirical eye, and to admit his own relationship to the material he is handling and the interpretations he is offering. This, it seems to me, is exactly what Norman Mailer has done, and why, despite varying performances, he is one of the most consistently relevant and revelatory writers about contemporary America. In dealing with grim facts he asserts the force of his own style; engaged in documentary work he reveals the presence of the registering, interpreting ego in the events, thus authenticating whatever version—no matter how idiosyncratic—he offers; and in his fiction he allows himself every form of licence, pushing invention as far as he can. In his various applications and extensions of his own particular genre, which we might call the demonized documentary, Mailer has shown a continuous ability to expose himself to what is going on and respond with some kind of vital lexical performance. In particular when he permits himself to operate in a frankly fictional dimension, where some people find him most outrageous, I think he is most successful.

At the end of Saul Bellow's *The Victim*, Leventhal cries out one last question to Albee: " 'What's your idea of who runs things.' " It is an apt question to conclude a book in which the persecutor and the paranoid are never quite sure which role they are playing at any particular moment. But more generally it could be said to be the question which occupies a large number of American novelists who, in one form or another, are obsessed with the problems and mysteries of power. It is certainly Mailer's central concern, and his first three novels can be seen as studies of three different kinds of power and their distinctive manifestations or modes of operation. In each, the geographic setting suggests an extra dimension of power outside the particular human power situation being studied. *The Naked and the Dead* (1948) is about men and war, and the temporary military installations are set in the jungle and surrounded by the sea. *Barbary Shore* (1951) is about men and politics, and the run-down boardinghouse in Brooklyn which contains most of the action is surrounded by the unfathomable density of the modern megalopolis. *The Deer Park* (1955) is about men and sex, and it takes place for the most part in an unreal annex of Hollywood called Desert D'Or. More real is the actual desert all around it. When he came to write *An American Dream* (1965), Mailer brought together these different geographies (either as actual settings or as metaphors) to make his most comprehensive exploration of the operations of power on many levels.

An interest in the mysteries of power necessarily involves a curiosity about the presence or absence of patterns and plots. This has been made abundantly clear in the course of this book. It is evident in Mailer's work from the start. In *The Naked and the Dead,* the American soldiers on the Pacific island often experience the feeling that, "It's a plot," or, "It's a trap." On one level this is an obvious reaction to being caught up in the exacting discipline of their own army, as well as being constantly vulnerable to sudden attacks by the Japanese. But the emotion is a response to something more than the force of contending armies. When the young soldier Hennessey is killed shortly after the beach landing, the reaction is not simply, *c'est la guerre.* One man, Red, has an awed sense that "someone, *something*" is behind it. "There was a pattern where there shouldn't be one." Another man, Croft, whose will to exercise his destructive power over the men is to be so decisive during the campaign, reacts with a strange feeling of omnipotence, since he feels that he controls the fate of his men. The death of Hennessey tantalizes him with "odd dreams and portents of power." Later on we are told of the feeling that the detached, cerebral Lieutenant Hearn experienced when he sailed for war. "Always there was the power that leaped at you, invited you." Determined to bring a wounded man back to base, another soldier, Brown, addresses his resolve to "whatever powers had formed him." The men share the same war, but each has his different experience or sense of the presence of more than human powers.

But the person most preoccupied with power is General Cummings, who is said to "control everything" on the island. Accused of being a reactionary by Hearn, he dismisses Hearn's narrow political frame of reference, and speaks of the coming "renaissance of real power." The war is not fought for ideals, it is simply "a power concentration"; to attempt to plan for a just society is foolish since " 'the only morality of the future is a power morality,' " and so on—the word is constantly on his lips. Cummings is a somewhat monstrous figure who commands a dark authority and feels himself in touch with the essential powers that run things. He is the first of many such figures, actual and fictional, from boxers to politicians, who are to absorb Mailer's attention in his subsequent work. As Cummings lies awake arranging his plans, he is sure that there is always a pattern if you know how to look for it. When he has ordered an attack he feels the thrill of total control. "The troops out in the jungle were disposed from the patterns in his mind. . . . All of it, all the violence, the dark coordination had sprung from his mind. In the night, at that moment, he felt such power that it was beyond joy. . . ." Later that same night, he tries to write down in his journal a comprehensive theory of how all power operates, to draw the curve which accurately defines the line of force as it rises and falls through human affairs. It is rather like Henry Adams's undertaking. But when it comes to drawing the definitive curve, he finds it is beyond him. "There was order but he could not reduce it to the form of a single curve. Things eluded him." This is borne out by what happens in the campaign, which is supposedly being run by him. His men do finally achieve victory, but he has a momentary recognition that he personally has had almost nothing to do with it: "It had been accomplished by a random play of vulgar good luck larded into a casual net of factors too large, too vague for him to comprehend." If there is a pattern it is beyond his grasp; the controller of the island is himself controlled in unfathomable ways. The master tactician has no idea who runs things, though he will go on pretending it is himself.

In connection with the delusory nature of man-made patterns, the setting is all important. While men consult the rule book, the moon exerts her mysterious force. The military concept of a "connected line" vanishes in the impenetrable jungle—"no army could live or move in it." The mountain which dominates the island dominates the men with its motionless hostility. The sea around them wears all things down and is full of death. The land itself becomes terrifying in its "somnolent brooding resistance." It seems as if there is a cosmic conspiracy against men, as if something working through the various forces of nature is seeking to bring them to a standstill, erase their identities, annihilate them altogether. The heaps of kelp on the beach remind Hearn of a lecture he had once heard on this seaweed. These plants live without movement in murky undersea jungles—"stationary, absorbed in their own nutriment." In storms they are heaped up as so much waste on the beaches, useful only as fertilizer. Their presence on the beaches of the island is a constant reminder that all things including men are worn down inexorably to some lowest common denominator of existence. It is the island which strips the men naked, leaving all of them exposed and many of them dead. Everything surrounding the men seems to presage some final immobility. If General Cummings had looked very carefully when he stood on the parapet peering into no-man's-land, this is the entropic pattern he would have discerned, the enemy he should have recognized. At the end of the book a foolish major is planning to lay a coordinate grid system over a picture of Betty Grable to "jazz up" his map-reading class. It is a last farcical reminder of the futility of imposing man-made patterns on the mysterious undulations of life.

The imposition of political patterns on the movements of history is experienced as ultimately futile in *Barbary Shore*. The pessimistic McLeod, who has moved beyond conflicting ideologies and is killed for such individual presumption, outlines a future of increasing chaos and conflict—" 'the deterioration continues until we are faced with mankind in barbary.' " The book contains a lot of political debate, with various ideological points of view advanced in some detail. Yet there seems to be a more mysterious power at work than that which is focused and applied by party conspiracies, and one indication of this is the presence of an unexplained secret object which the parties are trying to gain possession of. It could refer to some atomic secret plans, or more generally stand for that elusive mystery of power which men continually strive to appropriate and use. In the event McLeod hands it on to the narrator, along with the remnants of his socialist heritage, and the narrator is himself a man who will spend his time evading conscription into any particular party.

It is important that the narrator is a man who has lost his memory and hence all his connections with the past. He thus becomes a man who lives existentially, since he starts with no prior commitments or allegiances. He cannot reconstruct his identity, despite all his inquiries and studies of documents; he therefore has to create it anew. He has a recurrent fantasy of a traveller arriving at what he thinks is a familiar city, only to find that the architecture in it is strange, the clothing unfamiliar, the language of the signs indecipherable. He thinks that he must be dreaming, but the narrator imagines shouting to him. "You are wrong . . . this city is the real city, the material city, and your vehicle is history." It is because the narrator himself has to learn to comprehend what is to him an alien city, and formulate a role for himself in it, that he is attracted to the patterns and clarifications offered by politics. But by the end he has moved beyond all groups, like so many American heroes. He is alone, but his isolation is given meaning by his possession of the mysterious object, a moral act, as McLeod defined it, since as long as a single individual has the object, no party or country can exploit it. At the end, the narrator foresees a life of continual moving on, using flexibility to avoid destructive conscriptions, dodging and weaving from the hostile pre-emptive forces of the modern world. Mailer ends his novel with an inverted echo of the end of *The Great Gatsby,* heavy with pessimistic predictions of the coming chaos and destruction—"the storm approaches its thunderhead, and it is apparent that the boat drifts ever closer to the shore. So the blind will lead the blind, and the deaf shout warnings to one another until their voices are lost." The drift is towards Barbary Shore, and the hero's one aim is to resist the drift at least in his own person—politics and parties and countries and armies seem only to hasten it.

The Deer Park is set in the town of Desert D'Or, close to the capital of cinema in Southern California. Hollywood, and California in general, are situated on the edge of the Pacific. Desert D'Or is on the edge of the desert. In the last century it was a shanty town round an oasis from which prospectors set out to look for gold. They called it Desert Door. Now it has been completely rebuilt. It is "all new." In giving us these details of the setting on page one, Mailer outlines the main subject of his novel. People come west searching for dream gold; every age will define the dream gold it seeks. The quest brings many people to some kind of extreme edge, where they may be confronted with a door through which they might push to some new dimension of experience. Or they may discover that dream gold is fool's gold, and wake up to the actual mess of their lives which becomes clear as the power of fantasy wanes. Once again, the location of the Hollywood dream factory on the western edge of the continent has struck an American novelist with its irresistible suggestiveness.

On the narrative level, the novel is an account by an ex-serviceman named Sergius O'Shaugnessy who plunges into the life of Desert D'Or. He not only has problems about his own identity, but some temporary blocks in the creative realm— both sexual and literary. After various adventures or entangle- ments—mainly in the rather unreal area in which sex is inextricable from cinema—he finally leaves Desert D'Or for Mexico where he recovers sufficient potency to learn some of the rudiments of bull-fighting, and sleeps with a bull-fighter's mistress. From there he goes to New York where he achieves full literary potency and writes his book—which will be *The Deer Park*.

Another important inhabitant of Desert D'Or is Marion Faye. A pimp and drug addict who seems to go in for delib- erate degradation of self and others, he is in his own way a quester. He wants to "push to the end . . . and come out . . . he did not know where, but there was experience beyond experience, there was something. Of that, he was certain." The nature of his quest is perhaps best indicated by his delib- erate act of not locking his door, thus metaphorically leaving himself open to the dreads which come in from the desert and the more literal threats of his many enemies in town. Most people in Desert D'Or live with their doors locked in every sense. The houses have walls round them to keep out the sight of the real desert. At the same time they have extrava- gant interior settings and extensive mirrors, so that life achieves the sustained unreality of prolonged narcissism in theatrical conditions. The bars are made to look like jungles, grottos, cinema lounges—life becomes an indefinite extension of the film sets close by. In these conditions people can only play roles and sex becomes a desolate game; where fantasy is everywhere, there is no chance for truly productive relation- ships. It is not surprising that more than one character, includ- ing Sergius, gets locked up sexually, unable to perform the creative act.

Such a world is, to Marion Faye, a world of "slobs." He is trying to find the door which opens to some authentic ex- perience which he feels can only be had at the extreme edge of reality. It is one of his pleasures to drive with great speed out into the desert to a small summit from which he can look out, not only over the desert, but also to the gambling city and the atomic testing grounds which are both situated out there. He feels contempt and distaste for the way politicians and army officers produce verbal justifications for these great experiments with destructive power—"for the words belonged to the slobs, and the slobs hid the world with words." But Marion Faye does not regret the coming destruction which he foresees; rather he longs for it. He yearns for the great explosion which will erase the rot and stench of civilization as he knows it—"let it come for all of everywhere, just so it comes and the world stands clear in the white dead dawn." It is an authentic vision, but its purity is nihilistic: it seems appropriate that Marion Faye should finally involve himself in a nasty road accident. It is obviously imperative somehow to exit from the unreality of Desert D'Or, but the book suggests that Marion Faye has taken the wrong door out. Is there a right one?

This of course is the problem for Sergius O'Shaugnessy. In Desert D'Or he has rented a house "on the edge of the desert," and, like many other American heroes, he has good reason for pitching his habitation in such a border area, for his experience has taught him that there are two worlds and he has seen enough of both to realize that one has to negotiate a perilous existence somewhere between them. "I had the idea that there were two worlds. There was a real world as I called it . . . and this real world was a world where orphans burned orphans. It was better not even to think of this. I liked the other world in which almost everybody lived. The imaginary world." What his experience in Desert D'Or teaches him is that the imaginary world can have its own ruination and destructiveness. At the end of the novel, Sergius imagines a friend of his named Eitel (a film director who has lost his integrity) sending a silent message to him. In it Eitel confesses that he lost the true drive and desire of the artist, which is the conviction that whatever happens " 'there still remains that world we may create, more real to us, more real to others, than the mummery of what happens, passes, and is gone.' " He then urges Sergius to " 'try for that other world, the real world, where orphans burn orphans and nothing is more difficult to discover than a simple fact. And with the pride of the artist, you must blow against the walls of every power that exists, the small trumpet of your defiance.' " This is potentially ambiguous, but the feeling that emerges is as follows. From the world of brutal facts—wars and orphanages—Sergius has moved into the realm of Technicolored air-conditioned fantasies. But there is a further move to make. The imaginary world not only covers the world in which people live isolated in their own dreams and illusions; it also points to the truly creative world of art through which the artist may find a way into the secrets of reality. For Sergius, writing is the right door out of Desert D'Or—and all the puns are functional.

Having touched bottom, Sergius finds the strength to leave Desert D'Or, and his subsequent travels in Mexico and then to New York mark stages in his liberation. At the very end he seems to have arrived at a point beyond all politics and religions to put his trust in sex, for he hears from God that sex is time and time is "the connection of new circuits." The important transferences and linkings of power will in future be very private affairs, with the ostensibly important power circuits of society counting for less than the mysterious forces which work behind and through them. This is one of the terminal suggestions of the book.

In the ten years before he published his next novel, Mailer spent much of his time writing the various essays which he gathered together with some fragments of fiction in the two books *Advertisements for Myself* (1959) and *The Presidential Papers* (1963). One may note in passing that the two titles suggest a range of interest from the self-assertive power of the writer's own ego right up to the most powerful man in America. In a famous essay entitled "The White Negro" Mailer wrote that no matter how horrifying the twentieth cenury is, it is very exciting "for its tendency to reduce all of life to its ultimate alternatives." When Sergious started to find his feet as a writer he tells us that he started to think in "couples," such as love and hate, victory and defeat, and so on, and his binary reduction or schematization of life is much in evidence in Mailer's own subsequent journalism and occasional writing. "Today the enemy is vague," he also said in an early essay, and one can see that throughout his work he has tried to dissipate that vagueness by postulating pairs of opposed extremes—assassins and victims; conformists and outlaws; the cancerous forces of malign control resisted by the bravery and health of the hero as hipster; the black magician versus the good artist (see his classic account of the Liston-Patterson fight); love and death; being and nothingness; cannibals and Christians—and finally God and the Devil. These are just some of the "couples" that Mailer has deployed in his essays, and obviously he feels the excitement of going after extreme alternatives.

Looking back at those essays one can detect an increasing preference for images drawn from biology, from diseases and from primitive superstitions. Like Burroughs he sees cancer as an appropriate symbol of the forces of death which are gaining on us. He refers to the "cancer of the power that governs us"; the F.B.I. is a faceless "plague-like" evil force; totalitarianism is a spreading disease; the nation is "collectively sick." Few people resist this spreading disease, "the slow deadening of our best possibilities." There are just a few individuals—Kennedy, Castro, beats, hipsters, Negroes, psychopaths, who can assert their own inner energy and independent vision of reality against the prevailing forces. Such figures are resisting the overall drive towards death which is the dominant conspiracy. Mailer has a "dynamic view of existence" which sees every individual as "moving individually through each moment of life forward into growth or backward into death." And what is going on in the universe as a whole is a battle between an existential God and a principle of Evil "whose joy is to waste substance." The confrontation is comparable to that outlined by Burroughs, and we recognize the principle of Evil as entropy turned Manichaean. What Mailer feels is that somehow we have lost the ability to respond to this awesome confrontation. "The primitive understanding of dread—that one was caught in a dialogue with gods, devils, and spirits, and so was naturally consumed with awe, shame, and terror has been all but forgotten." Among other things, his next novel was to be about a man who seeks to recapture an adequate sense of dread.

In another coupling, from one of the Presidential Papers, Mailer suggests that Americans have been leading a double life: "Our history has moved on two rivers, one visible, the other underground; there has been the history of politics which is concrete, practical, and unbelievably dull . . . and there is the subterranean river of untapped, ferocious, lonely and romantic desires, that concentration of ecstasy and violence which is the dream life of the nation." The writer must be in touch with both, with all levels of American life, and able to swim in all its rivers: it is almost a direct prescription for Mailer's next novel. Having complained that "the life of politics and the life of myth had diverged too far" he would create in it a character who experienced their point of convergence—and separation.

The title, *An American Dream* (1965), might suggest that in this novel Mailer decided to leave the surface river of American life and plunge into the subterranean river to explore "that concentration of ecstasy and violence which is the dream life of the nation." And it is true that the hero of the book, Stephen Rojack, is twice very close to a literal plunge from lighted rooms in high buildings to dark streets below. Early in the book during the course of a party, he goes to the balcony to vomit out his rising nausea (that familiar act which he performs more than once, well aware of its ritual cleansing significance). The moon seems to be calling to him to jump from the balcony, and he does in fact start to climb over. He is "half on the balcony, half off" when "the formal part" of his brain tells him that he cannot die yet as he has work to do. Outside—the moon, strange influences in the darkness, superstitious promptings, the possibility of a descent which confusingly suggests itself as an ascent, an ambiguous summoning to liberation which may be death. Behind—the constricting and debased routines of a society out of love with itself and engaged in petty power plays and empty sexual games. Poised between them—the Mailer hero, caught in the paradox that while the summons from the moon seems more authentic and important than the voices from the party, to obey the moon would be to abandon form for formlessness, consciousness for unconsciousness, life for death. In this little incident Mailer adumbrates the subject of the whole novel, and anticipates the crucial scene when Rojack walks round the parapet of a high balcony, later in the book.

If you regard this novel simply as a narrative of incidents—as some critics did, and found it outrageous*—what happens is this. Stephen Rojack, an ex-war hero, had wanted to get into politics and, partly with this in mind, he had married Deborah Kelly who was socially influential and whose father wielded extraordinary, and nameless, powers. But having had a very intense experience of the mystery of death during the war when he killed some Germans in a desolate moonlit landscape, Rojack finds that the political game comes to seem like an unreal distraction in which the real private self is swallowed up in a fabricated public appearance. Rojack departs from politics to continue his "secret frightened romance with the phases of the moon." By the same token he is leaving the mental enclosures of bourgeois society and venturing into a new kind of power area in which the supernatural, the irrational and the demonic hold sway. This step out of society is marked by his murder of Deborah. He manages to make the murder look like suicide, and afterwards he finds that he has dropped out of respectable society and has entered a strange

---

*The best answer to these critics, and a brilliant comment on the novel as a whole, is to be found in a short piece by Leo Bersani in *Partisan Review* (Fall, 1965), entitled "The Interpretation of Dreams." Among other things he reminds us that the telling of the story is Rojack's invention and that its exuberance is a calculated effect—"we should be admiring the power of extravagance in Rojack's tall story instead of upholding the faded banner of verisimilitude."

underworld. The geography shifts from fashionable uptown New York to the Village, Harlem, the Lower East Side; the atmosphere becomes darker and more confused; he is pursued by police and criminals and is involved in power maneuvers which he cannot fathom. He has to fight for his life—psychically with a gang of hoodlums; physically with the Negro Shago Martin. He has, in effect, taken that plunge to the lower level of American life.

On that lower level he also finds true love with a singer named Cherry, an authentic passional relationship which had not been possible in the confines of society. But that lower level is also the place of death, and Cherry is pointlessly and brutally murdered. It is done in error, but there is no clear light at this level and everyone is prey to confusions. After this Rojack leaves New York, first of all going to make a lot of money in Las Vegas, and at the very end of the book heading for the jungles of Guatemala and Yucatan, away from the United States and towards the most primeval area left on the whole American continent. He is by this time well beyond the constituted power of the law, and the unconstituted powers of the lawless inhabitants of the lower level—indeed it might be said that he is beyond the United States of America altogether. It would seem that his apparent escape from the powers of retribution was very upsetting for some reviewers who felt that wife-murderers should not get off so easily. But taken as a vivid exploration of a man's relationship to the different orders of American reality, the novel is much more interesting and complex than any gesture of *épater le bourgeois*—which many reviewers took it to be.

Although the novel takes place in contemporary America, through the use of metaphor it opens on to every kind of pre-social reality—the jungle, the forest, the desert, the swamp, the ocean-bed. This metaphorical activity in the writing is so insistent that it provides a dimension of experience as real as that provided by the very detailed documentation of settings and scenes in contemporary New York. People are described in animal terms throughout. In addition the constant emphasis on all sorts of odors emanating from people, places, things, bespeaking growth or, more usually, decay, suggests a regression to a more primitive mode of perception and orientation. Language is efficient only on one level; elsewhere it is often safer to follow your nose.

In addition to touching on those powers and drives which operate on the many natural levels below society, language and consciousness (the three are obviously linked), the book tries to point inclusively to those supernatural powers which transcend this distinctively human trilogy. Starting with the moon, we encounter a widening range of references to evil spirits, vampires, demons, voodoo, magic, Zen, grace, and all those strange powers which the individual experiences as an *'it'* working *through* him, but not originating within him (this reminds one of Burroughs's universe). The thesis of Rojack's great work—for he is in effect the writer Sergius set out to become—is that "magic, dread, and the perception of death were the roots of motivation." As he says, he has come to believe in witches, spirits, demons, devils, warlocks, omens, wizards, fiends, incubi and succubi—"in grace and the lack of it, in the long finger of God and the swish of the Devil." One statement imputed to him is that "God's engaged in a war with the Devil, and God may lose." The implications of this are potentially pessimistic, for it reduces man to an incidental point of intersection of warring supernatural powers, a helpless pawn in a larger battle, susceptible to voodoo, desperate for grace. Rojack sees civilization itself as a disturbance of two orders. Primitive man had an instinctive sense of dread in his relationship with non-human nature; civilized man has disrupted this by believing himself to be permanently elevated above animals and the jungle. As a result that sense of dread which is requisite for psychic and spiritual health has been greatly attenuated. Related to this is civilization's "invasion of the supernatural" which takes the form of denying powers which it cannot see. The price of this, he thinks, is to accelerate our sense of some indefinable but imminent disaster. If a man becomes aware of those dimensions of nature and super-nature from which he feels that the rest of society has resolutely closed itself off, where does that leave him standing? By analogy we might say on an edge as precarious as the parapet round a balcony.

I will return to this analogy, but first let us consider the plot line of the novel, this time thinking of it as an almost allegorical exploration of different levels of mystery, different areas of power, different orderings of reality. One could simply say that Rojack moves through the three different worlds of Mailer's first three novels—war, politics and sexual experience, encountering different forms of death in each world. But a little more detail is called for. The world of Deborah Kelly and her father is centered on Park Avenue and is connected with all kinds of political power. The Kellys are involved in a power web which reaches not only to President Kennedy, but to the C.I.A., the Mafia and unspecified spy rings and international agents. Entering this world in an attempt to gain political power, Rojack finds himself very much its prisoner: he is manipulated and preempted by its far-ranging coercive resources, he is in danger of being trapped in its version of reality. When he murders Deborah, he is breaking free not just from a destructive woman, but from the picture of reality imposed by her world. As he is strangling her he feels he is opening a door, and he glimpses what lies "on the other side of the door, and heaven was there, some quiver of jewelled cities shining in the glow of a tropical dusk, and I thrust against the door once more . . . and *crack* the door flew open . . . and I was through the door . . . I was floating. I was as far into myself as I had ever been and universes wheeled in a dream." The image obviously recalls the attempts of Sergius to find the right door out of Desert D'Or, and among other things Rojack has broken out of the conventional novel into a realm of dream—one should take the hint. The question which interests us is what he finds on the other side of that door. Does Rojack find heaven, the jewelled cities, or is he drawn on by a mirage? Is his journey away from society and down finally to the ancient center of America an analogue for some deep descent into his own self?

He has the vision of a jewelled city on two further occasions, both times as an accompaniment to sexual orgasm. The first occurs with Ruta, Deborah's maid, with whom Rojack has intercourse immediately after the murder. During intercourse, he alternates between vaginal and anal penetration. The detail of this scene is offensive to some, but for Mailer it is quite clearly an analogue to a more metaphysical ambiguity. For just as one kind of intercourse is procreative, and the other kind quite the reverse, so Rojack cannot be sure whether he has broken through to some of the true mysteries of creativity after the sterile world of politics, or whether he has unwittingly aligned himself with the Satanic forces of waste. With Ruta the resultant vision of the mysterious city is desolate and dead. It seems like a place in the desert or on the moon, and everything in it looks as unreal as plastic.

Having left the political world, Rojack finds himself in a demonized world of invisible powers and strange portents, of rampant superstition and accurate magics. In moving away from Park Avenue both to Harlem and to the Lower East Side, Rojack is in effect leaving established society and conventional modes of consciousness for darker areas of experience, hidden at the heart or forgotten at the edge—of the city, of the mind. And in this world Rojack experiences a visionary orgasm with Cherry. This time it is purposefully and successfully procreative (he throws away her diaphragm as a signal of his intent). As a reward the vision is not of an arid, plastic place, but one of rich undersea mystery. "I was passing through a grotto of curious lights, like colored lanterns beneath the sea, a glimpse of that quiver of jewelled arrows, that heavenly city which had appeared as Deborah was expiring. . . ." It scarcely matters whether we feel this to be Jungian or not. In sinking or plunging down to the depths (the second river of American life), Rojack has reestablished contact with the secret source of life. It is as near heaven as he gets.

In the depths, authentic passion is inseparable from authentic violence, for this is the subconscious (or slum area) in which all the basic intensities are freed from the control of the socialized consciousness (or the uptown authorities). Rojack's intensely private moments of happiness with Cherry are foredoomed, and while Shago Martin is being beaten to death in Harlem, Cherry is being murdered in her Lower East Side hideaway. This area is full of its own threats and manipulations, and Rojack does not find it wholly liberating to be in an area in which the older dreads and magics connected both with the jungle and the moon have full play. Here death seems to strike more often than love.

Leaving New York, Rojack comes to Las Vegas and before setting off for Guatemala and Yucatan, he walks out into the desert to look up at the moon and back at the city. "There was a jewelled city on the horizon, spires rising in the night, but the jewels were diadems of electric and the spires were the neon of signs ten stories high. I was not good enough to climb up and pull them down." This has various implications. The two kinds of "jewelled city" he glimpsed while in union with Ruta and Cherry may indicate the two aspects of the creative-destructive dream which man has imposed on the American continent in his continuing loving and raping of the land. Given Rojack's response to Las Vegas it would seem that the destructive element has been realized and the original American "dream" has turned into this plastic and neon reality in the desert, deceptively brilliant from a distance. In his search for the true heavenly city, Rojack will have to keep on moving. Perhaps it is like Gatsby's green light, the orgiastic future which recedes as it is pursued. Perhaps it can only ever be a private vision, never to be realized but occasionally to be glimpsed in the rich depths of the imagination. In any case, Rojack leaves Las Vegas, which after all is only a distillation of the corruptions and violences he has encountered in New York. After talking to Cherry (in Heaven) on a disused rusty phone—for when a man is standing between the desert and the moon, the customary circuits do not obtain and new kinds of communication are possible—Rojack heads south in space and back in time, aiming perhaps to penetrate the secret center of his own, and America's identity.

The crucial last chapter is entitled "At the Lion and the Serpent" (Rojack's exodus from society through Las Vegas and towards South America is contained in an Epilogue, which suggests that the critical and decisive moment is passed). In terms of the plot, the situation in the chapter is as follows. Kelly has summoned Rojack to the Waldorf Towers on Park Avenue to question him about the death of his daughter and other matters. Rojack sets out with the conscious intention of keeping the appointment. But as he is travelling there he is aware of a subconscious voice telling him to " 'Go to Harlem' " if he wants to save Cherry. (In addition, Shago Martin's umbrella which Rojack has brought with him seems to be twitching with signals in his lap—telepathy and animism are common in Harlem.) He has earlier referred to the magician who lives in the "gaming rooms of the unconscious" and who sends messages up to "the tower of the brain," and the irrational summons to the dark depths of Harlem which challenges his more rational resolve to go to the Towers on Park Avenue obviously comes from that source. Once again, the two parts of New York serve as projections for different levels of consciousness. Rojack's uncertainty as to which part of New York he should head for at this moment of crisis offers an analogue for Mailer's uncertainty as to which part of the psyche he should rely on in trying to cope with the mystery of America— the empirical or the demonic, the formal decisions of reason or the formless promptings of dream.

In the Waldorf everything suggests death; even the real flowers look plastic. In Kelly's room, the ageing mobster Ganucci seems to reek of the cancer which is devouring him: decay is everywhere in the air. At the same time, the room is a center of political power, with lines reaching to the White House, the C.I.A., the Mafia and other unspecified organizations. Kelly himself, though he works through political agencies, seems like an elemental force or principle to Rojack. He smells of animal power, and, although his furniture is composed of expensive antiques and art works, Rojack has the sense of "vegetation working in the night" and experiences the civilized apartment as being something between a dark corner of the jungle and an ante-chamber of hell. Kelly tells him, " 'There's nothing but magic at the top,' " and one is made to feel that all the magic he draws on, as he manipulates the political levels of reality so cynically, is black. The forces he commands serve to extend the empire of death, just as his deepest sexual drive is incestuous (with his daughter), his aids and agents are cancerous (Ganucci), and his cities are plastic (he is a big power in Las Vegas). The power passing through Kelly is on the side of entropy.

Early on during this evening encounter Rojack goes out to the parapet of the balcony. Standing half on the edge, strange intuitions and suggestions come to him: to jump would be a cleansing act after the foulness of the room he has just left; it would be for Cherry; God exists, he suddenly feels as he looks down. But he also realizes that the fall to the street would mean a death as sharp and certain as that threatened by Shago Martin's knife—an important connection of ideas because it relates the notion of the jump to the Harlem side of Rojack's experience. At this stage Rojack climbs down from the parapet and returns for his long conversation with Kelly, but he returns to it at the end of the conversation because—" 'I was caught.' " He is caught between the deathly force emanating almost irresistibly from Kelly and the disturbing dreads which seem to be reaching him from Harlem. He is caught up among encircling and opposing demonisms which he cannot control nor clearly understand, or perhaps between the Devil and the Lord who have however lost their consolingly familiar theological identities to become names uncertainly applied to gusts and currents of power which drive unpredictably through the air. And Rojack decides— "I wanted to be free of magic. . . . But I could not move." It is at this point that he decides he must walk round the parapet of the terrace. Once up on the parapet he is poised between "the chasm of the drop" and "the tower behind me" or, as we might say, between rigid architecture and formless darkness. The jump into the authentic darkness, down to the street, would be as literally fatal as the return to the room would be symbolically a succumbing to Kelly. Both Park Avenue and Harlem would destroy Rojack, just as we have seen that too much form (fixity) and pure formlessness (flow) alike threaten to obliterate the identity of the American hero. Both rivers of American life promise drowning.

This is why Rojack has to walk round the parapet. He has to prove that he can negotiate that edge where the worlds meet—capitulating neither to a political nor to a demonized ordering of reality, avoiding the traps of social architecture and the chaotic dissolutions of the pre-social or sub-social dark. To be able to keep his balance is to achieve some degree of liberation from the coercive powers of both worlds—and after his walk Rojack strikes down Kelly and then throws Shago Martin's demon-charged umbrella over the parapet. He is temporarily free from both magics, and in terms of the plot it is this symbolic demonstration of his ability to keep that precarious balance on the edge which frees Rojack and effectively allows him to move beyond the two kinds of power exerted by the tower and the chasm. Earlier in the book he had described himself as feeling like a creature locked by fear to the border between earth and water who finally "took a leap over the edge of mutation so that now and at last it was something new." Passing through doors, moving across changing terrains, Rojack feels like a "new breed" of man and is once described as a "new soul." Whether or not he actually becomes a new breed of man, and what the novelty consists of, the book may fairly be said to leave ambiguous. But it does make clear that he is a man who has to live at the edge, trying to hold on to his identity between two threatening realms. If he does finally take a leap, it is not from one realm or atmosphere or river into the other, but rather into some third or new area beyond the existing alternatives formulated by North America. Yucatan is, one feels, as temporary a destination as Sweden was for Yossarian.

Rojack is really moving out beyond the world's mirror towards some placeless city of his own imagination.

In this connection it is interesting to note the frontispiece of Mailer's next book, *Cannibals and Christians* (1966). It depicts a model of a possible vertical city of the future and was designed by Mailer himself. The whole section in the book devoted to "Architectural Excerpts" is extremely relevant in considering *An American Dream,* and I will quote a fragment.

> Perhaps we live on the edge of a great divide in history and so are divided ourselves between the desire for a gracious, intimate, detailed and highly particular landscape and an urge less articulate to voyage out on explorations not yet made. Perhaps the blank faceless quality of our modern architecture is a reflection of the anxiety we feel before the void. . . . [*CC*, p. 235]

Since man is caught between old architecture and the void of space, as Rojack was caught between the tower and chasm, Mailer has designed a sort of dream city which will rise up into the sky and sway there like a ship in oceans of space. This is obviously again a sort of third area, between old architecture and unknown space. It is really the city of his own style.

With the mention of style, we have come to the last aspect of the book I wish to consider. I have stated previously that I think we can often detect a significantly analogous relationship between the situation of the character in the plot and the author in his language. Just so, when Rojack is moving in the world of politics and policemen, Mailer tends to employ a mainly documentary style, full of empirical notations and transcriptions of recognizably realistic dialogue. But when Rojack has broken out of this world into an area in which both the pre-social and the supernatural seem to hold sway, so that life is experienced more as a jungle full of magics, then Mailer calls on every kind of mythic, religious, superstitious reference, and metaphors drawn from every level of existence, to provide a style which is adequate to Rojack's novel experience. The documentary is extended to incorporate the demonic. A nice example of the confrontation of styles comes when the police are interrogating Rojack about the death of his wife. Rojack, fabricating his version of Deborah's death, explains that she committed suicide because she felt haunted by demons. " 'I don't know how to put demons on a police report,' " says Roberts. The police report is the equivalent of a style which only credits empirically perceived facts, a narrow naturalism. Rojack is quite sure that there are more things in heaven and earth than can be contained in a police report, and his vocabulary (which is Mailer's style) has been enlarged accordingly. One policeman is convinced he knows the facts of the matter. He asserts that Rojack killed her with a silk stocking—that is how it is usually done. Even so-called empirical realism has its own predetermining fantasies which it imposes on the given data. One of Rojack's struggles is against the inadequate fantasy patternings of reality implicit in the policeman's narrow and clichéd terminology; and it reflects Mailer's sense of his own struggle with available, inadequate, literary styles. Rojack's ability to defy the police and to negotiate that haunted violent part of New York connected with his Harlem and Lower East Side experiences is linked to Mailer's ability to break out of an old style and negotiate that new territory linguistically.

But just as Rojack finds that the second level of American life has its own way of trapping people in its version of the world, and he finally gets away from that area too, so Mailer has no wish to exchange naturalism for supernaturalism and commit himself henceforth to a purely demonic mode of writing—for that too is only a version, a fixed reading. He needs his demonology to give some definition to Rojack's confused perceptions of the realities of the dark world of Harlem, dream, chaos and old night. But if he went over to this style exclusively then he would become a prisoner in his own system. Just as Rojack walks the edge of the parapet to signify his intention to remain unclaimed by both sides, so Mailer walks a stylistic edge. He touches continually on two worlds—the inner and the outer, the demonic and the political, the dreaming and the waking, the structured and the flowing—and tries to be stylistically adequate to all without being trapped by any one.

As the plot of the novel thickens, or perhaps one should say multiplies, Rojack experiences that familiar American sense of "mysteries revolving into mysteries like galaxies forming themselves." Later, as he is driving through New York, he feels a growing nausea at the realization that although he is aware of plots and mystery revolving around him,

> I did not know if it was a hard precise mystery with a detailed solution, or a mystery fathered by the collision of larger mysteries, something so hopeless to determine as the edge of a cloud, or could it be, was it a mystery even worse, something between the two, some hopeless no-man's land from which nothing could return but exhaustion? [*AD*, p. 153]

If the mystery is a political, social one then Mailer can meet it with his more naturalistic style and the surface plot—Kelly, C.I.A., Mafia, and so on. If it is a larger mystery then Mailer will try to meet it with his rhetoric of myth, demons and dread. It may be a mystery in between, however. In which case, Mailer shows himself grappling with it, tottering on that vertiginous edge where the two kinds of mystery meet, a no-man's-land (into which General Cummings timidly peered, seeing nothing) which perhaps only the artist can fathom without falling. Unlike Cummings, Rojack has a sense of the powers on both sides of the parapet. Rojack learns that the secret of sanity is "the ability to hold the maximum of impossible combinations in one's mind," and Mailer's work represents an attempt to show, stylistically, how this may be done.

Ralph Ellison has the narrator of *The Invisible Man* declare: "Step outside the narrow borders of what men call reality and you step into chaos . . . or imagination." When Hawthorne's Wakefield stepped out of the "system" he stepped into a void. Rojack on the parapet is stepping *out* without stepping *over*. The parapet constitutes that third area so eagerly sought by American heroes, and using Ellison's terms we can identify it as the area of imagination—a territory not already marked out by contemporary society, but created by a personal energy of style. By asserting his own unique style, the writer on the edge resists imposed patterns (or pattern-lessness) from both sides. Ellison's Invisible Man, we remember, wrote his book in a "border area," withdrawn from uptown politics and plots, and from Harlem chaos, creating an identity with the illuminations of his own writing. William Burroughs's figure, Lee, writing from the other side of the world's mirror, and John Hawkes's Skipper, writing on his magic floating island, both seem to me to offer situational metaphors which can be compared with Rojack's parapet and Ellison's border area—all of them indicating a desire to find some third area beyond conditioning, avoiding both fixity and flow (or prison and jelly), where they can create without being controlled. It is an area from which the contemporary world is still intensely visible, but inside which the world's coercions and impositions are transformed into material which can be fashioned on the writer's own terms. It is the City of Words.

In *Why Are We in Vietnam?* (1967) Mailer continued his explorations into the mystery and source of power, trying to find the intersection point where the pure pre-moral force of nonhuman nature enters into, affects, or works through the human agencies of society. The narrative occasion is a hunting expedition into Alaska which takes a group from Texas into the northern wilderness. Vietnam is not mentioned until the last page, but the book is effectively trying to answer the question posed by the title. Is there a force of negation emanating from the northern ice which works through the "higher" orders of nature (animals and men), causing them to extend its empire of non-being by awakening impulses of destruction in them? Is there something in the American continent itself which touched the men who settled there, transforming creative impulses into periodic dark rages of annihilation which were turned not only on the original inhabitants, the animals, and the land itself, but which also now reach out as far as the jungles of Vietnam? Was the evil there waiting in the land, as Burroughs has said? Burroughs is mentioned by name more than once, and in fact this is Mailer's most Burroughs-like book inasmuch as it tries to examine the operational modes of whatever power it is that seems to be working to bring organic life back to the crystalline fixity of ice. The narrator refers to himself ironically as a Manichee and we could say that the novel is another approach to that nightmare of entropy turned Manichaean which seems to obsess American writers.

The narrator is a voice which identifies itself as D.J. He gives an account of the expedition to shoot bear which was organized by his father, Rusty, a powerful, brutal, Texan business man. D.J. is accompanied by his close friend Tex, and when the bear-shooting is over they take a walk together as far into the northern snow as they can, not to kill but to open themselves up to the mystery and dread of this geographical extreme. The book seems to include a deliberate evocation of Faulkner's classic story "The Bear." There a boy is initiated into "the wilderness' concordant generality" of which the bear is experienced as the ancient presiding spirit. In Faulkner's story the forest of course contains its danger and its violence, and the chilling snake encountered in the closing paragraphs of the story is also part of the spirit of the woods. Even so, it is fair to say that Faulkner allows one to feel that there is an ancient integrity and value and wisdom in untouched nature which the encroachments of civilization are systematically destroying. As a result something precious and irreplaceable is lost. Mailer, writing some twenty-five years later and from an urban background, seems to want to suggest that this traditional dichotomy between nature and civilization which is so dear to American literature and is enshrined in Faulkner's classic tale, needs to be questioned. Man does indeed despoil the beauties of nature, cuts himself off from its prime mysteries, devotes himself to corporations like the Pentagon, collects guns and contracts cancer, invents helicopters to defoliate and decimate, lives inside the deadening impurities of industrial and mental smog, and is curiously attracted to death—all this and more is touched on by Mailer's novel. But it generates the further suggestion that the original prompting for this compulsion to waste substance was not brought by man into the unspoiled realms of nature but rather contracted there—whether in the jungle, the desert, or at the polar ice cap. This is one reason why Mailer's book can be felt to be confusing. Because on the one hand he does make it seem wonderfully purifying to leave all the foul mess of society behind and "shed" the "corporation layers" to come into contact with the clean authenticity of the northern wilderness. On the other hand, having experienced this "purification," D.J. leaves for Vietnam with something approaching exhilaration. It is thus an ambiguous ceremony of initiation.

D.J. believes that we are all agents of Satan and the Lord, and that America is "run by a mysterious hidden mastermind"—sentiments familiar from Burroughs's work, to go no further afield. In moving out beyond society, D.J. is trying to get at the power anterior to all society. First the hunters move into a special camp, a "collision area marginated halfway" between civilization and nature. With guns and helicopters, they do their hunting with one foot firmly lodged in the land of technology which they have only half left behind. Thus the encounters with wild nature are usually ugly, messy woundings which maim the animals and shame the hunters. Not until they have left their arms and the rest of the expedition behind can D.J. and Tex experience the pure unrefracted mystery and power of the north, the animals, the lights and the awesome ice peaks. Not surprisingly they pause "on the edge" of the snow line; once more the American hero has brought himself to an edge. And in stepping over that edge, they make a temporary venture into undifferentiation, the "wilderness' concordant generality" in Faulkner's terms, "the endless non-contemplative powers" of pre-conscious nature in Mailer's own words. Significantly, it is also a temporary step beyond language. The narrator's language is throughout usually obscene, as many reviewers noted, but the following statement offers an important clarification. Having recorded their last dialogue, the narrator explains that they were "in such a haste to get all the mixed glut and sludge out of their systems that they're heating up all the foul talk to get rid of it in a hurry like bad air going up the flue and so be ready to enjoy good air and nature, cause don't forget they are up in God's attic." Cleansed of society's mores, weapons and words, they are ready to receive God's message, and tune into the secret of His power. And in the silence D.J. first experiences Him as a great beast, summoning him up into the darker north to die; then, as he resists this summoning (as Rojack resisted the moon's summons to jump from the parapet), God becomes a beast whispering, "Fulfill my will, go forth and kill." This seems to be the last message from the north.

However, all that I have said about the novel depends on accepting the narrator as a reliable delineator of his own experiences, and treating his account as a coherent version. But this the voice itself continuously, aggressively and mockingly discourages us from doing. It reminds us that we can never really know the identity which lies behind the written or spoken word. The voice tells us that it might belong to a crazed Harlem Negro who is hallucinating that he is a rich white boy in Texas, or precisely the reverse—a shade dreaming of being a spade, as he puts it. We are told that, one, we cannot be sure "whose consciousness" we are getting, and two, "there is no security in this consciousness." Notions of stable narration are dissolved in reminders of the problematical relationship between stream-of-consciousness, memory, imagination, fantasy (plus the possibility of drug-induced hallucination), documentary and the arbitrary fabrications of a processed tape recording. The whole thing could be a sportive program put out by the self-styled Disc Jockey; or it could be the twitchings of an "expiring consciousness," the "unwinding and unravelings of a nervous constellation just now executed." The voice aims at exploiting all the available speech levels of America, from the obscenities of Harlem slang to the pedantries of academe. We cannot possibly "fix" the identity of this narrator, and this manically maintained mysteriousness is a demonstration of a larger truth. "You never know what vision has been humping you through the night." We have encountered many American protagonists who are exceedingly anxious and uncertain about both the source and the nature of various versions of reality which they feel are being more or less subtly imposed on them. In this novel Mailer transfers that condition to the reader.

In one sense, then, we as readers are beset by the multiple voice of the American dream life made articulate. This voice has internalized so many of America's hidden desires and compulsions and power drives, just as it has assimilated so many of America's languages and sub-languages, that one has the disturbing sensation of tuning into many wavelengths at once. Like the work of Burroughs, this is another book which calls into question many of McLuhan's more sanguine aphorisms, for this voice comes from a consciousness picking up and transmitting a density of mixed messages which cannot be reduced to coherence nor reassembled into verifiable versions. What one can never know from the book is whether the narrative account comes from a victor or a victim. Thus, one could indeed hear the voice as coming from a consciousness which has been so conditioned and dazed by the onslaught of contemporary America that when it does get beyond the Arctic Circle it can never really "clear" all the static or sludge out of itself, but simply projects on to the god of the northern ice an exhortation to destruction which had in fact been fed into it since childhood by the power circuits of American society. Despite its manic assertiveness, this voice may just be frantic from excessive "input" which has inflamed rationality to the point of incoherence.

On the other hand one could say that the voice does at least avoid being trapped in any one version of patterning of reality—an abiding American aspiration as we have seen. It calls into question its own theories, it mocks its own metaphors and notions of magic—many of these close to Mailer's own, so there is the incidental possibility of self-parody here.

Whatever else it is, this narrating voice is counter-crystalline, since it refuses to be "fixed" and will never rest in the stasis of a single configuration. In a book which at one level is about ice, the narrative voice itself is constantly melting and refusing terminal forms. Of course, this leaves us with no one version, or interpretation, to hold on to; indeed it calls the whole range of narrating and interpreting activities of consciousness into question. The book removes itself to a plane of pure ambiguity. Perhaps, as Burroughs recommended, the narrator is getting all the accumulated junk of consciousness down on tape and playing it back just to get rid of it: perhaps, like Cabot Wright, he feels that when he has put all the versions down before him he can be free of them all, eluding all patterns to be finally alone with his non-self. Or perhaps he *is* trying to get at some deep truths about the source and nature of power in America, at the same time desperately avoiding the temptation to believe in any one definitive account. There is after all great energy manifested in and through the writing, whereas the sense of the difficulties involved in offering narrative accounts has led a writer like John Barth more in the direction of paralysis. Among these possibilities and others, we can never decide. D.J. does not walk a parapet but the book itself exists on a precarious edge where it is difficult to discriminate the status of winner and loser, just as the operations of Satan and the Lord seem almost indistinguishable. On that edge, however, it manages to communicate with unusual vividness something of what it is like to be a vexed and struggling consciousness in contemporary America. One could perhaps regard the book as being rather like one of Browning's dramatic monologues in which, as Walter Bagehot so admirably remarked, we are confronted by *"mind in difficulties* . . . amid the circumstances least favorable to it, just while it is struggling with obstacles, just where it is encumbered with incongruities."

In some of his more recent journalism, *The Armies of the Night* (1968) and *Miami and the Siege of Chicago* (1968), Mailer's material seems to polarize itself into convenient oppositions in a rather too predictable manner. It suggests that he is beginning to write in accordance with his own established formulae, and the consideration prompts itself that even Norman Mailer must confront the danger of becoming fixed in his own patternings. But it would be unfair and misleading to dwell on the weaknesses of Mailer's most recent work. The main point is that for most of the past two decades he has constantly sought to expose himself to the influences at work in America without capitulating to any of them, and as constantly sought for appropriate modes of utterance to project his responses to those influences and transform reaction into style. We may think back to Rojack walking round the parapet, while the powers around him push and tug at his precarious balance. It is perhaps only a personal dare, a private test of courage, in a way a rather preposterous performance. Yet it is only by this performance that he achieves a "provisional sanity" and secures at least a temporary freedom from the oppressive magics circulating around him. Some lines from Robert Browning's "Bishop Blougram's Apology" seem to me relevant here.

> You see lads walk the street
> Sixty the minute; what's to note in that?
> You see one lad o'erstride a chimney-stack;
> Him you must watch—he's sure to fall, yet stands!
> Our interest's on the dangerous edge of things.
> The honest thief, the tender murderer,
> The superstitious atheist . . .
> We watch while these in equilibrium keep
> The giddy line midway: one step aside,
> They're classed and done with.

If the boy on the chimney-stack, or Rojack on the parapet, take one step either way, they are "classed" and, indeed, "done with." Mailer's main achievement has been to keep an equilibrium on "the dangerous edge of things" through the resources of his own style. Norman Mailer on his parapet is doing what many other American writers are doing, or trying to do, in their own way—resisting classification, pre-

serving a tottering freedom by not capitulating to the patterns and powers on either side of him, walking his own line
in a bid to defy conditioning. It is perhaps the most characteristic stance of the American writer during the last two
decades.

1. *The Hell's Angels* (Random House, New York, 1967; Allen Lane, The
   Penguin Press, London, 1967).
2. In *Ramparts,* March, 1967.

POET

Barry H. Leeds

"Deaths for the Ladies and Other Disasters"

... The most painful disappointment to someone interested in Mailer's work (but who does not wish to assume the role of Mailer apologist) is his poetry. Almost every poem Mailer has ever written appears in a volume entitled *Deaths for the Ladies and Other Disasters*,[1] although many of these poems and a few new ones are sprinkled through the nonfiction collections, and one or two are worked into *The Deer Park* and *An American Dream*.

Deaths for the Ladies is one book which it appears Mailer was more foolhardy than brave to publish, for there is no significant literary merit anywhere in it. The few worthwhile poems which are included are not worthy of an entire volume, and most of the pieces are not worthy of the entire page which each occupies. It is certain that no major American publishing house would have considered the book without the benefit of Mailer's name to help sell it. Nonetheless, it is unfortunate that the book is pejoratively associated with Mailer's reputation but not usually associated with his other work; for it is only in the context of the entire body of his writing that the poetry assumes any interest. Just as *An American Dream* (which may seem at first to some readers a sloppy, self-indulgent fantasy) appears clearer in purpose and execution when read in light of what precedes it, *Deaths for the Ladies* is largely incomprehensible without extensive reading in Mailer's prose. But unlike *An American Dream,* it cannot be justified as a significant book even after careful study has unearthed some coherence in the patterns it presents.

For what it is or isn't worth, the book is conceived as a whole, an intention which is partially implemented by the device of omitting any pagination.[2] Refrains and echoes of early pages reappear later in the book, suggesting that Mailer is attempting to erect and reinforce a structure from his grab-bag of minor perceptions, epigrams, and personal horrors. In order not to overemphasize the very limited extent to which this attempt is successful, I would first like to establish some perspective by quoting a few of the more precious poems. (Mailer calls them "short hairs.")

A few attempt to explain the nature of the book itself, as:

> The art of
> the
> short hair
> is that
> it
> don't
> go on
> for
> too long.

And:

> This is
> genteel
> poetry.
> One thought
> at a time.

But the clearest insight into the form of this poetry and into Mailer's own attitude toward its publication comes from this poem:

A writer who
has power
should use it
to extract
such benefits
from his
publisher

as
give
his
words

room

to

breathe
I
w
a
n
t
m
y
l
i
n
e
t
o
s
t
r
i
k
e   e
l   k
i   a
k   n
e   s
a

A snake
can't strike
in a box

The poem suggests that Mailer is waggishly aware of the fact that it is the power of his name rather than the merit of his poetry which has persuaded the publisher to allow him *carte blanche* in presenting this material. This poem is also a good example of Mailer's derivative use of the devices of other poets. On the next page, he acknowledges the influence of e. e. cummings evident here:

you break

up your

line

like

ee

cum

mings

I notice

n

o   heb   re a

ksitu   pd

iffe

r

e

nt

*   *   *

r)

ette

besi desh e'sb

And on the following page, within his own poem, he italicizes this echo of Wallace Stevens:

> *the emperor is the*
> *emperor of ice cream*

Other literary influences are advertised as well. For example, Mailer uses a quotation from T. S. Eliot as an epigraph to a poem and dedicates two "wanderings in prose" to Hemingway. The latter are highly personal and rather poignant pieces about Mailer's own life. And in "Farewell to Arms Revisited," Mailer deals wittily with how Catherine and Frederick Henry would feel had they been married for twelve years.

Some of the individual poems are interesting in themselves, worth a chuckle or a wince:

Cheerleader

She
went to
Southern
Baptist
U
but
somehow
she nev-
er did
find out
who
John
the Bap-
tist was.

*   *   *

Definition of a Hero:

He
thrives
in
dikes.

*   *   *

Exodus

goodbye America,
    Jesus said.
Come back, *boy!*[3]
    we cried
    too late.

    *   *   *

       If
Harry Golden
is the gentile's
Jew
    can I be-
come the Golden
Goy?

    *   *   *

Men
who are not
    married
    and grow beards
    are insecure,
    said the CIA
    before
    it went
    to Cuba.

The most serious artistic attempt which Mailer seems to be making in this uneven book is to present the entire volume as one continuing experience. The device upon which this attempt at structure and continuity rests is the use of fugue-like repetitions from one part of the book to another. One of these provides a particularly good example of the way in which repetition establishes and reinforces a thematic statement:

doing the limbo bit
doing the limbo bit
      it's good enough
        for me

This bit of doggerel, taken from a popular song, appears several times, at intervals. Two primary associations occur immediately, and are reinforced by the monotony of repetition. First, the obvious derivation of the poem from a particularly mindless example of popular entertainment implies that our popular culture is tasteless and without meaning. Secondly, the speaker, in "doing the limbo bit," is saying in popular parlance that he is in a limbo (although the song itself means literally that he is doing the dance called the limbo). Both of these associations are encompassed by the intentional irony of the last line, "it's good enough for me," in which the speaker makes it clear that he is quite willing to accept the status quo of a personal limbo within a vacuous society.

Within the structure established by such repetitions, Mailer introduces a number of themes to which he returns throughout the book. One of these is the metaphor of cancer (already dealt with above in terms of the novels), which is viewed in a number of contexts, as:

Cancer Gulch

What's
    he got?
    (Made
    a little
    money
Lost
    a little
    love)

Miami.

Cancer has been shown previously to be a metaphor of particular importance to Mailer, one which recurs throughout his work. And the title, "Cancer Gulch," is a favorite Mailer term for the geographical or mental situations in America which are most artificial, most antipathetic to true emotion. Thus, the playland of Miami comes to represent the false, materialistic values of those who visit it, and by implication, those of most Americans. Other poems about cancer include:

Circumcision

They say
 that
 women
 don't get
 cancer
 of the
 cervix
 as much
 from Jewish
  men.

They don't.

They give
 it
 to
 Jewish
  men.

and:

Cancer
is growing
ivy
professor
which spreads
like college

and:

You have
so many
poems
about
cancer

It's me.
or
my readers.

The first of these poems ties into several other thematic patterns in the book. It reinforces Mailer's usual theory that cancer comes from stifled emotion; it provides another in a series of perceptions about the sexual identity problems of Jewish males (an issue dealt with more here than in any other of Mailer's books, despite the fact that he is himself Jewish); and it is related to the theme of disappointment in marriage which informs many of the poems. The other cancer poems quoted above further emphasize Mailer's contention that every aspect of American culture (even the academy) and most of the populace are touched by the cancer of stagnance and falsity.

If the numerous themes treated briefly (and sometimes rather superficially) by Mailer in this book are obviously representative of his cerebral preoccupations in the early nineteen-sixties, it should be no surprise that many of them correspond to those which govern *An American Dream*, which Mailer was to write two years later. Actually, this book might serve as a companion volume to *An American Dream* (although the juxtaposition certainly would not do Mailer's reputation any good in those quarters where the novel was badly received). Not only does the poetry reveal Mailer's earlier concern with themes and metaphors which appear in *An American Dream*, but sometimes actual plot situations are previewed, such as:

One
nerve
screams
before
you
fall
said
the
ledge
on
the
window
in
the
nineteenth
floor

and:

something
about
the
smell
of a cop
when he's
groping
you

And even Rojack's note to Cherry upon leaving her asleep appears first here:

Hey—
you
sleep
deep—
but what a sight
see
you
soon
beautiful
I hope

Other themes and metaphors in the poetry which figure in Mailer's prose works include witches, cannibals, urine, and the smell of corporation. But the most effective development of a theme within a single poem occurs at the end of *Deaths for the Ladies,* in the long poem entitled "The Inaugural Ball."

1.

There was a time
  when fornication
  was titanic
and the Devil
  had to work
  to cheat a womb.

  (pride of his teeth
    on a root
    long enough
        to
    pluck it out
    the green wet sea
    of the pussy slue
    and down a falling
        flight
    of cellar stairs
    hard, dark, deep
    into the maiden brown
    rooting out the bowels
    which fell
    like assassins
        upon the white foam
        of God's arrow)

*   *   *

3.

But now the devil
        smokes a cigar
        and has his nose
        up U.S. Phar-
        maceutical
The assassins
        who fall on God's
        white arrow
        give off the fumes
        of chemical
        killer bedded
        in vaseline
        as heroic
        in its odor
        as the exhaust
        which comes off a
        New York City
        Transportation
        System Bus.

There is more to the poem, but this will suffice. The first
section quoted above presents in abstract form the bedroom
scene between Rojack and Ruta in *An American Dream,* and
the central metaphor established by that scene: the conflict
between God and the Devil as represented in the choice between Ruta's two orifices. The second excerpt carries the idea
further, by implying that the American experience, conditioned by the influence of mass technology, has further stacked
the odds against the victory of the fertile forces of God. In
the fourth and final section of this poem, Mailer looks to the
future, hoping that the contest will once again become an
equal one. The central metaphor is effectively developed here,
perhaps better than in any other of his poems. Yet the idea
is much more precisely and effectively given literary form in
the Ruta passage of *An American Dream.* And this is a

judgment which I feel extends to all Mailer's poetry. *Deaths for the Ladies and Other Disasters* is a strange and uneven book, sometimes witty, often merely cute. But even in its better aspects, the few good individual poems and Mailer's intention to make the book one cumulative experience, the experiment falls far short of the achievement of Mailer's prose. It is certainly less than one would like to expect from him.

NOTES

1. New York: G. P. Putnam's Sons, 1962.
2. Where it seems relevant, it will be made clear whether a poem precedes or follows another, or whether it appears early or late in the book.
3. The emphasis on the italicized word *boy*, the traditional Southern term of address for a Negro, makes plain Mailer's condemnation of American arrogance and moral blindness.

PLAYWRIGHT

Gerald Weales

The Park in the Playhouse

When Norman Mailer published his novel *The Deer Park* in 1955, he used as epigraph Gide's "Please do not understand me too quickly." Shortly before the stage version of *The Deer Park* opened at the Theatre de Lys, he wrote the traditional philosopho-advertising Sunday article for the *New York Times,* in which, commenting on how hard it is for the first-night reviewer to respond to "an exciting, difficult play," he asked for the same forbearance.

At the risk of being too quick, I will assume that both the novel and the play, which follows the novel very closely, use the professional fraudulence of Hollywood and the commercial artificiality of Desert D'Or, the resort setting for the action, as masks for the pretenses, conscious and unconscious, that men use in their sexual, political, and artistic lives. Although the sex is used satirically and Mailer beats society with a priapic weapon as though he were Juvenal, both novel and play assume that beyond the pretense is a painful truth about the relationship of man to woman and man to his own possibilities which is finally comforting. I cannot take seriously Sergius O'Shaugnessy, Mailer's narrator-hero, but I suspect that the author does and that he really means that "to have heard that sex was time and time the connection of new circuits was a part of the poor odd dialogues which give hope to us noble humans for more than one night." Whether this summary of *The Deer Park* is a critical understanding or misunderstanding will not change the fact that, aside from some successful comedy, the play is dull, sentimental, and flatulent.

The comedy lies primarily in the character of Herman Teppis, the caricature of a studio head, who—particularly as Will Lee plays him—suggests Louis B. Mayer, at least the Mayer that Lillian Ross invented. It is not surprising that Teppis, the most memorable character in the novel, should become the commanding figure on stage. Mailer uses him not only in extended scenes, as in the novel, but also in brief verbal spots sometimes no more than a sentence long, garbled platitudes that work like revue one-liners: lights up, joke, comic expression, blackout.

Since Teppis spends most of the evening on a platform above the action, sitting on a throne (which turns out to be a throne in the slang sense of the word), Mailer presumably intends to suggest some kind of God–king–studio-head analogy, but the character works primarily as relief. Lee plays him very broadly and endearingly, which surely must not be the intention; but he is funny, and whenever the lights went down on him and up on still another of the passion-and-palaver sequences, I wanted to cry out, in Teppis's words, "Let's not get off the sidetrack."

As for the troubles on the main track, they have to do with both the subject matter and Mailer's conception of a play. In the *Times* article, he talked about traditional plot as though it were a kind of intellectual spoon-feeding, the playwright's way of leading a shy audience to that last big scene. "Why not," he asked, "write a play which went from explosion to explosion . . . from one moment of intensity or reality . . . to the next—a play which went at full throttle all the way." Had he really written such a play, the result might have been exciting, but would surely have been self-defeating: when there are no non-explosions to measure the explosions by, the pow-pow-pow turns into a hum.

Not counting the mechanical attempts at artificial res-
piration by means of flashing lights and ringing bells, Mailer
uses three kinds of "explosions": comic, verbal, and dramatic.
The first kind works because the lines are funny and the
caricatures easily recognizable. The second fails because it
involves extended speeches, sometimes metaphorical, that
build to one of the four-letter words which many of us use
casually in ordinary conversation and which the actors at the
de Lys speak as though they were surrounded by exclamation
points.

The dramatic scenes fail primarily because of that old
devil plot. For all his avowals, Mailer has retained the three
main plots of the novel, although Sergius's search for a soul
and the romantic and studio problems of Lulu Meyers, movie
star and sex symbol, have been moved to the periphery so that
Charles Francis Eitel can take center stage with his artistic
and political struggle, seen obliquely through his affair with
Elena. While Mailer uses the devices of non-naturalistic
theatre, his dramatic scenes—those moments of intensity—
are apparently supposed to work realistically. They cannot
do so because the scenes depend for their power not on what
is immediately happening but on the people to whom it is
happening, and Mailer never creates those people. If the scenes
were to be simply a dance of masks, that might be acceptable;
but they seem to be inviting us to be touched, to be moved,
even to be annoyed. In his attempt to give the characters
validity, Mailer moves great hunks of expositional material
from the novel to the play, taking thoughts from his characters' minds and putting them into their mouths, where they
certainly do not belong. The result is extended self-analysis
—played often at a shrill whine—so clumsy that it makes the
psychological plays of the 1950's seem austere and guarded.
The Deer Park is stocked with garrulous stick figures.

The art, the politics, and the sex in the play are no more
believable than the characters. In the first two instances, that
is because the play is a period piece passing itself off as a
contemporary drama. Mailer updates some of Eitel's problems

a bit, but the director is still beset by a Communist-hunting Congressional committee and an industry blacklist and he is still the willing victim of a studio system that is at once an oppression and a comfort. Mailer must have been aware that most of the play's overtones were from the mid-1950's, for there is a note in the program explaining that the play is set in an unspecified time that "offers us echoes of all the decades." Even though the old Hollywood studio system is dead and the old Hollywood blacklists whitewashed, there is no reason why these images cannot seem relevant today (as they do when one rereads the novel), but in a play that is vaguely set in the right-now they are hardly believable villains.

The difficulty with the sex is not that it is old-fashioned, which it is, but that it is a sentimental bore. Almost everyone in the play goes on and on and on about who is good with whom and how. Yet the mechanics are not specified but clucked over lyrically: "Charley, you're the king." Not that so much talk about sex would be any less boring if details were supplied, but at least it might sound less like a ladies'-magazine view of the lurid life. Kathleen Norris is not dead; she's alive in Norman Mailer.

Wait a minute. Maybe I did understand Mailer too quickly. There are two movie scripts in *The Deer Park*. One is the serious one that Eitel is presumably writing, the story of a TV personality who, driven by compassion, becomes a secular saint who does only harm when he wants to do good. The other is the version of Eitel's script refashioned by a canny producer to fit the presumed market, with an upbeat ending in which the hero becomes a priest against a background of angelic voices. In the novel, Eitel's original script is, in a way, his own story. The revised script may be more important to the play, where the lines from the novel become somehow portentous ("Sergius, what does one ever do with one's life? Are you one of those who know?"), where the malevolent pimp is given conventional motivation, where Eitel is nicely finished off with a heart attack, where Sergius relights the sexual-spiritual torch Eitel has let go out and

Sergius has his final talk with God. *The Deer Park* may even be a joke about that type of movie, which would explain why the comedy is obvious and the rest at once unlikely and dull. This is the interpretation that surpasseth understanding.

FILMMAKER

Leo Braudy

"Maidstone: A Mystery"

In the late fall of 1967 Norman Mailer spoke at Yale. The Law School auditorium was packed with a nervous audience, many of whom had never read a word Mailer had written, but all eagerly waiting for a show, knowing that he always made a spectacle of himself. Mailer didn't let them down. Rocking back and forth towards the microphone as though unwilling to rest too close or too far from his audience, he began a rambling series of good jokes and bad ones, sly attacks on Yale at the expense of Harvard, and casually slipped in obscenities.

Soon the audience began to feel that it wasn't getting its money's worth. (Admission was free.) Rolled-up wads of paper pelted the authorial presence. More pointed obscenities followed. The audience relaxed cheerfully. But then another stretch of rhetorical dead space brought forth another barrage of paper.

"The next person who hits me will be invited onto the stage for an existential confrontation," announced Mailer with the mock-heroic solemnity of Falstaff challenging an innkeeper. The challenge was quickly picked up, the challenger invited to the stage, insults were traded, and the challenger was finally forced to leave the auditorium in order to prove his assertion that Mailer wasn't worth listening to.

The filming of *Maidstone,* whose background, script and metaphysic take up Mailer's latest book [fall, 1971] is similarly described as "the advanced course in existentialism." To make this third of his movies (after "Wild 90" and "Beyond the Law") Mailer in the early summer of 1968 took almost a hundred people out to a series of Long Island estates for five days and nights of filming during which they were to become "a bunch of enforced existentialists."

This literary twin of *Maidstone,* the movie, is compounded of three different approaches to those five days on Long Island: first, a descriptive introduction to the scene of production woven from articles written at the time by J. Anthony Lukas (*The New York Times*), Sally Beauman (*New York* magazine) and James Toback (*Esquire*). Then comes the "script" itself, that is, a transcript of the final film with Mailer's Shavian stage directions and comments (there was no shooting script). Then finally there is *A Course in Filmmaking,* Mailer's part-metaphysical, part-descriptive account of the process that led to the finished film. A cast list, technical credits and stills fill out the book.

Like anything Mailer undertakes, the resulting mélange of journalism, film and speculation is fascinating, with a labyrinth of data and fancy presented in the tones of that whimsical didacticism Mailer has fashioned for his literary voice since *Advertisements for Myself.* Two ideas of filmmaking battle against each other in Mailer's theory: the desire to release the untapped "existential" potential in his (largely) unprofessional cast; and the belief that the film director is like a general, somehow coordinating a mass of conflicting desires and details into a successful campaign. To combat the director's tendency to extract meaning that he himself had already placed into a scene, Mailer allowed the actors to improvise their lines and set loose several camera crews to film scenes simultaneously so that his own presence would not be continually inhibiting.

But, as Mailer recounts it in *A Course in Filmmaking,* the film he had hoped for never emerged from the 45 hours of film he shot. *A Course in Filmmaking* in fact has little of the originality and suggestiveness of an earlier essay on "Wild 90" Mailer published in *Esquire* in 1967. Its true interest lies much more in its account of Mailer's esthetic failures than his successes. *Maidstone: A Mystery* reveals a story in the film that its author never expected, and so, after a long section "On the Theory," Mailer throws away his theoretic ladder and proceeds to "In the Practice."

Only after watching the rushes for many hours does he realize that the attack on him by Rip Torn (which now ends the film) was the film's true realization and represented a more profound conception of what was going on in the film than he himself realized. Whatever his own interest in releasing existial potential in his actors, in fact his own personality, expressed either as Norman T. Kingsley the movie director/ Presidential candidate (in the film) or Norman Mailer the movie director/noted author (in the film as well), had manipulated them into what turned out to be often not very interesting postures. But one of the marionettes revolted, appropriately enough Rip Torn, the only professional actor in a main role. His revolt makes *Maidstone* one of the few films one ought to see at least twice, since the ending, with no indication of being a cheap reversal, makes the viewer immediately want to re-evaluate what came before, so authentic is the emotion released.

Now, with the printed script, it is fascinating to see how the film inevitably, but also surprisingly, leads up to the attack. Kingsley/Mailer boxes with his sparring partner and tells him not to go for the head. Mailer/Kingsley pedagogically instructs his cast and crew about the levels of reality they are plumbing. Torn's hammer on Mailer's head does not complete the plot of the film so much as it completes the esthetic of the film, the odd balance beween control and uncertainty that Mailer was searching for. One wonders if in the back of Torn's own head was Mailer's remark in *Advertisements for Myself* that the reader of James Baldwin felt a need "to take a hammer to his detachment, smash the perfumed dome of his ego."

In its esthetic play with the levels of reality *Maidstone* is a marriage of the violent dislocations of Godard's *Weekend* with the playful theatricality of *A Midsummer Night's Dream*. Once again, the theoretical aspect is less congenial than what finally emerged. Mailer at the end of *A Course in Filmmaking* concludes that in the search for reality "the ineluctable ore of the authentic is our only key to the lock," and too often in his essay the "authentic" seems to have something to do with the documentary. Mailer scorns *cinéma verité* (although less cogently than in his earlier essay) because people do not do so well playing themselves. Yet the process of filmmaking he describes sounds very much in accord with *cinéma verité* beliefs: Set up as many cameras as possible for as much time as possible, and then with judicious cutting, the "real" will appear. The form of *Maidstone: A Mystery* seems to repeat that formula: the "objective" reportorial views of the filming, the emergent script, and the director's meditation.

Mailer claims that his main impulse in making the film was to get away from the merciless collectivity and rigorous schedules of the Hollywood product. Yet he is uncertain about his own fixing of the line between spontaneity and control. Film may be an individual dream, in contrast to the social ritual of theater. But he also says that in his dreams an individual adds to his own vast social novel, and Mailer alternately refers to his cast and crew as an army and a party. The army floundering into success in *The Naked and the Dead*? The party proposed in *Advertisements for Myself* that will be recounted by a dead man?*

Coming beween *The Armies of the Night* and *Miami and the Siege of Chicago* in Mailer's work, *Maidstone* (and *Maidstone: A Mystery*) continues that as yet incomplete process of dismantling that Mailer is performing on the public

*See "Advertisements for Myself on the Way Out." [Editor's Note.]

ego that has served him so well over the years; it is a prelude to the political uncertainty of *Miami and Chicago* and the "loss of ego" that begins *Of a Fire on the Moon,* as well as the defense of his literary integrity and style in *The Prisoner of Sex.* I like the film *Maidstone* very much, its wit, its frequent visual beauty and its unique infusion of emotion into what might have otherwise been dry Pirandellian exercises. *Maidstone: A Mystery* is more important for the light it casts on Mailer's other work. It is a staging ground for later experiments with narrative method, for example, the emphasis on mood in *Of a Fire on the Moon.*

But what remains compelling about both film and book derives less from Mailer's theory than from his acute sense of deception and self-deception in the characters of others and especially in his own, and his willingness to change his preconceptions. At one point in the film Mailer as Kingsley the director is interviewing an actress and asks her to do some Shakespeare. She begins to speak, but his attention is distracted and he never quite hears or recognizes what she recites. It is Titania's speech when she wakes and sees Bottom with his ass's head standing before her. At its best *Maidstone: A Mystery* explores with charm and power one of Mailer's great themes, the potentialities of human character. Like Bottom's dream it is an exploration that has no bottom.

JOURNALIST

Michael L. Johnson

Norman Mailer

Besides being a novelist, Norman Mailer has done a great deal of journalistic writing in the last fifteen years. Much of his writing for *Esquire* and other magazines during the early 1960's was in the vanguard of good journalistic writing. The earliest piece which foreshadows clearly his leaning toward the New Journalism he helped to found is "Superman Comes to the Supermarket," a report on Kennedy's candidacy published by *Esquire* in November of 1960; and one may find other examples in *The Presidential Papers of Norman Mailer* (1963) or in other collections of his work, such as *Cannibals and Christians* (1966). However, it was his 90,000-word piece, "The Steps of the Pentagon," concerning the Pentagon demonstration in October 1967, published in *Harper's,* March 1968, that marked his coming of age as a New Journalist. It, along with his more objective history of and final reflections on the demonstration, "The Battle of the Pentagon," published in *Commentary,* April 1968, was published later that year in book form as *The Armies of the Night.*

In the subtitle of the book Mailer describes his purpose: *History as a Novel, The Novel as History,* an idea which aligns him with Capote and Wolfe as a genre-maker. Unlike Capote and Wolfe, he features himself as the novel's neo-Jamesian perceiver and Mailerian protagonist, speaking of this character in a self-conscious third person as "Mailer." What Mailer writes of concerning the Pentagon demonstration is not simply the event itself but also the larger aberrations and motivations of the American psyche he sees operating there, a task he had undertaken earlier through the electronic-scatological metaphors of his novel *Why Are We in Vietnam?* (1967). Having pushed a fictional exploration of the contemporary American psyche about as far as he could in that book, he turned his energies to the larger, perhaps more complex task of exploring the activities of that psyche, and of his own, in the frenetic reality of events: history is the raw material of the novelist's art; and the novel is essentially a historical-narrative or, here, journalistic genre.

"History as a Novel: The Steps of the Pentagon," the first part of the book, is concerned with the activities of the demonstration itself: the parties and speeches beforehand, the Lincoln Memorial rally, the herd-like march across the Potomac by way of one crowded bridge, the taunting of the guard around the Pentagon and on the top of the machine-gun-armed building, the arrests of those (including Mailer) who attempted to storm the guard lines, the night in jail—all told with the immediacy, breath-taking cadence, and symbolic sense of detail one associates with Mailer's writing. And through it all Mailer is honest and confessional about his feeling toward the people and the events they were creating. His portraits of Dwight Macdonald, Paul Goodman, Robert Lowell, and other personages involved are memorable, accurate, and revealing of both Mailer and his subjects, for his jealousies and dislikes come freely into play. He says of Robert Lowell, for instance, that he "gave off at times the unwilling haunted saintliness of a man who was repaying the moral debts of ten generations of ancestors"[1]—a description which catches him exactly and at the same time reveals subtly some of Mailer's uneasiness about the greatness of Lowell's talent.

Also, though their styles differ in many ways, Mailer resembles Wolfe in his ability to recreate the feeling, the

mythical and psychological ambience, of an event. As an
example, consider his description of the gathering before the
Lincoln Memorial:

> And from the north and the east, from the direction of the
> White House and the Smithsonian and the Capitol, from
> Union Station and the Department of Justice the troops were
> coming in, the volunteers were answering the call. They came
> walking up in all sizes, a citizens' army not ranked yet by
> height, an army of both sexes in numbers almost equal, and
> of all ages, although most were young. Some were well-
> dressed, some were poor, many were conventional in appear-
> ance, as often were not. The hippies were there in great num-
> ber, perambulating down the hill, many dressed like the
> legions of Sgt. Pepper's Band, some were gotten up like Arab
> sheiks, or in Park Avenue's doormen's greatcoats, others like
> Rogers and Clark of the West, Wyatt Earp, Kit Carson,
> Daniel Boone in buckskin, some had grown mustaches to look
> like *Have Gun, Will Travel*—Paladin's surrogate was here!
> —and wild Indians with feathers, a hippie gotten up like Bat-
> man, another like Claude Rains in *The Invisible Man*—his
> face wrapped in a turban of bandages and he wore a black
> satin top hat. [108]

Or he can communicate very effectively the pressure and
presence of the crowd and the close, physical character of the
event, as in this passage where the demonstration moves from
Lincoln Memorial to cross the Arlington Memorial Bridge:

> Picture then this mass, bored for hours by speeches, now
> elated at the beginning of the March, now made irritable by
> delay, now compressed, all old latent pips of claustrophobia
> popping out of the crush, and picture them as they stepped
> out toward the bridge, monitors in the lead, hollow square
> behind, next the line of notables with tens, then hundreds of
> lines squeezing up behind, helicopters overhead, police gun-
> ning motorcycles, cameras spinning their gears like the wing-
> ing of horseflies, TV car bursting seams with hysterically
> overworked technicians, sun beating overhead—this huge
> avalanche of people rumbled forward thirty feet and came to
> a stop in disorder, the lines breaking and warping and melding
> into themselves to make a crowd not a parade, and some
> jam-up at the front, just what no one knew, now they were
> moving again. Forty more feet. They stopped. At this rate

it would take six hours to reach the Pentagon. And a murmur
came up from behind of huge discontent, not huge yet, huge
in the potential of its discontent. "Let's get going," people in
the front lines were calling out. [126]

Both passages have a cinematic, or TV-camera, kind of visual
presence, with the addition of imagination in the first and a
sense of strain and impatience in the second.

Mailer shifts from the excited narration of events into
long reflective passages with ease, apologizing that it is "one
of the oldest devices of the novelist" (152); and these passages, feverishly insightful, usually derive directly from and
illuminate magically the described event they follow. After
telling of his wait on the police bus following his arrest, Mailer
ascends into the rich, sweeping, metaphorical style, the
driving cadences and moral quandaries of *Why Are We in
Vietnam?* The Arnoldian overtones of the title begin to be
explored: why do men wage war; why this particular war,
that must be opposed by the "armies" of the humane and
conscientious? For Mailer, the war in Vietnam, like the
Pentagon demonstration and his own way of perceiving and
recording it, is peculiarly American and must be seen in that
way, as it was in *Why Are We in Vietnam?* His reportage of
his arrest leads him to darker thoughts:

> One did not have to look for who would work in the
> concentration camps and the liquidation centers—the garri-
> son would be filled with applicants from the pages of a
> hundred American novels, from *Day of the Locust* and *Naked
> Lunch* and *The Magic Christian,* one could enlist half the
> marshals outside this bus, simple, honest, hard-working gov-
> ernment law-enforcement agents, yeah! There was something
> at loose now in American life, the poet's beast slinking to the
> marketplace. The country had always been wild. It had always
> been harsh and hard, it had always had a fever—when life in
> one American town grew insupportable, one could travel, the
> fever to travel was in the American blood, so said all, but
> now the fever had left the blood, it was in the cells, the cells
> traveled, and the cells were as insane as Grandma with orange
> hair [from a reference previously to a senile Las Vegas type
> —reminiscent of Wolfe]. The small towns were disappearing

in the by-passes and the supermarkets and the shopping centers, the small town in America was losing its sense of the
knuckle, the herb, and the root, the walking sticks were no
longer cut from trees, nor were they cured, the schools did
not have crazy old teachers now but teaching aids, and in the
libraries, *National Geographic* gave way to *TV Guide* . . .
the American small town grew out of itself. . . . It had grown
out of itself again and again, its cells traveled, worked for
government, found security through wars in foreign lands,
and the nightmares which passed on the winds in the old small
towns now traveled on the nozzle tip of the flame thrower,
no dreams now of barbarian lusts, slaughtered villages, battles
of blood, no, nor any need for them—technology had driven
insanity out of the wind and out of the attic, and out of all
the lost primitive places: one had to find it now wherever
fever, force, and machines could come together, in Vegas, at
the race track, in pro football, race riots for the Negro, sub-
urban orgies—none of it was enough—one had to find it in
Vietnam; that was where the small town had gone to get its
kicks. [172–174]

This line of commentary comes to a head later in the first
part: "He came to the saddest conclusion of them all for it
went beyond the war in Vietnam. He had come to decide that
the center of America might be insane" [211].

Mailer's journalism, as can be seen from the passages
above, is frequently poetic, and that poetic quality sharpens
the edge of his observations and speculations, giving them
the vitality of a dawning consciousness in the reader. Faustian-
Falstaffian Mailer uses the poetry as a kind of electricity to
charge the described events with the significance and energy
they had when originally experienced and to transform them
into a central mythology of the present age. The effectiveness
of *The Armies of the Night* as journalism is due largely to
Mailer's remarkable ability to combine poetry and objectivity
into a greater whole. In the reportage of the first part he re-
tains a heuristic, exploratory attitude throughout, so that by
the time he finishes "History as a Novel: The Steps of the Pentagon," he is "delivered a discovery of what the March on the
Pentagon has finally meant" and so is ready "to write a most

concise Short History, a veritable précis of a collective novel, which here now, in the remaining pages, will seek as History, no, rather as some Novel of History, to elucidate the mysterious character of that Quintessentially American event" (241).

The second part of the book, "The Novel as History: The Battle of the Pentagon," considerably shorter than the first, is a more objective piece. It narrates the history of preparation for the march and many events of which Mailer learned but had not directly experienced, including some of the "battles" between Pentagon guards and demonstrators which resulted in an incredible lot of brutality and arrests, as well as some touching moments of communication between the guards and the people demonstrating. Mailer's analysis of events leads to criticisms about the demonstration and how it might have been better handled, and the conclusion is a bleak portrait of America's sickness and totalitarianism. It is a much less personal document than the first part, less poetic, and to that exent more conventionally journalistic. However, Mailer strikes another blow for New Journalism in his criticism of the established press's reportage of the event as inaccurate, insensitive, and politically biased. When he wants reliable newspaper reporting for evidence in constructing his history, he turns to the Washington *Free Press,* an underground paper, not the Washington *Post* or *Time,* although he does find the Washington *Star* accurate at one point. Indeed, returning to the beginning of the first part of the book, one remembers that Mailer began his narrative with a report from *Time* of his own predemonstration speech in Washington's Ambassador Theater, asserting, after quoting *Time's* report, that what followed would be "what happened" in reality (14). So the whole book is an attempt to give to the public the kind of coverage Mailer knew the established press would never offer, and the second part is to a great extent an attempt to correct the so called "objectivity" of that press's reportage.

The first part is essential to the second, for through it we know the character of the journalist-historian of the second:

we know what he has experienced, what he has not, and how he responds to what he experiences:

> So the Novelist working in secret collaboration with the Historian has perhaps tried to build with his novel a tower fully equipped with telescopes to study—at the greatest advantage—our own horizon. Of course, the tower is crooked, and the telescopes warped, but the instruments of all sciences —history so much as physics—are always constructed in small or large error; what supports the use of them now is that our intimacy with the master builder of the tower, and the lens grinder of the telescopes (yes, even the machinist of the barrels) has given some advantage for correcting the error of the instruments and the imbalance of his tower. May that be claimed of many histories? . . .
>
> The method is then exposed. The mass media which surrounded the March on the Pentagon created a forest of inaccuracy which would blind the efforts of an historian; our novel has provided us with the possibility, no, even the instrument to view our facts and conceivably study them in that field of light a labor of lens-grinding has produced. [245–246]

That is Mailer's esthetic. It is primarily a historical and artistic esthetic, and it is one that is a key to the success of much of the New Journalism. It involves a bringing into play of the full power of the reporter's imagination and sensibility as essential to anything like an honest and relevant, if necessarily imperfect, journalism.

In *Miami and the Siege of Chicago* (1968) Mailer continues his examination of the American psyche, again in a political context, the most obvious one of all—the conventions. He subtitles the book *An Informal History of the Republican and Democratic Conventions of 1968*. Declaring in the first part, "Nixon in Miami," that *New York Times* reporters are not instructed that "there is no history without nuance,"[2] Mailer discloses his approach: he is writing a history *with* nuance, watching for, recording, and assessing the significance of gestures, peripheral events (as well as central ones), and attitudes. Stylistically, this book is similar to *The Armies of the Night*, which was also a "history with nuance." Again

Mailer reveals his keen eye for details, his ability to react to those details and to communicate his reactions vividly, accurately, openly, and, frequently, with poetic grace and depth. However, *Miami and the Siege of Chicago* is journalistically more like "The Battle of the Pentagon" than the first part of the previous book, for Mailer is less introspective and exhibitionistic. Identifying himself as "the reporter," he tries to be objective and interpretive, although he does, occasionally, inject personal reflections, particularly those concerning his sense of political affiliation as an evaluation of events. Thus, he shifts from a conservative radical role to that of a kind of cultural aristocrat, through others, until, after the Chicago convention he speculates that he wouldn't cast his vote—"not unless it was for Eldridge Cleaver" (223). He is trying to narrate honestly the changes of political attitude any man experiences in witnessing the conventions. At any rate, this is probably the best report of the 1968 conventions in print.

Mailer's rapid writing—this book took two weeks—and his heuristic-dialectic manner of imaginatively feeling his way through events give his work a fantastic immediacy, as if the reader were embarked with him on a frenetic voyage of discovery, where the final boundaries, the settled character of things, can't be fully assessed—a task which is left to the stodgy historians of the future; what we are experiencing on the voyage, as Scholes says, is "hystory," something maniacally of the moment, uncertain, and difficult to document. Mailer's style, which is a product of a desire to pull together the telling facts of a situation, of a genius for transfiguring those facts into truth, and of a habit of writing rapidly, holding slow intellection to a minimum, is his secret as a writer; and, as Peter Shaw notes in his review of *Miami and the Siege of Chicago,* it links him to a classical tradition in American writing—which suggests some more of the historical roots of the New Journalism:

> Writing at high speed, he has time only to comprehend people and events imaginatively, in the novelist's way. As it turns out, in the frenetic form of the last two books, Mailer has found for himself a way to approximate the accomplishments

of the classic American writers. They too had much to fear from giving a subject too much thought. Brooders like Hawthorne, Melville, and Mark Twain knew that they could destroy themselves and their work with too much intellection, and Hawthorne took that danger for the theme of many of his stories, in which excessive brooders destroyed their own works of art and even their loved ones.

When we think of the great achievements in American writing we tend to think of symbolism and fantasy, of the romantic and the farfetched: the white whale, the dream world of Huckleberry Finn and Jim on the magic river, Hawthorne's dark puritan forests of symbols. But the other side of the American imagination has been just as important in its very different function of dealing with facts in order somehow to illuminate them. Mailer is not the first American novelist to revel in the role of reporter, gatherer of facts. I am thinking not only of Stephen Crane and Ernest Hemingway, but of the other side of *Moby Dick* and *Huckleberry Finn* themselves, where not fantasy but *things* reign. Even more to the point, for Mailer's is a book about Chicago and about hotels, is Dreiser, who also could breathe life into the dross of America's gilt existence.[3]

I think Shaw's observation about the writer's, or Mailer's, attempt to avoid "brooding," over-intellection (not to say he doesn't think intelligently), or self-consciousness is quite true. That attempt is central to the salvation of literary art, including good journalism, in an incredibly self-conscious age. Mailer's shifting around of his protagonist's roles, of narrator identities, from "Mailer" to "the reporter" to "Aquarius" in his more recent work for *Life, Of a Fire on the Moon,* is an indication of his desire to avoid becoming too self-consciously present in his work—although, in a way, it makes him more so. Also, he clearly wants to avoid freezing his exploratory attitude into any kind of dogmatism; he wants to keep his ideas free, changing, his mind open to the forces of the moment. He wants, in short, to be a journalist, not a philosopher.

In "Nixon in Miami," the first part of *Miami and the Siege of Chicago,* Mailer tries to give life and significance to what was "the dullest convention anyone could remember" (15), and in many ways he succeeds beautifully, primarily because of his ability to see its placid events for what they really were: emblems of the vagaries of the American psyche. Consider, for example, his reportage of the place of the convention as an allegory of the Republican mentality:

> . . . the Republicans, Grand Old Party with a philosophy rather than a program, had chosen what must certainly be the materialist capital of the world for their convention. Las Vegas might offer competition, but Las Vegas was materialism in the service of electricity—fortunes could be in the spark of the dice. Miami was materialism baking in the sun, then stepping back to air-conditioned caverns where ice could nestle in the fur. It was the first of a hundred curiosities— that in a year when the Republic hovered on the edge of revolution, nihilism, and lines of police on the edge of the horizon, visions of future Vietnams in our own cities upon us, the party of conservatism and principle, of corporate wealth and personal frugality, the party of cleanliness, hygiene, and balanced budget, should have set down on a sultan's strip. [14]

The emblematic character of the convention and its irrelevant curiosities have changed the mood of the narrator from what it was at the Pentagon. Less boisterous and self-displaying, "the reporter" moves through the convention "quietly, as anonymously as possible, wan, depressed, troubled" (14).

This is not an event which obviously and typically attracts his energies, but one in which he must learn to discern the ambiguous subtleties beneath the clean, boring surface. Mailer's observations of people are extremely careful, even if heuristic and inconclusive. His portrait of Nixon at a press conference, for instance, reveals a complex range of feelings and suspicions, and it is accurate:

> There was something in his carefully shaven face—the dark jowls already showing the first overtones of thin gloomy blue at this early hour—some worry which gave promise of never leaving him, some hint of inner debate about his value before eternity which spoke of precisely the sort of improvement that comes upon a man when he shifts in appearance from looking like an undertaker's assistant to looking like an old con seriously determined to go respectable. The Old Nixon, which

is to say the young Nixon, used to look, on clasping his hands in front of him, like a church usher (of the variety who would twist a boy's ear after removing him from church). The older Nixon before the Press now—the *new* Nixon—had finally acquired some of the dignity of the old athlete and the old con. . . . [44]

Gaining a sense of the convention's place, of Nixon and the other candidates, of the delegates and their gatherings, Mailer moves to a point where he begins to discern the importance of Nixon and his followers and, on the basis of his observations, formulates some journalistic speculations which have since been proven true prophecy:

> How could there be, after all, a greater passion in a man like Nixon, so universally half-despised, than to show the center of history itself that he was not without greatness. What a dream for such a man! . . . It was possible, even likely, even necessary, that the WASP must enter the center of our history again. . . . They were the most powerful force in America, and yet they were a psychic island. If they did not find a bridge, they could only grow more insane each year, like a rich nobleman in an empty castle chasing elves and ogres with his stick. They had every power but the one they needed—which was to attach their philosophy to history. . . . One could predict: their budgeting would prove insane, their righteousness would prove insane, their love for order and clear-thinking would be twisted through many a wry neck, the intellectual foundations of their anti-Communism would split into its separate parts. And the small-town faith in small free enterprise would run smash into the corporate jugger-nauts of technology land; their love of polite culture would collide with the mad esthetics of the new America; their livid passion for military superiority would smash its nose on the impossibility of having such superiority without more govern-ment spending; their love of nature would have to take up arms against the despoiling foe, themselves, their own greed, their own big business. [62–63]

If the event itself was dull and largely uneventful, Mail-er's journalistic style and vision made it, at least, prophetic. The convention was also a kind of strange comedy, a fact which Mailer illustrates occasionally, partly by noticing its comic aspects, partly through a style of writing reminiscent of Wolfe's comic-esthetic point of view but colored with a moral darkness:

> At large on the ocean, would people yet pray for Nixon and wish him strength as once they had wished strength to old Hindenburg and Dollfuss and Schuschnigg and Von Papen? Oom-pah went the tuba, starts! went the horn. Blood and shit might soon be flying like the red and brown of a *verboten* flag. It had had black in it as well. For death perhaps. Areas of white for purity. They would talk yet of purity. They always did. And shave the shorn. God give strength to Richard Nixon, and a nose for the real news. Oom-pah went the tuba, *farts* went the horn. [66]

Perhaps the comedy itself was the prophecy, and Mailer left Miami for Chicago with "no idea at all if God was in the land or the Devil played the tune" (82).

The second part, "The Siege of Chicago," opens with a portrait of Chicago. Mailer conjures up the aura of the city, its relation to his own Brooklyn, its geography. His portrait of the stockyards is a microcosmic orgy of Chicago violence that forecasts the future of the convention, and it is a good example of Mailer at his best. It is also inaccurate, as the stockyards are now more modern than he thinks; the operators use tranquilizers on the animals and are a smaller business than they used to be. Many of the facts are wrong, but, as Raymond Mungo would say, the truth is there nonetheless. Mailer captures the spirit of the violence that was brought down on the heads of demonstrators and innocent bystanders in the streets of Chicago, and he portrays the people and their way of life:

> In the slaughterhouse, during the day, a carnage worthy of the Disasters of War took place each morning and afternoon. . . . What an awful odor the fear of absolute and unavoidable death gave to the stool and stuffing and pure vomitous shit of beasts waiting in the pens in the stockyard, what a sweat of hell-leather, and yet the odor, no, the titanic stench, which rose from the yards was not so simple as the collective diarrhetics of an hysterical army of beasts, no, for after the throats were cut and the blood ran in rich

gutters, red light on the sweating back of the red throat-cutters, the dying and some just dead animals clanked along the overhead, arterial blood spurting like the nip-ups of a little boy urinating in public, the red-hot carcass quickly encountered another Black or Hunkie with a long knife on a long stick who would cut the belly from the chest to groin and a stew and a stink of two hundred pounds of stomach, lungs, intestines . . . and general gag-all would flop and slither over the floor, the man with the knife getting a good blood-splatting as he dug and twisted with his blade to liberate the roots of the organ, intestine and impedimenta still integrated into the meat and bone of the excavated existence he was working on. . . .

Yes, Chicago was a town where nobody could ever forget how the money was made. It was picked up from floors still slippery with blood. . . . So something of the entrails and the secrets of the gut got into the faces of native Chicagoans. . . . It was the last of the great American cities, and people had great faces, carnal as blood, greedy, direct, too impatient for hypocrisy, in love with honest plunder. [88–90]

In this renovation of Sandburg, Mailer is suggesting the psychic landscape of the convention and city controlled by Mayor Richard Daley and, at a powerful remove, Lyndon Johnson. As in other passages in this part, Mailer seems more attracted to than repelled by the violence he observes here and condemns later when it is directed against demonstrators as well as reporters and innocent bystanders; and it is this peculiar attraction which allows him to write about it so well, directly and without euphemisms—a journalistic attitude which is tuned to the directness and brutal honesty he associates with the city he describes.

With the appetite of a journalist, Mailer collects the data that he forms into the backdrop of the Chicago drama. Then, with the sensibility and imagination of the novelist, he plays his characters and episodes against that backdrop, which serves as a measuring stick for the people involved, a context and reason for the events. Senator Eugene McCarthy and his followers, for instance, have "thin noses, and thin . . . nostrils" compared to the face of Chicago, which "might be reduced to a broad fleshy nose with nostrils open wide to stench, stink, power, a pretty day, a well-stacked broad, and the beauties of a dirty buck . . . " (90-91). Humphrey, on the other hand, is adapted to the environment: "The Mafia loved Humphrey . . . and there was big money behind Humphrey, . . . in the Hilton called the Hubaret . . . you needed a scorecard to separate the trade-union leaders from the Maf . . ." (110). McGovern, "reminiscent of Henry Fonda" (122), does not blend well. The protestors, violent or Gandhian, are clearly in the land of the enemy. Mayor Daley is clearly in his element, controlling the convention directly from the floor, controlling the streets through hundreds of Chicago-hardened policemen who are also in their element, though many were fearful and maniacal enough to riot under Daley's command.

Mailer is continuously broadening the context of the Chicago convention by drawing in Bobby Kennedy's assassination (as well as his detailed personal reaction), Martin Luther King's, or Valerie Solanas' near-fatal shooting of Andy Warhol. He spins out the context of American violence until, after the convention and riots, the reader perceives clearly that a good journalist of this country's politics has to embrace and articulate a large and very complex universe of events, with Mayor Daley's jowl as "the soft underbelly of the new American axis" (223). Although Mailer spends much of his time inside the convention hall, witnessing a less physical violence than that in the streets (although it was physical inside as well, as many newsmen will testify), he portrays the street violence as having a meaning central to that of the convention and its country; and he supplements his view from the nineteenth floor of the Conrad Hilton with coverage from the *Village Voice,* as well as the *New York Times* and the *Washington Post,* whose reporters, like all media people, were commonly at odds with the frenzied police and National Guard.

There were two armies in the streets: those who were committed to transforming the convention into a significant turn in recent American history or to destroying it, revealing its brutality and hypocrisy; and those who were committed to crushing dissent, keeping the convention as the seemingly polite meeting of wheeler-dealers, hangers-on, and hack politicians that it largely was, and holding the walls of Daley's fortress. Abbie Hoffman and Allen Ginsberg, yippies and hippies listening to speeches and rock music or yelling "Dump the Hump," "these children like filthy Christians sitting quietly in the grass" (143), the New Left and concerned middle-aged middle-classers, as well as militant or peaceful blacks—all attacked by herds of policemen, each in another situation, perhaps, trying "to solve his violence by blanketing it with a uniform" (174), but in the streets of a frightened convention city "a true criminal force, chaotic, improvisational, undisciplined and finally—sufficiently aroused—uncontrollable" (175). In contrast to Wolfe, Mailer is implicitly moralistic throughout his account of the convention, particularly in his coverage of the riots where the two armies meet (although, as he admits, his nineteenth-floor view allowed an unreal kind of esthetic detachment):

> The police cut through the crowd one way, then cut through them another. They chased people into the park, ran them down, beat them up; they cut through the intersection at Michigan and Balbo like a razor cutting a channel through a head of hair, and then drove columns of new police into the channel who in turn pushed out, clubs flailing, on each side, to cut new channels, and new ones again. As demonstrators ran, they reformed in new groups only to be chased by the police again. The action went on for ten minutes, fifteen minutes, with the absolute ferocity of a tropical storm, and watching it from a window on the nineteenth floor, there was something of the detachment of studying a storm at evening through a glass, the light was a lovely gray-blue, the police had uniforms of sky-blue, even the ferocity had an abstract elemental play of forces of nature at battle with other forces, as if sheets of tropical rain were driving across the street in patterns. . . . The reporter . . . could understand now how Mussolini's son-in-law had once been able to find the bombs he dropped from his airplane beautiful as they burst, yes, children, and youths, and middle-

aged men and women were being pounded and clubbed and gassed and beaten, hunted and driven, sent scattering in all directions by teams of policemen who had exploded out of their restraints like the bursting of a boil. . . .

A great stillness rose from the street through all the small noise of clubbing and cries, small sirens, sigh of loaded arrest vans as off they pulled, shouts of police as they wheeled in larger circles, the intersection clearing further, then further, a stillness rose through the steel and stone of the hotel, congregating in the shocked centers of every room where delegates and wives and Press and campaign workers innocent until now of the intimate working of social force, looked down now into the murderous paradigm of Vietnam there beneath them at this huge intersection of this great city. [169–172]

In 1965 Mailer said that novelists were "no longer writing about the beast but, as in the case of Hemingway, . . . about the paw of the beast, or in Faulkner about the dreams of the beast."[4] In *Miami and the Siege of Chicago* he has recorded as a journalist what he created fictionally as a novelist: the movements, the actuality, of the beast at the heart of American politics. Even if Mailer is somehow limited psychologically by his posing as a tough-guy intellectual—especially near the end of the book—the reader occasionally put off by his musing on his own cowardice and compromised existence, and the events of Chicago partly transcendent to the imagination of a writer slightly displaced from the present activist generation, who is perhaps ironically better attuned to the slow-paced subtleties of the Miami convention, it is also true that he has written an admirable piece of imaginative personal journalism. The political events of the present demand a tremendous effort of anyone to comprehend, and they involve, as Mailer says, "large thoughts for a reporter to have" (188).

Mailer spent his time after the conventions making movies at his own expense and running in the Democratic primary for mayor of New York City. In the spring of 1969, during the campaign, he was contracted by *Life* to write a book-length series of articles about the U.S. space program. The first installment, "A Fire on the Moon," concerning the Apollo 11 flight, appeared in the 29 August issue. It was following by a second, "The Psychology of Astronauts," written after the Apollo 11 astronauts' return, which appeared 14 November, and a third, "A Dream of the Future's Face," 9 January 1970.[5] Mailer's account is easily the best of its kind I have read. It is a *tour de force* in journalistic writing about contemporary technology, science, and their human and political milieu.[6] I would like to discuss the first two installments, as representative of his work, in some detail, omitting consideration of the third, which, though good, is more speculative than reportorial.

In "A Fire on the Moon," Mailer takes as his starting point the suicide of Ernest Hemingway and construes it as an emblem of the end of a romanticism that survived into an age of dread, now become an age of space technology which must be understood:

> We are obliged after all to comprehend the astronauts. If we approach our subject via Aquarius, it is because he is a detective of sorts, and different in spirit from eight years ago. He has learned to live with questions. Of course, as always, he has little to do with the immediate spirit of the time. Which is why Norman on this occasion may call himself Aquarius. Born January 31, he is entitled to the name, but he thinks it a fine irony that we now enter the Aquarian Period since he has never had less sense of possessing the age. He feels in fact little more than a decent spirit, somewhat shunted to the side. It is the best possible position for detective work. [25–26]

There is here some of the feeling of Henry Adams, the nineteenth-century man, encountering the dynamo of the twentieth century, as Adams recorded it in his autobiography, *The Education of Henry Adams*. There is additional support for the idea that the events of the Chicago convention may have partly transcended Mailer's imagination; but here, as there, and as in Adams' own case, the displacement, no matter what its extent, is used to the advantage of gaining perspective. Here it places Mailer in the position of a detective, a man who must work through the displacement to articulate the mystery, who will communicate to us a record of his discoveries.

Again he creates a name, "Aquarius," from a third-person point of view, for his protagonist. Again he tries to place himself properly in relation to the narrative that follows: to be *in* enough that the story will be personal and tuned to his own present sensibility, but *out* enough that he will avoid the chains of self-consciousness and the temptation of exhibitionism. With the Democratic primary for mayor over (he having come in fourth out of five), Mailer considers himself superbly ready for the assignment at hand, "For he was detached this season from the imperial demands of his ego; he could think about astronauts, space, space programs, and the moon, quite free of the fact that none of these heroes, presences, and forces were by any necessity friendly to him" (26). Thus prepared, he reflects on his technique as a journalist:

> He preferred to divine an event through his senses—since he was as nearsighted as he was vain, he tended to sniff out the center of a situation from a distance. So his mind often stayed out of contact with the workings of his brain for days at a time. When it was time, lo and behold, he seemed to have comprehended the event. That was one advantage of using the nose—technology had not yet succeeded in elaborating a science of smell. [26]

Mailer, perhaps resolving the Eliotic "dissociation of sensibility," approaches his subject with a kind of childlike sense of wonder and openness—a starting point for any really good journalist—which he tempers with moral judgment and esthetic control derived from experience.

Here, in the world of the space program, he is in new territory, but his senses are open, his mind articulate; and he tends to evaluate and define through an awareness of the people he encounters and through a sixth sense about the political logic of all large American events. In a swamp of technological happenings and terminology Mailer picks up the vibrations of the people. He notices, for instance, the "absolute lack of surface provocation, or idiosyncrasy of personality, which characterizes physicists, engineering students, statisticians, computer technicians, and many a young man of science" (27). Personality is an important key in unlocking the mythology of astronautics. Consider his portrait of Wernher von Braun, for instance:

> Yes, Von Braun most definitely was not like other men. Curiously shifty, as if to show his eyes in full would give away too much, a man who wheeled whole complexes of cautions into every gesture—he was after all an engineer who put massive explosives into adjoining tanks and then was obliged to worry about leaks. What is plumbing after all but the prevention of treachery in closed systems? So he would never give anything away he did not have to, but the secrets he held, the tensions he held, the very philosophical explosives he contained under such super-compression gave him an air of magic. He was a rocketeer. . . . Immediate reflection must tell you that a man who wishes to reach heavenly bodies is an agent of the Lord or Mephisto. In fact, Von Braun, with his handsome spoiled face, massive chin, and long and highly articulated nose, had a fair resemblance to Goethe. (Albeit none of the fine weatherings of the Old Master's head.) But brood on it: . . . What went on in Von Braun's mind during a dream? [34]

Mailer, trained in his youth as an engineer, is also at home with much of the technology, although he admits that, like most world citizens of his generation, he is unable to comprehend the whole character of the change it has wrought. The Vehicle Assembly Building he sees as "the first cathedral of the age of technology"—a kind of metaphorical knowledge that distinguishes him as a writer—but "this emergence of a ship to travel the ether, thrust across a vacuum, was no event he could measure by any philosophy he had yet put together in his brain" (30). Nonetheless, his awe at the largeness of the event, combined with his talent as a writer, makes his account of the launching a memorable piece of journalism. He sees the rising ship as a "slim angelic mysterious ship of stages . . . slow as Melville's Leviathan might swim" (40). His final note, however, is moral, for the event is not unambiguously moral—

that much of its technological implications Mailer comprehends as he quotes Reverend Abernathy after the launch:
"This is really holy ground. And it will be more holy once we
feed the hungry, care for the sick, and provide for those who
do not have houses" (40).

In the second installment, "The Psychology of Astronauts," Mailer applies himself to the problem of journalistically
presenting the astronauts by reporting and analyzing their
comments on the technicalities of the flight, by exploring his
own complex reactions to the men, and by relating their
psychology to the historical context and mythology of the
Apollo 11 event. He sees Aldrin as "all meat and stone, . . .
a man of solid presentation, dependable as a tractor, but
suggesting the strength of a tank, dull, almost ponderous, yet
with the hint of unpredictability" (53). Collins, in contrast to
Aldrin, "moved easily; Collins was cool. Collins was the man
nearly everybody was glad to see at a party, for he was the
living spirit of good and graceful manners" (54). Armstrong,
however, is an enigma:

> So Armstrong seemed of all the astronauts the man nearest
> to being saintly, yet there was something as hard, small-town
> and used in his face as the look of a cashier over pennies. . . .
> He could be an angel, he could be the town's most unsavory
> devil. You could not penetrate the flash of the smile—all of
> America's bounty was in it. Readiness to serve, innocence,
> competence, modesty, sly humor, and then a lopsided yawn-
> ing slide of a dumb smile at the gulf of one's own ignorance,
> like oops am I small-town dumb!—that was also in it. [55]

All three of the astronauts are finally, for Mailer, men who are
contradictory in character. What he has learned of them leads
to the final commentary:

> It was the most soul-destroying and apocalyptic of centuries.
> So in their turn the astronauts had personalities of unequaled
> banality and apocalyptic dignity. So they suggested in their
> contradictions the power of the century to live with its own
> incredible contradictions and yet release some of the untold
> energies of the earth. A century devoted to the rationality
> of technique was also a century so irrational as to open in

every mind the real possibility of global destruction. . . . As one had only to listen to an astronaut speak for a few minutes to know that his comprehension of unconscious impulses was technical, not carnal, so did the century suggest that its tendency was unconscious of itself. The itch was to accelerate—the metaphysical direction unknown. [63]

To know an age is to know its men. Mailer, as a writer, understands the significance of that idea; and, as a New Journalist, he knows that one writes of the world and its men through one's own reaction to them, whether that reaction be called objective or personal. For Mailer journalism is fundamentally an art, creative and honest, and he has contributed a great deal toward its future development.

I have devoted this chapter* to Capote, Wolfe, and Mailer as three major stylists of the New Journalism because I think they fill those roles, at least during the decade of the 1960's with which we are concerned. They defined and pursued new stylistic directions, and they have influenced many other journalists within the last few years. That is not to say that they are absolutely the most important journalists of the 1960's— though in many ways they are—for there are many others who have been influential in changing the style of traditional journalism who are also important and articulate writers, such as John Hersey, Jimmy Breslin, Dan Wakefield, and Hunter Thompson.

If Robert Scholes is right in his theory, that the realistic novel or, more generally, realistic fiction is splitting into two new forms, "fabulous non-realistic fiction" and a "creative journalism," then many of the New Journalists, especially those considered in this chapter, are creating a literary genre of the future, as well as recording and assessing an age more richly than has ever been done before. And I would expand his theory to the point of saying that many of the literarily important works of long narrative length in the near future

*This selection is excerpted from Johnson's book *The New Journalism.*

will probably be journalistic, stylistic experiments in the communication of actual events; whereas, on the other hand, much important fiction will be in the form of short, episodic prose pieces, largely fabulous, as he suggests, or fantastic, science-fictional, poetic or hallucinatory, "stoned." (And there may be a subtle significance in the fact that the short prose piece is in some ways a prototypical journalistic form).

NOTES

1. (New York: New American Library, 1968), p. 99. Further quotations from this New American Library paperback edition will be cited by page number in the text.

2. (New York, 1968), p. 56. Further quotations from this New American Library paperback edition will be cited by page number in the text.

3. "The Conventions, 1968," *Commentary,* December 1968, p. 93.

4. From a paper read at the Modern Language Association meeting and published in *Commentary,* March 1966, pp. 39 ff. I am quoting here from Robert Langbaum's essay "Mailer's New Style" in his book *The Modern Spirit: Essays on the Continuity of Nineteenth- and Twentieth-Century Literature* (New York: Oxford University Press, 1970), p. 148. Langbaum is helpful with the novels, but he is only briefly concerned with Mailer's journalism.

5. Pp. 24–41, 51–63, 57–74, respectively. I will cite quotations by page number in the text. These articles, with additional material, have been incorporated into Mailer's recent book *Of a Fire on the Moon* (Boston: Little, Brown & Co., 1970), the end product of the *Life* contract.

6. There are few books about scientific endeavor that are really well written. Mailer's work on the astronauts thus helps to fill a gap and also to bridge some of the points of separation of C. P. Snow's "two cultures," science and humanism. Another scientific book which is written very largely as a kind of personal journalism is *The Double,* James D. Watson's account of the people and events surrounding the discovery of the structure of DNA. Watson's book is only somewhat obliquely a part of the New Journalism, but it is pretty well written and, like Mailer's, portrays the human situations behind what seem on the surface to be accomplished, cold events.

POLITICIAN

Jane O'Reilly

Diary of a Mailer Trailer

One fine Sunday morning last May [1969] I got into a car with a photographer from *Life,* a literary columnist from Chicago, a reporter from the *Yale Daily News,* and a person who in political campaigns is known as The Driver, and we all rode out to the Howard Beach Jewish Community Center to hear Norman Mailer, Pulitzer prize-winning author and candidate for mayor of the city of New York. Howard Beach is on the line between Brooklyn and Queens. The houses look as though they were built for a showroom out of toothpicks and bits of styrofoam and balsa wood. It is a place where the developers rolled incredible, possibly plastic grass out over the dunes of Jamaica Bay, plopped identical houses in rows on top of each square of the incorruptible turf, and planted spotlights amidst the shrubbery for nighttime revelations of the proud achievement of the owners of these $18,000 villas.

It was ten o'clock in the morning, and they were serving bagels and lox and cream cheese. Perhaps forty men and a few wives were waiting for Mailer and his running mate, James Breslin, political columnist and candidate for City Council president.

One of the men told the columnist from Chicago that what New York needed was a mayor like Daley. Accountants

and schoolteachers and appliance-store managers live in Howard Beach, and they are strong on the law-and-order issue.
Breslin spoke first. He is a big man, and he worries a lot, and
is often moved to outrage. He looks at his audience sideways,
as though he isn't sure they, or he, can take what he has to say.
This morning it is too early for him to comfort them with his
famous humor, he lays it on straight: "They are lying to you.
They say what we need is more police. The police aren't going
to solve this problem. We must control our lives. As long as
everything is centralized, nothing will happen."

Mailer is introduced and politely applauded. He is
dressed in a marvelously tailored pinstriped suit, a white,
rather old-fashioned shirt—his campaign clothes—and he isn't
sure of the early-morning vibrations in this prefabricated syn-
agogue-*cum*-community center. One hand in a coat pocket,
standing three quarters to the microphone—his usual fighting
posture, both exhortive and combative—he says: "What we
have in New York, what has come to New York first, is the
problem of the technological age. The problem of the society
which is built on a machine rather than a conception of the
human spirit."

After he spoke, the audience asked questions: political
questions about Mailer and Breslin's program and how it could
work. They didn't ask why they were running, or if they were
serious, and they apparently didn't think they were listening to
a literary curiosity come to entertain them on a spring morning. They treated Mailer and Breslin as candidates who might
have an answer to some of their problems. There were nine
more campaign stops that day, and those questions would be
asked at other places, but mostly in the press car. We actually
were spending a fine spring day observing this literary curiosity, the writer as candidate (MAILER as candidate), and it
was our professional duty to wonder why and what for and
what did it all really mean?

About a month before, in mid-April, when Mailer decided to run for mayor, he was quoted (which is usually a very
different thing from saying "he said") as saying: "This is a

dangerous thing for a writer to do, I'm going to try to think creatively in public, out in front." Mailer isn't just any writer, and the press came pouring into town, partly on the wise assumption that there might be something said worth listening to, and partly to catch the show--Free Mailer, Come and Get It! Always good copy!

The show toured the five boroughs daily, and I caught it whenever I could from the back of the campaign car. Let other people write about the impossible Mailer, the "fireworks salesman," the mean drunk. By the June primary, Mailer had become My Hero, and it pleases me to portray him as flawless. Mailer is the man who is permanently out in front, the scout for our times, always miles ahead down the path testing the trail for traps and false prophets and illusions, confronting with his own spirit the villains and fakers and wrong turnings; always ahead, dimly glowing with evangelical fervor, exhorting us to come on, press on: stop sniveling and posturing; stand up and march like men with souls.

The day that began at Howard Beach I was not inclined to admire him. No middle-aged Bronx housewife had a more tight-lipped image of Mailer as Public Sinner albeit Greatest Living American Writer. In retreat from the sure sense that things are indeed getting worse, I had been reading the comforting cadences of Jane Austen, and not Norman Mailer. But, media glutted, I read *about* him; newspaper accounts of marriages and binges; highly reasoned and tortuously wordy literary essays by other New York writers, who essentially complain that Mailer's behemoth personality is burning up all the creative oxygen around. "Norman," not the real Mailer but some secondhand version, is a constant whisper at New York cocktail parties—someone has always just been to Provincetown, or to a party at the fabled penthouse in Brooklyn Heights. Girls are constantly sighing: "Oh, Norman Mailer, I met him once, I made such a fool of myself." There is something about him—a combination of charm and shyness and fierceness and fame—that makes people, men and women, fling themselves into his presence like moths into a candle. There is no real evidence that Mailer continuously invites or enjoys these physical and mental challenges. He does not suffer fools gladly, but he has such sympathy for the spectacle of someone making a fool of himself, that if he can, by sheer magnetic force, he will make him stop. Some of his friends are people no one else can tolerate, and one of the reasons is, they are tolerable around him. He insists on his own perception of a person, and some people respond by improving. Others markedly do not.

That first day on the campaign I would ordinarily have made a fool of myself, and asked a lot of dumb and bitchy questions, except that by good fortune I had such a terrible toothache I couldn't talk. Also, I was terrified of Mailer. I had seen him twice before, and neither was a soothing experience. The first time was in April, when I went, in a mood of tentative mockery, to a campaign organizational meeting. There were dozens of people milling around busily, all energetically carrying on overlapping conversations and repeating directions and committee allocations to each other. There were some former Kennedy people, and some former McCarthy people, some people who would work for anybody with an idea, some writers, and some people to whom it was important to pretend that they know the "real" Norman better than anyone.

The real Norman looked just like his pictures, maybe a little fatter. His eyes are so intense that the expression shows even in a photograph. But his voice was surprising: words rumble and bubble and jump out, in a variety of accents; New York, faintly southern, all g's dropped (as in "Ahm talkin' ") when he is particularly shy. Rising from his chair occasionally, he tried to give encouraging directives to the oblivious workers. "We have got to get some sense of everything moving upward in this campaign. We will levitate at some point . . . or we won't." "We are going to allow these people to find some interest in their lives." "New York either gets an imagination, or it dies." He then snarled, an icy snarl, at one of his most efficient campaign aides: "DON'T TALK WHILE I AM TALKING."

I sniffed, and went home muttering about the liberal

death wish and the fate of New York intellectuals who have no grasp on the realities of life. People even dumber than I was were saying, "He's a writer, and writers should write." Smarter people were calling up to ask if they could help. A week later I went to the press conference Mailer and Breslin held to announce their candidacy. Very nice, very straightforward, very interesting. New York should be the fifty-first state and get out from under Albany's thumb. Power to the neighborhoods. Fine.

Then, on May 7, there was a rally at the Village Gate, which was very hard to explain away to the "Norman Mailer couldn't possibly be serious because obviously he is off on the ultimate ego trip" skeptics. The rally began at midnight, $5.00 admission, and the place was jammed. Campaign buttons saying "Vote the Rascals In" and "The *other* guys are the joke" and "No More Bull Shit" were all around. Jimmy Breslin, looking especially anguished, made a very funny speech. "What brings fat James Breslin to the Gate on a night when he could be in a smaller bar with fewer people who couldn't check his lies? People ask if we are serious. The first day I thought we were doing a little dealing in politics between books. The second day I thought it was a good way to straighten out. The third day, Norman arrives with a TIE on. This city is run by people who think everything is o.k. if things are o.k. on Wall Street, in the 17th Congressional District . . . while the East Bronx falls down." And, "Our claim is that we're going to put the English language back into politics."

Mailer had been to some earlier fund-raising parties. By the time he got up to speak, his mood, and the audience's mood, had soured. Other speakers had not been as gently outraged as Breslin, and at least half the crowd was there for blood. The Greenwich Village cannibals, the "Fang Club" somebody called them, like the mechanical dolls in *Barbarella* with sharp little pointed-steel teeth clicking and snapping, they were there to tear Mailer apart; just as they tear him apart at dinners and cocktails and in small literary reviews.

He attacked back, in the style that later in the campaign came to be known as "The Old Mailer." "Listen to me, 'cause I'm talkin' hard," he said, hard, his nose twitching with distaste. "If you're comin' to work—WORK. Leave your ego at the door. Keep quiet! . . . Don't come to be entertained, we're in this very deep."

There was a girl crouched on the floor beneath the platform, like a particularly hideous illustration from an underground newspaper. She was beating steadily on the stage with a huge stick and shouting FUCK FUCK FUCK in rhythm with the stick. She was obscene, and so was Mailer, and the half of the audience that had come to see vintage Mailer roared and hissed and spit back. The other half of the audience, the ones Norman was addressing when he talked about "If you are coming to work—WORK," was perfectly respectable, dimly do-gooder, willing to donate bits of money and time, but essentially unrelating to the city or the crisis except in the most comfortable way. They had given little dinners for each other before the benefit, and they were shocked and embarrassed. Later, Mailer's campaign staff laboriously explained to him that he had hurt the people who were really working for him, and he apologized and said he understood he was cruel to those rich pigs who came in late and—still later—he called it the night he made a fool of himself. But, what he said at the Gate was true, and for some there was catharsis in the insult.

The next day I called a friend who was working hard for Mailer, and I said: "What on earth is really going on?" She said, "We are doing it because the Democratic Party in New York is in a desperate situation and we need to spread some ideas around." But Mailer was running for mayor. He said: "I'm not running an educational campaign because I think an educational campaign saps the spirit and creates a false superiority in the defeated." He was right again, of course.

When we left Howard Beach I got into Mailer's car. The day was clear and springy, and we drove along the edge of Jamaica Bay, "Where particularly hardy New Yorkers go swimming," said Mailer. There were people riding horses along the water's edge, and Sunday fishermen, and people enjoying nature, just as they do in Cincinnati and Malibu Beach, but not at all the way they do in my Manhattan-bound image of New York City. All day we drove through neighborhoods in Brooklyn and Queens and the Bronx, through parts of the city where life has roots and continuity. There are miles and miles and miles of New York, and every possible life style, except agricultural. (No, even that, there are still farms on Staten Island.) The city is governed by Albany, where, said Breslin: "They think Bedford-Stuyvesant is a new breed of dairy cattle." If New York City were a separate state, it would be the sixth largest. Of course, I think to myself, what an obvious idea, how strange that none of the other candidates have suggested it.

We drove through a section of Brooklyn with small one- and two-story row houses; ugly, but friendly in the morning light, with careful aluminum awnings and silver balls in tiny front gardens, and orange-painted store fronts. Comfortable lower-middle class. "Now this is what I call a neighborhood," said Mailer. "This is the sort of place I grew up in." "You did?" I said, disappointed. He laughed. "You thought I grew up in some slum," he said. I certainly did, I thought EVERYBODY who grew up in New York had to fight their way out of a tangle of fire escapes. I thought the tree that grew in Brooklyn was the only tree.

Another synagogue. Everything in it is labeled, "Donated by . . ." The chairs donated by the Glick family, the window from the Goldstein family, the microphone from Mr. Schwartz. Mailer tells them: "We are running on a powerful notion, the notion of New York as the fifty-first state .We are offering the city a chance to reconsider, we are offering a chance to dig and explore, and debate and see where we are going. What we are saying, is, there is no need to destroy ourselves." A man in the audience says: "There are people, other people, who are trying to keep the city alive. I see complete ANARCHY in your neighborhood concept." Applause; *this* neighborhood's concept seems to be a sort of gang warfare with gun battles and street barricades against "them"—the people in Harlem and the South Bronx and Bedford-Stuyvesant. Mailer smiles, the smile of the emerging politician, and says; "OK. Now let's talk about it. I don't mean ALL power to the neighborhoods, I mean as much as is compatible with the needs of the city." By the time he leaves, they are still suspicious, but interested.

About five o'clock, Mailer dropped into two fund-raising parties. Afterwards, the whole pack of us, press, campaign manager, advance man, and candidate, went to a West Side hotel where, under different auspices, "Swinger's Socials" are regularly held. ("Passive man wants to meet two strong blond dominating women.") This evening some kind of Reform Democratic club, not swinging, was meeting in an airless, ugly room, filled with people who seemed to have taken literally the columnists' advice to lonely people: "Join your local political club and meet people, get involved." Mailer talked about the mechanics of Power to the Neighborhoods: "They will forge themselves, deliver their own forms out of their conflicting needs." Part of the Mailer-Breslin platform was a plan for a monorail around New York City, and free electric jitneys in Manhattan. No cars allowed. "It will give New Yorkers a certain sense of liberty swinging from one bus to another." There was polite laughter. New Yorkers right now have so little sense of liberty that they cannot even imagine the exhilaration of free buses. "This city either gets an imagination or it dies," the candidates keep repeating. Now I see what they mean. The meeting was followed by a tango-dance exhibition. We did not stay.

Political clubs all look the same: full of folding tables and ancient chairs, drifts of leaflets on the floors and ashtrays that have been forever full, little old ladies who bring boxes of cookies and packs of cigarettes and make nests in the desk drawers. That night we drove through the cool May twilight to another club, miles and miles into Queens along New York's version of the numbing All-American highway, Queens Boulevard. Endless blocks of pizza parlors, parking lots, automobile showrooms, chandelier modern. One reporter swore he had driven down it one night with Mailer, who was muttering to himself: "I don't want to be mayor of this evil, evil city."

Twelve midnight: We are going to a bar. Just a bar, not one of the in places where people whisper "NORMAN was here last night." Norman says he isn't too crazy about those. By now I'm calling him Norman. I'm very happy, there are six men and me, and it is very late and everyone feels justified in staying up later because we've all been through a long day together and, besides, while Norman keeps talking, we are theoretically still working. I keep drinking brandy—for my tooth—and I say something calculatedly self-deprecating about how I was pleased to be with the grownups, but I was afraid I had taken up somebody else's position in the car. With just the barest hint of a twinkle Norman says: "You are ageless . . . and without position." He grins fiendishly. Now I see why they say don't lie around him. Don't even adopt a slight, comforting little pose.

The men talk about stories they have done about athletes: Sonny Liston and Cassius Clay and Jim Brown. They talk about the sheer physical presence of those guys: All of them describe a moment of truth when they were plain scared. Mailer's presence has the same frightening effect on writers, male writers. "Norman's going to read this," they think, paralyzingly, their professional egos at stake. For women, it isn't such a challenge. We, the women I know working around him, and me, aren't even sure he takes us seriously anyway. "He exalts women spiritually and puts them down intellectually," somebody said. For some reason, with Mailer it is endearing instead of infuriating. Probably because we are so busy trying to meet his real challenge to us; we are trying to be prototypical WOMAN.

For men, getting Mailer down in words is like wrestling the big one into the boat. The results are often very contradictory, verging on incoherent. Probably the only person who can write about Mailer is Mailer. Even describing his face is like trying to capture exactly the effect of light on a particularly profound body of water. Sometimes he looks menacing, and his lip curls back like an angry dog as when he talks about the dis-ease (he pronounces words literally, as well as using them literally) of the twentieth century. And then, in the split second before Wolfman takes over, the lines around his eyes crinkle up and the threat is a joke, shared. In the course of one sentence he can be brilliant, obscure, naïve, kind, attacking, articulate, and demonic. He is deeply engrossing, terribly funny, and almost totally impossible to remember accurately when you are not with him. It makes complete accuracy in reporting difficult.

Still at the bar; two o'clock in the morning. One of the reporters, relentlessly searching for Mailer's essence, said: "HOW could you have written *Armies of the Night* without taking notes?" And Mailer said: "It's funny, when I checked my facts I found I had remembered most of the night. I didn't take any notes because I didn't plan to write anything. But when I got on the plane back to New York I had a sudden Epiphany." He grinned, and spread his arms, and we could see him sitting in the plane, expanding with a vision. We laughed and talked about how "Epiphany" would replace "existential" in intellectual slang, and we all planned to have creative Epiphanies as soon as possible.

May 26: A new girl is riding in the press car, tall, blonde, just back from free-lancing in Vietnam. Norman goes into his ritual ten-minute man-woman thing: "You look like you hunt, do you hunt?" he asks her, cozily. Yes, she hunts, with various kinds of guns. I hate her. "I fish," I say, hopefully. He laughs, his mood is good. All evening with petulant questioners, lightly, intuitively, truth through tact. It's the same night that Breslin faces a hostile, long-winded girl who questions him while her large dog howls. Jimmy resists his natural instincts, and inquires politely: "Madam, has that dog had his shots?" He deserves to carry the assembly district for that.

There is a brief unpleasantness during a small benefit appearance at the Electric Circus. Intellectual cannibals again, and Norman asks for questions instead of giving his rousing street-corner speech. "I hate the Electric Circus, I hate the architecture, I hate what it stands for. It's a trap." (A rather inconvenient aversion, since Village campaign headquarters are in the Electric Circus building.) "The whole Village is a trap, isn't it?" someone asks. "Well, it isn't nourishing," says Mailer. Out of six stops tonight, the *Times* tangentially covers only the Electric Circus appearance, with a drama page review: "First the audience . . . witnessed a psychodrama of another variety, 'The Campaign,' starring Norman Mailer. While TV cameras captured the bizarre scene . . ." Later, Breslin will say truthfully, "Most of the reporters in New York are $240 a week shipwrecks."

They are waiting for Mailer at the League of Women Voters. They are really with him, tolerating the other candidates in tonight's debate, but applauding wildly for Mailer. A man about thirty-five, with a drooping mustache, claps, and his mother, in stony disapproval, jabs him with her elbow. The son strokes his mustache fiercely, in defiance. Mailer begins: "The acquired experience of the past is useless for New York because New York is the first victim of the twentieth century, what I called the dis-ease of the technological society. To wit, all the ills of the world were assumed at one point by technology, which proceeded to pipe them out the back of the car in the form of exhaust and they've come back: the greed, the exploitation, the iniquity (spoken letter by letter, with fangs showing) of capitalism have come back to the city in the form of smog." Applause. There are many little old ladies here, with firm hats and firm opinions. They agree with Mailer on the Vietnam war—a subject he doesn't get into because this is a mayoral contest. If there are no votes here, there are no votes anywhere.

Memorial Day weekend the campaign went to Aqueduct Race Track and Coney Island. I missed it, but the tall beautiful blonde went. Today, June 3 (??) there is a lunch-hour walk around midtown Manhattan: from the CBS building to Rockefeller Center, up across Fifty-seventh Street and down Third Avenue to P. J. Clarke's pub. Jimmy and Norman, wearing bachelor's-buttons in their buttonholes—donated by the St. Patrick's Cathedral flower fair—walk down the street, hand out. Volunteers fan out around the block, leafleting, urging. "Come and meet Norman Mailer, Pulitzer prize-winning author and candidate for mayor. Come and meet Jimmy Breslin, candidate for City Council president."

At that hour, at that time of year, the people on Fifth Avenue are half Swedish models and Middle-Western tourists, but there are enough New Yorkers, and enough step up to shake hands. They have heard of Mailer, but KNOW Jimmy, who has spent years writing columns in their cause. His walk was one long series of regards sent to sisters-in-law, inquiries about the family back in Flushing. It sounded as though he had gone to high school with half the people on the street. "How's it goin' Jimmy," they said. "Not bad, same old thing," he said. "Say, he's a handsome guy isn't he? What a big fella," they said, pleased to meet Breslin and see that he was handsome. They were shyer about Mailer, asking for autographs and telling him they had read his books.

That day there were packs of reporters, several elite columnists, and at least two complete television crews. It was June 3, and finally the press seemed to have decided that this was a *serious* campaign. Up until then, the three local papers had been running stories, with a few excellent exceptions, that were inaccurate, misleading, out of context, and "made us look like monkeys," said Mailer.

Mailer was not easy to cover. He speaks so quickly there is no way to catch what he says exactly, and he speaks with such unexpected turns of language, a sort of shorthand of his writing, that he is impossible to paraphrase. And, unless he is carefully struggling through an interview, he often doesn't answer questions at all, throws off one-liners, or answers them four hours later.

He patiently suffered daily interviews, explaining slowly what he thought about the city, trying to answer tedious questions without snapping. If people tried to get his opinion on subjects other than the mayoral race, he referred them to his books, saying, "I've written about it so much better than I can say it here." One day, when I had collected a lot of questions, I tried to have a straight interview. He said: "Whose questions are those? They aren't real questions, they are dull, stupid questions. Why do you need an interview, you've been here two weeks. Why are you so greedy? You reporters all have tapeworm, and the tapeworm is dialogue." He had grown fangs again, but I copied down everything he said so dutifully that he laughed.

For most of the other reporters, he contained himself, not that it did much good. They would arrive, saying: "I guess they are always drunk, late, and obscene, huh? Crazy guys, what a wild idea." And then they would begin to dimly realize that this campaign was something between Norman Mailer and Jimmy Breslin and the people of New York. Rarely did they manage to carry their new perception back to the city desk. They would take the easy way and play it for laughs: "Norman Mailer considers the solution to crime to be spiritual: He is sort of the left-wing Billy Graham."

Verbally, Mailer was hard to catch. But the *concept* shouldn't have been beyond the reach of most journalists. Even so, one reputedly competent man murmured at the end of two weeks on the assignment: "But, WHY is he doing it?"

He was doing it, I think, for spiritual reasons, partly. "We are paying our dues to this city," he said, and Breslin said. The way to do it was to go out and challenge, personally, the disease of the twentieth century where it lived: by confronting the tired and numbed people and making them think and prodding them to get a sense of themselves. He gave more than he got, and he seemd to thrive on it. "I'm not tired," he said toward the end of the campaign. "My stamina is good and getting better all the time." Every day he seemed to be cheerier, happier, and firmer about what he was saying. There was suspicion that he had been bored before the campaign began.

On Fifth Avenue, the people were not yet greeting the candidates as saviors of their city. A woman darted up to

Breslin and said, hissing, "That's all we need, an illiterate for City Council president, and a pervert for mayor." She said it twice, to make sure. "Beautiful," said Breslin. She may have called Mailer a pervert because he has gone on record in favor of sex, and has had four wives. But everyone is entitled to at least two marriages these days, and certainly Norman Mailer is entitled to four. One of the press group's favorite things to cluck about (reporters are really old men at heart, gossips, all of them), was the fact that Norman's wives seem to get along with each other. As though that were undesirable and somehow shocking. But there he is, way out in front, once again.

The women on Fifth Avenue were frightening. They scuttled along, girded for war with the Return for Credit Department; eyelids painted brilliant green over the webs of age. Once in Queens, Mailer said: "The women out here are real women, their lives center on their home and children." I thought that was Mailer, the Last of the Great Romantics, speaking. He didn't seem to notice their fingernails bitten down to the quick, or their wigs at ten in the morning, or the petulance that had settled on their faces. But when I really looked at the examples of womanhood on Fifth Avenue, stared them in the face while I urged them to shake the candidate's hand, I saw what he meant. They were ravening beasts compared to the house-bound ladies of Queens. Norman Mailer is a cumulative experience.

Lunch at P. J. Clarke's. There is a long table full of reporters and campaign aides, and Norman and Jimmy pick up the bill—again. People seem to think this is a Rockefeller running. A grizzled city-desk type is hunched over the end of the table, interviewing Norman. "I'm not looking for a revolution at all," he says. "I'm looking for its exact opposite. I'm lookin' for a way to give people in this city a sense of their own political power. Until we give power back to the neighborhoods, nobody will have a sense of what it is to gain or lose. I say I'm running as a left-conservative: It means the conservatives are right that man must solve his problems through his own agency, but you can't ask the other half to do it until they have their own agency. I'm talking about economic funding for the other half, and that's left."

That afternoon Mailer speaks at a special meeting for *Time-Life* employees. He is really rolling along, by now he REALLY knows what he would want to do if he were mayor, and he moves through the subjects of welfare and discriminating trade unions and finally to crime as a result of the greater evils of society. "Crime becomes a way of life, it becomes the one way a man may express himself." They ask about his position on CCNY. Mailer was the only mayoral candidate who spoke out in favor of the black students at CCNY who were demanding, last spring, separate and open enrollment for blacks. ("I didn't even have to think about it," said Mailer at the time. "It seemed right.") It was a position that shocked the fair, liberal-white sensibilities of the people who learned those liberal sentiments at CCNY in its great days during the depression. Beneath the liberal facade, they simply believed that letting in many black students would SPOIL the university. "Lower standards."

Mailer said, to *Time-Life:* "Well, you all are *very* serious about CCNY. The idea of the pearl having its standards adulterated, eh?" He stopped, and said as an aside, "It's awful to think of a pearl having its standards adulterated." Earlier, another night, he had said, "These black people have been promised in the last twenty years over and over and over and over that they would be given opportunities to have education, free education, for their needs. They were denied, cheated, and tricked for two centuries in this country. Finally they seized the opportunity, they *forced* that recognition that they should have double admission at the college, and I say fine, I cheer. What no one says is, what are they going to do if those kids don't go to college? Let 'em stand on the street and shake their dice and wait and jive talk and figure out how they can spoil the city? They have the wit and want to get into college and I say bless 'em." To *Time,* he added: "We have to recognize that everybody in this city is paying for the sins of their fathers. And, realize, when WHITE boys can't get into CCNY, then we finally get those community colleges, and not before."

Outside the lecture room at *Time* there was a reception room with a yellow-and-black-tile floor, and long tables spread out with drinks. No one standing outside the hall touched a drink until Mailer finished. There were ripples of girls going through: special *Time-Life* girls with Hampton tans and very short skirts. One of the photographers said: "They made me want to just grab hold with both hands and bite their thighs." I asked Norman what he thought of their fuckability quotient, if the question didn't offend him. He said: "Yes, it would offend my notion of the mystery."

The day's campaigning continued. A fund-raising party in a too carefully decorated West Side apartment. A debate on the Lower East Side where the people were stolid, welcoming. There were sleeping children in the audience, and a few hippies, and some who looked as though they had come over from the old country in 1860. Norman liked it there, it reminded him of another part of his childhood, and when he had to leave to go uptown to another meeting, he hurried through it and raced back downtown. "I think I can get 'em," he said. "The devils are running in this campaign," he was saying to the audience, as one of the devils walked in through the stage door. The poor man never had a chance. In response to Mailer he said things like: "I don't use liberal in the pejorative sense. We don't need simplistic nonsense. We are in a crisis of liberalism. If competent, tough, effective liberalism doesn't work, then we are in trouble." I don't think the people he was speaking to had actually realized that liberalism had already failed until that moment.

"I'm not a liberal," said Mailer. "I don't believe in gentle progressive steps. This city is half insane by now and we have to do something. John Lindsay is a nice fellow, but he is too good for this city. He is so tall and we are all so small and ugly. He should be president, the problems would be simpler." He talked about Sweet Sunday: "Since at bottom I'm a mystic, I'm still for shutting off the electricity, but it won't happen until New Yorkers get their heads cleared, and get tired of TV."

Afterwards, outside, it was dark, and it was good. A man came up in the crowd, wearing a yarmulke and work clothes, and said: "Mr. Mailer, would you give me your autograph, and your favorite verse from the Old Testament? I've read a couple of your books and they have given me a lot of pleasure in life." The crowd gathered around to see if Mailer could do it. He wrote something slowly in Hebrew, and then he corrected the end, and they sighed with relief. Later, in the car, he said he had written, "In the beginning."

On June 5 I met Mailer and Breslin in Joe's Restaurant in downtown Brooklyn. Jimmy was swearing under his breath at some political enemies sitting across the room. Norman had gotten up at six to shake hands outside subway entrances. Norman and I were supposed to have an interview, but that was the day he snarled about tapeworm, so I sat there and ate their olives and asked about the beginning of the campaign.

In April ("My God," said Breslin, "do you know how long ago that seems?") they had gone to about fifteen local colleges to see if they had any support. They said: "We are feeling around, if you want us to go for it, we will." At Union Theological Seminary, Jimmy made them feel ashamed of their education, they felt guilty at not having street smarts. They asked Norman to read aloud the passage from *Miami and the Siege of Chicago* where he describes the Republicans, ("They scourged themselves with WASP self-Hate," said somebody who was at UTS).

At Queens College, Mailer and Breslin climbed up fourteen floors to talk to the kids who had seized the building. In Queens, one of the big political issues in the campaign was the fact that the snow had not been removed for two weeks after last winter's blizzard. "What would you have done about it?" they asked Mailer. Imbued with the revolutionary spirit of the fourteenth floor, Mailer put his hand on his hip, leaned

forward and said: "I would have PISSED on it." Somehow in
print that doesn't look as captivating as it was.

I wondered if he was ever asked questions about his
books, his "body of work," his philosophy. "They don't treat
me as a walking body of knowledge because there is no reason
why they should. I'm a frightfully ignorant man. I'm an ama-
teur philosopher," he said, scowling. One of Mailer's favorite
mottoes is "Once—a philosopher, twice—a pervert." He says
a girl told it to him, he thinks it is from Voltaire, and he is
pleased thinking so, and he trots it out prefaced by "I would
remind you that . . . " But he delivers it with an emphasis
that reads as though he meant once upon a time a philosopher,
sure to end up a pervert twice. The recipient of this philosophical nugget usually stands up nodding in bewilderment, which
gives Mailer a chance to get away.

After Joe's Restaurant, we went to Bedford-Stuyvesant,
the particular ghetto section of Brooklyn that was the center
of Robert Kennedy's prototypical slum program. It is a really
beautiful part of New York, full of trees and magnificent old
brownstones, which Mailer took great pleasure in pointing
out. Brownstones can be saved he said, housing projects simply
crush the soul. The group, press, and/or leaflet passers, stood
on a central street corner, in front of the Club Baby Grand.
I had never noticed before that we were all white, or at least
we were that particular afternoon.

Norman had said: "We are scarcely a household word
in BedStuy," but then, almost none of the other candidates
ever appeared there at all. People, mostly young black men,
stopped and talked and wanted to know what about it. Norman, who was shorter than most of the men, looked straight
into their eyes and spoke levelly, straight ahead, which was
physically impossible. His face was compassionate, concerned,
he told them what he would do and what they would be able to
do if there was neighborhood control. Everywhere he spoke,
the middle class stood up and said, "If the neighborhoods
have control, what about BedStuy? What's to keep them
from getting most of the money?" He answered: "The idea

won't work unless black neighborhoods get more at first, in order to build their own economies. The liberal and the left in New York have to consider over and over that the black communities have to have the chance to get their thing together."

So there the candidates were, on a June afternoon, explaining what it would be like if the firemen and policemen and garbage men were from the community, and if the community could decide for itself what to do about its schools and its parks and its traffic. They talked about their platform which called for the community to take over the renewal of dilapidated housing, to train itself to do the work (which would also by-pass discriminating trade unions). A very tall black man, wearing an African robe, asked Jimmy a question about police. Breslin stood very close to him and looked up into his face, craning his neck back and said, very low, pushing the words into the man, pushing the reality, the recognition out between them where it might do some good: "You know by now the white man isn't going to do *anything* for you. You've got to have your own police." The man nodded. He knew, but he didn't know anyone else knew.

That day I was carrying a copy of *Armies of the Night*. We were all constantly sneaking around with unread Mailer works. Norman offered to autograph it, and I was pleased. As we drove to his house, he thought and fidgeted, and finally wrote down: "To Jane, with all fine lights to the lady, Norman." Thank you, I said, what does it mean?

"I thought it sounded nice," said Norman. My Pulitzer prize-winning autograph.

The best thing about being a Mailer Trailer, aside from my life being changed, my perceptions unclogged, and my knowledge of New York extended beyond the surrealistic and dis-eased island of Manhattan, was that Norman did, indeed, make me feel like a lady. That afternoon, he was on his way home to change and then drive out to Rutgers to receive his first honorary degree. He asked if I would like to come up. I had once heard him describe another candidate as "a gentleman, someone I would invite to my home." I felt privileged.

Everybody at headquarters that afternoon was absolutely outraged by what they called the Pulitzer prize-winning jingle. Someone had donated money for radio spots and the staff wrote a series that they considered sharp, impressive, educational, and moving. Norman threw them all out and insisted on using his jingle which had been partially inspired by a man who had pressed a small piece of paper into his hand on the street in Bedford-Stuyvesant, on which was written, "You've seen the rest, now vote the best, Mailer-Breslin and the fifty-first state."

Canvassers were out ringing doorbells, carrying notes from the major position papers, and some directions, one of which was: "Under the present status of this city, the same style of life is being forced on both the lion and the ox, and that, as the poet Blake said, is oppression." At their last press conference, Mailer and Breslin presented a "Miscellany of Ideas for the 51st State." Vest-pocket neighborhood colleges. Free bicycles in all city parks. A referendum calling for the fifty-first state and subsequent consitutional convention. Day-care centers and nurseries. A central farmer's market offering ethnic foods of all varieties. Rebuilding our dilapidated neighborhood water fronts as water-front housing. Investigation and abolishment of loan companies and city marshals. Craftsman training in gardening. And so on. Think about it. People laughed and laughed, as though civilizing steps were forever beyond them, but as one of the slogans said: "If you think the 51st state is a joke, New York may die laughing."

They didn't win of course. Mailer came in fourth in a field of five. Jimmy ran well. They had hoped to do somewhat better. The night of the primary, people came to headquarters. "It wasn't the sort of party that Norman Mailer usually attends," said one of the newspapers. They were always saying things like that. How did they know? One time a reporter asked: "Don't you find this grubby: aren't these people you would avoid in your personal life?"

"It isn't the same," he said patiently. "You see a blank stare when they meet you. Then you tell them who you are and what you are trying to do, and their eyes light, and you know you are relating and somehow it all seems to matter."

Mailer and Breslin thanked the volunteers. Norman said: "I came up with the fifty-first state idea. I thought it was a powerful idea. I'll see if it has real growth potential." Jimmy said: "I will now drink in public. I am mortified to have been part of a process which required the closing of the bars." And then he said: "Please don't stop here. I think most of you know what you have to do."

The next day Norman went back to editing his movie, *Maidstone,* and then went to Houston for the moon flight. Jimmy went to Westhampton to write.

After one of the meetings in a synagogue, two men who had been standing in the back started laughing and shaking their heads. "They are really crazy with that power to the neighborhoods stuff," said one. "Imagine giving power to Harlem!"

"No, wait a minute, Herbie," said the other man, "he's talking about giving power back to us too." Mailer and Breslin, by sheer force of will and argument, had opened up that one person, that day, to a new idea. I guess that's what we all have to do.

MALE CHAUVINIST?

Joyce Carol Oates

Out of the Machine

> . . . a day had to come when women shattered the pearl of their love for pristine and feminine will and found the man, yes that man in the million who could become the point of the seed which would give an egg back to nature, and let the woman return with a babe who came from the root of God's desire. . . .
>
> *The Prisoner of Sex*

It is appropriate that Norman Mailer has become the central target of the fiercest and cruelest of Women's Liberation attacks, not because Mailer is prejudiced against women, or bullying about them, not even because he claims to know much about them, but because he is so dangerous a visionary, a poet, a mystic—he is shameless in his passion for women, and one is led to believe anything he says because he says it so well. He is so puritanical, so easily and deeply shocked, like any hero, that his arguments, which approach the fluidity and senselessness of music, have the effect of making the dehumanized aspects of womanhood appear attractive.

Here is Mailer: ". . . Why not begin to think of the ovum as a specialized production, as even an artistic creation?" And: "Yes, through history, there must have been every variation of the power to conceive or not to conceive —it was finally an expression of the character of the

216

woman, perhaps the deepest expression of her character—"
What, are artistic creation and the expression of character, for women, not detachable from their bodies? From the
mechanism of their bodies? It is terrible to be told, in 1971,
that we belong to something called a species, and that we
had, throughout centuries, a mystical "power to conceive or
not to conceive." Why didn't we know about this power?

No matter if we protest that sexual identity is the least
significant aspect of our lives. No matter if we hope, not
absurdly in this era, that technology might make our lives
less physical and more spiritual. None of this matters for, to
Norman Mailer, "the prime responsibility of a woman is
probably to be on earth long enough to find the best mate
possible for herself, and conceive children who will improve
the species."

But we don't know what the *species* is. A post-Darwinist
name for "God"? A scientific concept? A mystical concept?
A word? An identity? An essence? Do we locate ourselves in
it, or does it push through us, blindly, with the affection of a
stampeding crowd? And how long is "long enough"? Should
we remain on earth for twenty years, or forty, or dare we hope
for an extravagant eighty years, though our last several
decades will be unproductive and therefore unjustified? The
machine of the female body is thought by some to be a sacred
vessel, designed to bring other sacred vessels into the world,
for the glory of God; but it is also thought to be rather foul,
as in Lear's words:

> But to the girdle do the gods inherit,
> Beneath is all the fiend's.
> There's hell, there's darkness, there's the sulphurous pit;
> burning, scalding, stench, consumption. . . .

It is also considered a means of improving the species, that is,
a machine designed to improve the quality of other machines;
and the proper artistic creation of a woman is not a novel, a
symphony, not a political theory, certainly, but the cultivation
of her womb. The "power to conceive or not to conceive" is,

after all, the "deepest expression of [a woman's] character. . . . Not one kind of expression, not even the most pragmatic expression, but the deepest expression! One sees why the mystic is the most dangerous of human beings.

There is a famous remark of Freud's that ends with the question, "What does a woman want?" A good question. And a woman is inclined to ask, with the same exasperation. "What does a man want?" Indeed, a woman must ask, "What does a *woman* want?" The question is a good one, but it is fraudulent. It suggests that there is a single answer—a single "want"—for a multitude of human personalities that happen to be female. Many women are angry today because they are only women; that is, they possess the bodies of women, the mechanisms for reproducing the species, and they are therefore defined simply as "women." But there is no reality to the class of "women," just as there is no emotional reality to the "species." There are only individuals. The individual may be compartmentalized into any number of compartments, the absurd boxes of the poll-taker (the "Irish Catholic," the "suburbanite, affluent," the "35-year-old divorcée," etc.), but he exists in none of these compartments, and his personality will reject them. The only reality is personality. Not sex. Not sexual identity. No categories can contain or define us, and that is why we draw back from the female chauvinists who claim a biological sisterhood with us, just as we draw back from the male chauvinists who have attempted to define us in the past.

"If we are going to be liberated," says Dana Densmore, in a pamphlet called "Sex Roles and Female Oppression," which is quoted in the Mailer article, "we must reject the false image that makes men love us, and this will make men cease to love us." But this viewpoint is not acceptable. It assumes that men demand a false image, that all men demand false images. It does not distinguish between one man and another man. And it assumes that women do not demand, from men, images that are occasionally false. Can an "image" be anything but false? The perfect mate of the toiling, distraught housewife is not a free, marauding male, but a husband stuck to a job that is probably as demeaning as housework, but more grating on the nerves because it is played out in a field of competition. If the woman has become trapped in a biological machine, the man has become trapped in an economic machine that pits him against other men, and for mysterious and shabby rewards. Man's fate may be to languish in imaginary roles, wearing the distorted masks of ideal images, but he can at least improve the quality of these roles by using his intelligence and imagination. But only by breaking the machine. Only by abandoning and climbing out of the machine, the traps of "maleness" and "femaleness."

Freud has been attacked from all sides as a representative of typical male prejudice, but his views on the subject are always worthwhile. In that wise, complex essay *Civilization and its Discontents,* he speaks of sex as "a biological fact which, although it is of extraordinary importance in mental life, is hard to grasp psychologically . . . though anatomy, it is true, can point out the characteristics of maleness and femaleness, psychology cannot. For psychology the contrast between the sexes fades away into one between activity and passivity, in which we far too readily identify activity with maleness and passivity with femaleness." Obviously, the distinctions are not simple.

For if the female finds herself locked in a physical machine marked "passive," the male is as tragically locked in a machine marked "active." As Sylvia Plath says, ironically, "Every woman loves a fascist." What is left, then, but for the man to play the role of a brute? What is masculinity in any popular sense, except the playing of this stupid, dead-end role? In our culture men do not dare cry, they do not dare to be less than "men"—whatever that means.

The mechanical fact of possessing a certain body must no longer determine the role of the spirit, the personality. If Women's Liberation accomplishes no more than this it will have accomplished nearly everything.

But there are further problems, further areas of masculine

uneasiness. Mailer criticizes Kate Millett for believing in "the liberal use of technology for any solution to human pain." Yes, that sounds like heretical belief so long as human pain is valued as sacred, or important as an expression of personality, or helpful for salvation . . . or even conversation. But it isn't. It is nothing, it is a waste, a handicap, a mistake. What good is human pain? We are all going to experience it soon enough, regardless of technology's miracles, so there is no point in our ignoring it or romanticizing it. Human pain— the acceptance of a bodily machine without any rebellion— is a way of making us human, yes, but the rewards are chancy and might be as well accomplished by an act of the imagina· tion. Why shouldn't we ask of technology the release from as much pain as possible? Why not? Why not the disturbing Utopian dream/nightmares of the "extra-uterine conception and incubation"—if they are a means of diminishing pain? Mailer, like all heroic spirits, places a primitive value on suffering. And one feels that he would not shy away from suffering, even the suffering of childbirth, if that were a possibility for him. Yes, to suffer, to feel, to be changed—it is a way of realizing that we live. But it is also a way of becoming dehumanized, mechanized. In fact, a way of dying.

To be mechanically operated, to have one's body moving along in a process that the spirit cannot control, to have the spirit trapped in an unchosen physical predicament—this is a kind of death. It is life for the species, perhaps, but death for the individual. Throughout human history women have been machines for the production of babies. It was not possible for them to live imaginative, intellectual, fully human lives at all, if indeed they survived for very long. They lived long enough to find a mate, to have a number of children, many of whom would not survive . . . but it was the process that mattered, the blind, anonymous reproductive process that gave these women their identities.

In a little-known story by Herman Melville, "The Tartarus of Maids," young girls working in a paper factory are seen by a sympathetic narrator: "At rows of blank-looking counters sat rows of blank-looking girls, with blank, white folders in their blank hands, all blankly folding blank paper." They are the pulp that is turned into blank paper out of a certain "white, wet, woolly-looking stuff . . . like the albuminous part of an egg," in a room stifling with a "strange, blood-like, abdominal heat." The process takes only nine minutes, is presided over by a jovial young man named Cupid, and what terrifies is its relentlessness: it is an absolute process, a godly machine that cannot be stopped. "The pulp can't help going," the narrator is told smugly. And he thinks: "What made the thing I saw so specially terrible to me was the metallic necessity, the unbudging fatality which governed it." Melville, who seemed to have no interest at all in the relationship between men and women, and who created no memorable woman character in all his fiction, has given us the best metaphor for the existential predicament of most of the world's women.

No wonder that the feminists look to technology for deliverance! As they climb out of their machines they must find other, substitute machines to do the work of women. A body is no more than a machine, if it is not guided by a personality—so why not a surrogate machine, an actual machine, why not the escape from as much impersonal pain as possible?

Once we are delivered from the machine of our bodies, perhaps we will become truly spiritual.

Perhaps.

At the start of *The Prisoner of Sex,* Mailer speaks of having taken care of his large family for several weeks during the summer, cooking, cleaning, turning into a kind of house-wife, so exhausted with domestic chores that he had no time to write, to think, to contemplate his ego. *No time to contemplate his ego!* After a while, in such a frenzy, one loses his ego altogether . . . one misplaces his personality, and sinks into the routine frenzy of work that adds up to nothing, that comes to no conclusion, no climax. Is this a human life? Can one call an uncontemplated life really a "life" at all? Or is it merely brute existence? One has the time to contemplate his ego—to achieve a personality—only when he or she is liberated from the tyranny of physical burdens, whether they are external in the form of housework to be done eternally, or a commuting distance to be traveled, or whether they are internal, the processes of a body unaltered by technology and human choice. And what grief, what anger and dismay, for the women who—to "liberate" themselves and their men from the possibility of pregnancy—began taking the Pill on absolute faith, only to discover that the Pill carried with it mysterious disappointments and possible catastrophes of its own!—for Technology is probably male, in its most secret essence male.

The problem is: do we control nature, or will we be controlled by nature? A difficult question. A Faustian question. To accept technology and to create surrogate machines that will bear our children—this sounds like madness, perversity. Yet, to deny human choice in the matter of reproduction, as we would never do in the matter of, say, ordinary medicine or dentistry, seems an empty sentimentality.

But after all this, after all these considerations, we are still left with the rage of Women's Liberation. How to explain this anger? And we understand slowly that what is being liberated is really hatred. *Hatred of men.* Women have always been forbidden hatred. Certainly they have been forbidden the articulation of all base, aggressive desires, in a way that men have not. Aggression has been glorified in men, abhorred in women.

Now, the hatred is emerging. And such hatred! Such crude, vicious jokes at the expense of men! Most women, reading the accusations of certain feminists, will be as shocked and demoralized as Norman Mailer himself. Somehow, in spite of all the exploitation, the oppression, somehow . . . there are things about the private lives of men and women that should not be uttered, or at least we think they should not be uttered, they are so awful. Women have been the subjects of crude jokes for centuries, the objects of healthy male scorn, and now, as the revolution is upon us, men will become the objects of this scorn, this exaggerated disgust and comic sadism.

Nothing will stop the hatred, not the passage of legislation, not the friendliest of men eager to come out in support of Women's Liberation. It has just begun. It is going to get worse.

And yet, it will probably be short-lived. Hatred goes nowhere, has no goal, no energy. It has a certain use, but it has no beauty. There will be a place in our society for Mailer's heroic mysticism, at the point in history at which women can afford the same mysticism. Until then, it is better for us to contemplate the blank-faced horror of Melville's pulp factory, rather than the dreamy illogic of Mailer's "ovum-as-artistic-creation."

PERFORMER—1

Bruce Cook

Aquarius Rex

The man who comes through the gymnasium door at the Stony Brook campus of the State University of New York has the developed torso and the rolling, bandy-legged gait of a professional boxer (which he isn't, but would probably like to be), the keen quick glance of an intellectual (which he is, but often seems to wish not to be), and the assured manner of a celebrity (no doubt about that, and he clearly relishes the role).

He is Norman Mailer, perhaps the only writer in America today whose name and face would be recognizable to the vast majority who read no books at all. He is the writer-hero, the Hemingway of our age. And he is here tonight at this half-finished cluster of university buildings 60 miles out on the narrow sandspit they call Long Island to talk to the students and let them know just what he thinks about the Nov. 7 election [1972].

His student hosts meet Mailer at the entrance and whisk him off to a nearby room to wait for the gym to fill up. I catch up with him there in that makeshift Green Room, introduce myself, and remind him that we had agreed through his secretary to get together here. Mailer is on the move a lot these days, lecturing at universities and doing a bit of restrained pitching for his new book, *St. George and the Godfather*, and I have been a little uneasy about this meeting. Was he really expecting me?

His immediate smile and strong handshake reassure me. Mailer repeats my name. "Didn't we meet years ago in Chicago?" he asks. "An interview?" I'm amazed that he remembers that after 12 years, and I tell him so. But he shrugs it off and says simply that the name had stuck with him because he had spotted it on bylines afterward.

Suddenly I am uneasy. Bylines probably meant book reviews, and my enthusiasm for his books has not always been unqualified; one of them I did not like, and said so plainly. Maybe this was it, the awful day that every reviewer dreads, when those chickens come home to roost.

And I know that Mailer is remarkably sensitive about what is written about him and his work. He astonished millions of people when he appeared on the Dick Cavett show last spring opposite Gore Vidal and attacked the other writer —one is tempted to say *venomously*, but there is so little real poison in Mailer that he actually seemed bent on crushing Vidal python-style with abuse—all because of a particularly mean-spirited review Vidal had written of Mailer's *The Prisoner of Sex*.

Dick Cavett was shocked; Janet Flanner (the *New Yorker*'s Genet," who was also on the show) was shocked; *I*, sitting at home, was shocked. Why should Mailer, who is certainly the most important writer around today, care what anybody says about him in a book review? I found that bewildering and began to wonder if we were not given a public glimpse of some private collapse.

My fears have now been allayed. In the few months since that awful night he has attended the Democratic and Republican conventions and written a book about them. No writer who is cracking up can perform *that* gracefully under pressure. And here he is before me now, the Mailer of old, easy and confident, speaking to the students from a prepared text that, it turns out, is selected manuscript pages from his new book, then not yet on the stands.

He is acutely conscious of himself before an audience. He has a good sense of what he is about, easing into his material, kidding the students, kidding himself almost mercilessly, and finally beginning with a selection from the book on the choosing of the Vice President: "There were arts to picking a Vice President," he began, "and the first was the name. Your ticket became a company." It is a keen perception, and he develops it in good comic style as he takes us through the possible combinations and what they might suggets to voters: " . . . McGovern and Ribicoff as a product would be reminiscent of ambulance chasers."

The students love it. Everyone is feeling good. But what rude surprise has Mailer in store for them? Something, surely, for he wrote of himself in *The Armies of the Night*, "While there was no danger of Mailer ever becoming a demagog, since if the first idea he offered could appeal to a mob, the second in compensation would be sure to enrage them, he might nonetheless have made a fair country orator, for he loved to speak, he loved in fact to holler, and he liked to hear a crowd holler back." (Of how many New York intellectuals may that be said?)

And true to form tonight, Norman Mailer offers that second idea to enrage them: He reads them the long and brilliantly written section from *St. George and the Godfather* on the Democratic Women's Caucus views on abortion. It is heavy with the weight of apocalypse that Mailer seems to carry about as a burden. It broods darkly on the meaning of abortion and the nature of the movement that supports it: "Of course, Aquarius' real opinion was that at the bottom of Women's Liberation was all the explosive of alienated will, a will now so detached from any of the old female functions, and hence so autocratic, that insanity, cancer, or suicidal collapse might have to be the penalty if the will did not acquire huge social power. Totalitarian power." And so on.

That did it, of course. He broke off then and asked if there were "any questions from the floor on the scale and scheme of the values of the section I have just read." There were plenty. The crowd hollered back. You could tell he liked it. Standing with one shoulder cocked and a hand thrust into the pocket of his jeans, he said outrageous and eloquent things to them in response on the nature of sex and life and even the quality of the sex act that produced President Nixon.

He is talking over most of their heads. They begin to walk out on him. By the time he is back on the track and is reading sections—wise and witty stuff indeed—on republicanism and Richard Nixon, he has lost almost half of his audience. (Not *just* the female half—it doesn't break down quite that neatly.)

Why have they left? Not because they disagree with his incisive disparagement of Nixon. That is old stuff to them. There cannot be more than a dozen Nixonites among the hundreds there; Mailer verified this at one point by asking for a show of hands. No, they are clearly annoyed with him. He has had the temerity to disagree with them, to challenge them—*them*. The kids! Youth! And they thought he was on their side. Some of them show their displeasure by marching out loudly and slamming the doors behind them.

But Norman Mailer, even as a radical, has always been something of a maverick—and nowhere more than in *St. George and the Godfather*. Nobody, not even the hero, McGovern—the St. George of the title—escapes unscathed. And if he has made fun of Richard Nixon in the past, Mailer now takes him with deadly seriousness in his godfather analogy, suggesting that the Chief Executive really doesn't care how many are killed abroad as long as order is kept here at home. This, says Mailer, "is characteristic of a Mafialike society."

How does *St. George and the Godfather* compare with *Miami and the Siege of Chicago,* which covered the two conventions in 1968, and *The Armies of the Night,* his account of the 1967 Pentagon demonstration that brought him both the National Book Award and the Pulitzer Prize in 1969? It compares quite favorably with both. The eye for the moral nuance is still there, the lively intelligence is still at work on the real events of our time. In 1972, of course, the real events themselves are not nearly as exciting, and so if it lacks something of the fire of the two earlier books, it compensates by digging deeper in its analysis.

It is the 20th book by this almost incredibly prolific writer, and the second this year. ("I need all the money I get," he tells the roomful of students who join him for the rap session afterward. "No fooling. I'm in debt.") In addition, he has had three full-length critical books devoted to his work, as well as a collection of critical essays from various sources focusing on him. He will even appear as a character in a novel soon to be published.

(Or perhaps not. Mailer and his lawyer met recently with a novelist named Alan Lelchuk; representatives of Lelchuk's publisher, Farrar, Straus & Giroux; and their respective lawyers. Mailer objected to the use of his name for a character who appears in a brief scene in Lelchuk's forthcoming *American Mischief* and dies ignominiously with his pants down. What Lelchuk would do about it, says Mailer's attorney, is up to Lelchuk.)

The latest of the book-length studies of Mailer and his work is titled simply *Norman Mailer,* and it considers him in a series along with such writers and thinkers as Albert Camus, James Joyce, Sigmund Freud, and William Butler Yeats. In his conclusion to the study, Richard Poirier observes rather ominously that Mailer now seems to be at a crisis in his writing " equivalent . . . to the early period of exhaustion after *The Deer Park.*" But Poirier goes on to say that, "Mailer is uniquely situated to escape the entrapment that often turns American writers into imitators and finally into unconscious parodists of themselves."

Such expressions of concern and pledges of faith by critics treating Mailer's literary career have become almost traditional. The American literary establishment has a considerable investment in him. As far back as 1948, when *The Naked and the Dead*—the best novel to come out of World War II—was published, he was acknowledged as the crown prince. Sometime in the late '60s—fix it at 1968, the year that both *The Armies of the Night* and *Miami and the Siege of Chicago* were published—they crowned him king. As such has he reigned since.

There is some reason, however, for these expressions of anxiety. No writer in America today seems to live and work quite so close to the brink as Norman Mailer. He gave all the critics a turn when he suddenly got interested in making movies. Unstated in a study such as Poirier's, which barely mentions his three films—*Wild 90, Beyond the Law,* and *Maidstone*—is the obvious, fervent hope that Mailer has left all that behind him now.

Has he? I put the question to him as we settled down at the bar of his motel after leaving Stony Brook and the loyal many who had held him with questions for over an hour after his talk.

What I ask is, If someone were to hand him a script and guarantee financing (Mailer says his movies have cleaned him out) would he try again?

His response surprises me: "As a director or as an actor?"

"Well, er, as a director," I say. Somehow I had never really thought of Mailer as an actor, even though he played the central role in all three of his films.

He shrugs, not much taken with the idea. "Oh, I might be interested to try it one more time just to see if I could do it that way—but I'd love to play in a movie and not be the director. In fact, I was offered a role in one a year ago. It was going to have Eldridge Cleaver as a black revolutionary who kidnaps a Supreme Court Justice, which I was going to play. Mick Jagger was in it too, playing a rock star who is involved in it some way." He sighs. "I was looking forward to it, but it fell through."

What about a novel? I tell him that when I first tried

to arrange an interview with him I was told he was at work on one.

He nods. "Yes, there's a novel—which I won't talk about. I interrupted my work on it to do *St. George*. In general terms, though, I'll say it's related to the novel I announced 15 years ago."

It was to be a supernovel, a 10-years-in-the-writing novel. Back in 1959 he wrote of it in *Advertisements for Myself:* "If it is to have any effect, and I can hardly look forward to exhausting the next 10 years without hope of a deep explosion of effect, the book will be fired to its fuse by the rumor that once I pointed to the farthest fence and said that within 10 years I would try to hit the longest ball ever to go up into the accelerated hurricane air of our American letters." That was to be the novel—but then he turned to journalism and became king of the hill.

This last is not intended to diminish his achievement. I have the respect all journalists seem to share for Mailer's skill as a reporter. Like all the rest, too, I am interested in how he does it.

"Notebook, no tape recorder. We must be the last of the note-takers"—this to me directly as I make notes. *St. George and the Godfather* was written because I accepted an assignment from *Life* magazine and couldn't stop until I had had my say. It had to be written pretty quickly. It's about 80,000 or 85,000 words long. I did the first section on the Democratic convention for *Life* and then expanded it. There is a middle section of about 8,000 or 10,000 words on Washington between the conventions. I did that and the section on the Republican convention—a chunk of about 50,000 words—in two weeks."

I ask if the response tonight to the book—the walkout during his reading of the latter sections of *St. George and the Godfather*—bothered him. At one point he had seemed annoyed at the door slamming.

"A couple of years ago it was worse," he says. "Then I was looked on as some old fuddy-duddy conservative who was out in his own self-interest, a rich man talking Left. But now the confidence of the kids on the Left has evaporated. They don't have to agree with what I say, but they begin to find it intriguing. I think the '60s radical movement fell because it lacked radical ideas near the root. It may not have looked like much out there tonight, but I got nearer to them than I usually do."

What about the '60s movement? What shape is all that radical energy likely to take in the '70s? What shape should it take?

"The movement? Well, as one—how shall I put it?— who has had a fair share of acceptance, what I have been doing is working out every idea I have had for the past 10 years. And if I have a fundamental idea it's that people have to do their own work. I'm not prescribing. Not enough work went into the '60s movement. It doesn't matter what kind of society you create, if people are conned into it, it's going to be a bad society."

And the prospect before us? In spite of his obvious wish to the contrary, Norman Mailer seemed to concede before the Stony Brook students that a Nixon win is likely. If that happens, I ask, what can we expect the next four years?

"Well, I'm notoriously bad at predictions. And it's increasingly more difficult to look ahead now, because there's more going on at a greater rate. But I think we're going to start sinking into—well, totalitarianism is a word I've overworked, so call it a programmed society, a benign totalitarianism.

"Nixon has found that 65 per cent is quite enough to control completely. I think all the popular arts will begin to look like *Love Story* more and more. The revolution in film will slow down. And in books we'll have best-seller types and surrealistic literature with not much in between.

"I see the future as a kind of super-highway with a broad area of conformity in the center and some freakiness on the shoulders," Mailer muses. "And no. I don't think the war will continue. I think we lost the war more in the last four years when we were supposedly disengaging because we lost our moral fundament. We are not now finally and fundamentally a moral people."

PERFORMER—2

Richard Poirier

Mailer—Good Form and Bad

From the very beginning Norman Mailer has exhibited a literary ambition that can best be called imperialistic. He has wanted to translate his life into a literary career and then to translate that literary career into history. I say this not critically but descriptively. His is the kind of ambition, after all (regardless of whether one thinks he lives up to it), common to many of the great romantic writers: of Yeats, Conrad, Byron, Shelley, and Keats—of Coleridge, who lied about the actual dates of some of his writings so as to give his career and his life the dramatic development of a literary work.

Some years ago Gore Vidal made the point that Mailer is "a species of Bolingbroke," a usurper. Such an estimate, and it wasn't offered derogatorily, comes naturally enough to a writer who has no illusions, as Mailer does, about the differences between literary and, say, political careers. Committed to neoclassical ideas about the limits and proprieties of his own style and of the quite different demands made by each of the various forms in which he chooses to work, Vidal doesn't show in his writings or in his public manners those tremors of dissatisfaction that can be noted in whatever Mailer does. Unlike Mailer, Vidal does not confuse the rewards of writing with the rewards of winning public office, one kind of power with another kind. He would think it ludicrous to say, as Mailer has, that the power he exercises in managing the materials in a novel can be compared to the power of a general marshaling his forces in the field.

Some of these differences between Vidal and Mailer were displayed for everyone to see on Dick Cavett's show on the night of December 1, 1971, where they confronted one another in the company also of Janet Flanner, known for her sharply manicured reports from Paris to the *New Yorker*. It has been a bad memory for anyone who saw it. What is mostly remembered is Mailer's attack on Vidal and then on the audience, ending with a self-pitying, if blustering, public announcement that he was the only contender with the talent and the guts to become the literary champion of the world.

What is often forgotten is that the show was an embarrassment even before Mailer was introduced as the last guest. For one thing, Vidal's "inside" recollections about Eleanor Roosevelt (he once caught her storing flowers in the toilet bowl) exuded too much self-satisfaction, especially since he had just recently publicized the same anecdotes in the *New York Review of Books*. And Miss Flanner—gracious, husky, even craggy, quite happy to be there with the fellows, though apparently unable to grasp that Vidal was trying to initiate a political as well as a social discussion— had induced him into the sort of badinage meant to suggest how high-class literary folk really carry on when nobody's looking. Millions, unfortunately, were, and the condescension could have pleased very few.

A late-night show is scarcely the ideal place to create an image of the literary life as something exclusive and privileged. But it is precisely that kind of illusion, the illusion that we are being allowed to peep through the tube into somebody's salon, that the Cavett show depends upon. Vidal and Miss Flanner were, if anything, too good at it. Vidal, who always exercises a patrician ease and skepticism on such occasions, seemed willing to accept an alliance with Flanner and Cavett, as if in some anticipation of Mailer's attack. There was an audible effort to set a prevailing tone before Mailer could introduce his own. The results were cloying, the more so for Cavett's deferential boyishness, like some feisty dog anxious for affection. He has that Yalie manner in the presence of celebrities, as if to say that if *he,* who is after all comfortable with such people, is made to feel just a little shy tonight, then *we* ought to feel at least grateful.

Let it be said, then, that Mailer had a lot going for him when he waddled out like some nervous but bullish boy walking into the middle of a neighborhood gang. It was time, one felt, for a challenge to the pecking order, the calling of a bluff or two. Time even for the voice of the American family man, since Mailer is the devoted father of seven children, even if he has been the husband of four wives. Speaking out of that experience, he would perforce be listened to more confidently by the great American public on the issue of the sexes than Miss Flanner or Vidal. For sexuality and the sexes were to be the inevitable subject of the show. Vidal had written a long piece about sex and women's liberation, again for the *New York Review of Books,* which was for the most part brilliantly sane and witty. But he had been highly critical of Mailer both for his sexual attitudes and for his allegedly related taste for violence. In the process he had linked Mailer (and Henry Miller) with Charles Manson. And it was to this article that Mailer was ready to take strong, bitter, and understandable—but not very articulate—objection.

Linking Henry Miller with Manson makes so little sense as to suggest that the whole formulation occurred to Vidal because his customary discrimination was overwhelmed by his wit. He perhaps could not resist the dictates of alliteration, and I suspect that we would have been spared the connection had Manson been named Samson. The attempt to connect Mailer's wounding of his third* wife during a

*Actually, his second wife, Adele Morales. [Editor's Note.]

domestic quarrel with the fiendish, premeditated, systematic murders of a Manson was perhaps even more unfair than the guilt assigned to Miller by mere alliterative association.

Mailer, then, was from almost any point of view in a strong position for the confrontation with Vidal that he had elected to have. Why, then, did he proceed to botch his given opportunities? Why did he come off looking certainly no better, and to most viewers a lot worse, than the others?

One reason has to do with the format of a show such as Cavett's, with the form, that is, in which Mailer chose to express himself. It is a form that doesn't allow for any but the most trivial discussions, and it works best for people who are capable of putting their subtleties to one side for the occasion. Above all, such a show does not allow for the complex development of an idea or a position through that kind of dialectical interplay on which Mailer depends no matter where or how he is trying to explain his position on any subject.

To say that Vidal performs better than Mailer on a show of this kind does, indeed, say something about the marked differences between them as writers, the difference in the style by which each hopes to approximate in words and manner more or less what he thinks and how he feels. The difference is nicely clarified by something D. H. Lawrence once said about two painters, Albrecht Dürer and Antonio Correggio. "Dürer," he remarked, "starts with a sense of that which he does not know and would discover. Correggio with the sense of that which he has known and would re-create."

Mailer is obviously closer to Dürer, Vidal to Correggio. Which means that Vidal has a much sharper sense of the limits of literature, of its obligations to life-as-it-is, and of the extent to which the literary imagination is necessarily modified by forms that are independent of it. It means that Vidal is actively conscious of the circumscriptions and decorums of a literary career, especially in a world where other forms of expression are so much more conspicuously

powerful. Television is one of those forms. If your inclina-
tions are neoclassical like Vidal's—or even for that matter
like Janet Flanner's—you know better than to expect a talk
show to be easily hospitable to your impulses to self-expression,
your needs to vindicate yourself by elaborated and complex
explanations.

And this brings up a still more important and telling
difference between Mailer and the other guests on the show.
If, that is, the others were literary in a patronizing and genteel way, like members of a guild, Mailer (in quite another
way) was even more literary. He really thought his literary
and personal powers could dominate the nonliterary medium
in which he had agreed to express himself. He thought he
could make himself clear in a medium designed primarily
for the Correggios, which is not at all hospitable to anyone
"with a sense of that which he does not know and would
discover."

It is consistent with what I'm saying that Vidal so freely
used material from the *New York Review of Books* as if he
were not repeating himself, as if the audience for Dick
Cavett's show were not the audience for a journal of a cosmopolitan and academic intellectual elite. By contrast,
Mailer attacked Vidal for saying things about him in that
journal as if the millions watching the show already knew
what the article was all about. He assumed that any literary
controversy involving him, even as long ago as last July, was
still news, a part of history, a public event, whereas Vidal
and Miss Flanner knew that the best thing for them to do
was to re-create themselves, to adapt what was already known
about them to television.

If Mailer could make very little sense on the Cavett
show, except in the bare accusation that Vidal had sacrificed
his intellectual responsibilities by linking him to Manson, if
he could not deliver his mind within the conventions of a
late-night show, he nonetheless chose to be there, knowing
full well that he has almost never been any good at it. It is
pointless to disapprove of him for getting himself into these

situations, since it is now fairly clear that they are absolutely essential to him as a man and as a writer. So essential, in fact, that the form of his behavior on the Cavett show and on other such occasions can be seen to duplicate the form of some of his best writing and, indeed, the form he has given his literary career.

This form—of Mailer's public behavior, writing, and career—is shaped in roughly the following way: He finds himself as a participant in a situation, be it social, political, or literary that calls for conventional good manners. There follows an effort, sooner or later, to disassociate himself from other participants in the same enterprise. This act of disassociation very often requires of him a certain degree of intemperateness, or even obscenity. Then follows a period in which he angrily justifies this differentiation of himself until finally, by argument and self-persuasion, he arrives at the pleasurable sense of minority status. At this point he makes his most direct appeal to an audience—that it should regard him as a kind of culture hero. He is able to claim that his minority status, as against the prevailing social, political, or literary establishment, is what makes him the best, most imaginative figure in whatever group he happens to have placed himself. For one must remember that he is still participating in some sort of corporate literary, social, or political enterprise. He sees himself as the best part of this enterprise, the man who carries more of the burden of complication, more of the burden of imagination than anyone else. He becomes in effect the only man who deserves to be "the champ."

Such is the structure for example, of a book like *The Armies of the Night* and also of the experiences, as he recounts them, that went into that book. The same might be said of *Of a Fire on the Moon.* Each book begins with an account of how he has accepted an invitation to a gathering, how he joined in some large enterprise, how his conduct then set him apart from the other participants, how his view of things emerged as both more inclusive and more importantly complex than theirs, so that at the end his is therefore representative of the embattled Novelistic Imagination in a world that barely comprehends but has been obliged to tolerate him. In an elementary way this, too, is the outline of his career from his earliest work, with its heavy indebtedness to official, establishment literature that preceded him—as if he would join the company of Faulkner, Fitzgerald, Dos Passos, Hemingway—to the crisis of alienation from literature, politics, and society as described in *Advertisements for Myself,* to his joining these various elements of American life but at a different degree of assimilation and intensity. All this leads to work—in *The Armies of the Night* and *Why Are We in Vietnam?*—that truly is at a much higher level of originality and integration than any he had achieved before and than any of his contemporaries has yet to achieve.

Of all American writers perhaps since Henry James, Mailer is the most committed to the romantic view of the artist, the novelist, the creator of imaginative forms that can serve as alternatives to social, political, and linguistic forms proposed by non-artists. At the same time his mind is possessed of an unrelieved anxiety that he might be confused with someone else, especially another writer of any approximate similarity of position, that he might not decisively enough even exist, that his revolutionary stance will not appear wholly original. A telling incident, roughly similar to what happened on the Cavett show, occurs at the outset of *The Armies of the Night* when Mailer describes a party in Washington, D.C., for some of the people who are to march on the Pentagon. At the party with Mailer is Paul Goodman, and the book reveals Mailer's concern lest this semblance of alliance be mistaken for an identity of views. His objection to Goodman's politics and especially to his sexual attitudes is of a piece, finally, with his criticism of Goodman's writing. Speaking of himself in the third person, he complains, "But, oh, the style! It set Mailer's teeth on edge to read it; he was inclined to think that the body of students who followed Goodman must have something de-animalized to put up with the style, or at least such was Mailer's bigoted view."

What he means by "the style" is clarified somewhat later in a chapter called "In the Rhetoric" where, as in *Miami and the Siege of Chicago,* he reveals his distaste for the language of the American protest movement and of the young. As in his discussion of sex, his critique of language is ultimately a defense of neglected mysteries and visions of which liberal rationality takes no sufficient notice. The most offensive language smells

> like the storeroom of a pharmacology company's warehouse, doubtless productive of cancer over the long haul, but essential perhaps, perhaps! to a Left forever suffering from malnutrition. Mailer knew this attitude had nothing to do with reality—if names like SANE or Women Strike for Peace sounded like brand names, which could have been used as happily to sell aspirin, he could hardly think the same of SNCC or SDS or one or two of the others; now and again, remarkable young men sprang out of these alphabet soups. No, it was more that the Novelist begrudged the dimming of what was remarkable in the best of these young men because some part of their nervous system would have to attach vision and lust and dreams of power, glory, justice, sacrifice and future purchases on heaven to these deadening letters.

Behind the ostensible subjects of politics, sex, language, and style is the central concern about where Mailer the Novelist fits into the revolutionary alliance. More aptly, he is searching for the ways in which Mailer the Novelist does *not* fit into an easy alliance. How could he be expected to fit, being a Novelist responsible for values no other kind of writer necessarily has to care about—the Imagination, dread, awe, wonder, mystery. Thinking in Mailer is the function of his desperate need to imagine himself the savior of the imagination and, inevitably, in any circumstances, a minority figure.

All too often Mailer's ideas derive from his will to differentiate the lone Novelist from the mass of fellow journalists (as in *Of a Fire on the Moon*) or to isolate the lone Left-conservative from revolutionary poseurs (as in *The Prisoner*

of Sex). In *The Armies of the Night* he very willingly joins
a protest march, joins other dissenters or revolutionaries, and
all through it, even in jail, pictures himself as at odds with
his compatriots. Much more instinctively, he feels compatible
with those who are supposed to be his opponents: some of
the U.S. marshals; the judge he is so anxious to impress when
he is called before the bench; the badgered and exploited
soldiers who guard the Pentagon, against which the whole
march of collegians, intellectuals, and the privileged is directed. He is in the eloquently patriotic situation of a man
who feels the competing pulls of America in him, the worst
in the best and the best in the worst.

His situation is less important, of itself, than the language that emanates from it. He objects to thinking separated
from obscenity, sex separated from dreams of some ultimate
"scream and pinch of orgasm," vision separated from lust,
justice from love of power. In a quite laudable way he sets
out in his writing to restore these missing or neglected or
spurned qualities to what he considers their rightful and
seductive place in the scheme of things. To attain what he
considers the right balance, he must initially and inevitably
throw himself as well as everyone else off-balance. This is
notably true when his opposition to the prevailing mood
(particularly if it is a nice and vegetarian or genteel mood)
excites in him a distaste for those same qualities in himself,
especially since he has from the outset been at such pains to
disguise them. That "nice boy" whom Mailer remembers
with some embarrassment was only redeemed, after all, by
serving in an army quite unlike the one in which the Harvard
graduate and distinguished author now finds himself obliged
to march. In World War II Mailer served not in an army of
liberals and "drug-vitiated, jargon-mired children," but in an
army of mostly southern boys, average pals and buddies,
"real" American teen-agers. They were fellows to be loved
and admired with a proper wit. If the "army" marching on
the Pentagon is mostly of a quite different sort, if it is dominated by "concepts," the earlier one was redolent of "ob-

scenity," and Mailer, as he marches with one army against a later version of the other, still admits that he "never felt more like an American than when he was naturally obscene—all the gifts of the American language came out in the happy play of obscenity against concept, which enabled one to go back to concept again."

"Play" of this kind is often the effect of Mailer's own style, personal as well as literary. He provokes within himself some equivalent of the competing claims, the factionalisms of the whole country—the Brooklyn Jew, Harvard graduate, Army rifleman, novelist, dialectician, brawler, father, and, also, the husband who could write in 1968, "No, it could not be an altogether awful country because otherwise how would his wife, a southerner and an Army brat, have come out so subtle, so supple, so mysterious, so fine-skinned, so tender and wise."

It isn't too much to say that Mailer regards his achieved style (its mixture of "concept" and "obscenity," of intellectual jargons and hip vocabularies) as an image of America as well as of himself. Hence his fury when the audience at the Cavett show seemed to side with Vidal rather than with him. But when has he ever let a public gathering identify with him?

A rather startling instance of Mailer's failure to capture an audience's sympathy, or rather of his determination to reject that sympathy, occurred at the kickoff for his mayoralty campaign early in the summer of 1969. Again, the form of this rally was nearly identical to that of the Cavett show performance. Having circulated amiably throughout the group, he then took the platform; and within ten minutes, sensing that the audience of socialite supporters and prep-schooled, ivy-leagued hippies were taking him too much for granted, were assuming a too easy alliance between him and them, he abused them for their anticipated laziness. Then, body pushed out in schoolyard pugnacity, he stood shouting "Fuck you" to a chorus back of the same.

What is one to conclude from this? Only in writing can Mailer exist in a form that embraces his contradictions; only in writing about a historical occasion after it is over can he give form to feelings that, expressed at the time, threaten to multilate the form that he is searching for in the occasion. The time of his time probably has no historical equivalent, only a literary one. The form of history most tolerable to him is made of his own language existing in a kind of suspension, productive of a turmoil of meaning that public events are designed not to sustain but to ameliorate.

Men of great power and magnificent ambition, men who become presidents or champions of the world, are, if one could look into their heads, probably very much like Mailer. But they make a point of not letting us, as he does, look into their heads. They act more like Vidal. Their madness may be their motive, but it is not their image to the world. Mailer is fascinated by dialectical encounters in which hunger for power, fascination with mystery, and any kind of lust work to the possible destruction of opponents rather than the destruction of oneself. And yet it is he himself who gets hurt in public, and only in his writing can he arrive at anything like his true but still tense equilibrium. Dialectics are his hope of sanity. Existing uncomfortably as a mere person rather than what he calls a Being, a mere character—partial, moderated—his only alternative outside writing is to turn destructively on himself with scatology. Where Mailer is not, by virtue of the act of writing, able to control a situation, the hidden thrust of his energy is toward the sacrificial waste of himself.

BIBLIOGRAPHY

Works by Norman Mailer

Note: The publisher of the current paperback reprint is given in parentheses following the original date of publication.

The Naked And the Dead. New York: Holt, Rinehart & Winston, 1948 (Signet).

Barbary Shore. New York: Holt, Rinehart & Winston, 1951 (Signet).

The Deer Park (novel). New York: G. P. Putnam's Sons, 1955 (Berkley, Signet).

The White Negro. San Francisco: City Lights, 1957 (reprinted in *Advertisements for Myself*).

Advertisements for Myself. New York: G. P. Putnam's Sons, 1959 (Berkley).

Deaths for the Ladies, and Other Disasters. New York: G. P. Putnam's Sons, 1962 (Grove Press, Signet).

The Presidential Papers. New York: G. P. Putnam's Sons, 1963 (Berkley).

An American Dream. New York: The Dial Press, 1965 (Dell.)

Cannibals and Christians. New York: The Dial Press, 1966 (Delta, Dell).

The Bullfight: A Photographic Narrative with Text by Norman Mailer. New York: C.B.S. Legacy Books, distributed by the Macmillan Company, 1967.

The Deer Park (play), New York: The Dial Press, 1967 (Dell).

The Short Fiction of Norman Mailer. New York: Dell, 1967.

Why Are We in Vietnam? New York: G. P. Putnam's Sons, 1967 (Berkley).

Wild 90 (film). 1967.

The Armies of the Night. New York: New American Library, 1968 (Signet).

Beyond the Law (film). Distributed by New Line Cinema. 1968.

The Idol and the Octopus. New York: Dell, 1968.

Miami and the Siege of Chicago. New York: New American Library, 1968 (Signet).

Maidstone (film). Distributed by New Line Cinema. 1970.

Of a Fire on the Moon. Boston: Little, Brown, 1970 (Signet).

"King of the Hill." New York: Signet, 1971.

Maidstone: A Mystery. New York: Signet, 1971.

The Prisoner of Sex. Boston: Little, Brown, 1971 (Signet).

Existential Errands. Boston: Little, Brown, 1972.

St. George and the Godfather. New York: New American Library, 1972.

Marilyn, New York, Grosset & Dunlap, 1973.

Uncollected Pieces by Norman Mailer

"Right Shoe on Left Foot." *Harvard Advocate,* May, 1942, pp. 12-18, 30-33.

"Do Professors Have Rights?" *New York Post,* October 8, 1948, pp. 5, 34.

"What I Think of Artistic Freedom." *Dissent,* Spring, 1955, pp. 98, 192-93.

"Quickly." *The Village Voice* (weekly column January 11-May 2, 1956):

February 1, pp. 5, 11.   March 21, pp. 5, 11.
February 8, p. 5.   March 28, pp. 5, 11.
February 15, pp. 5, 10.   April 4, p. 5.
February 22, pp. 4, 5, 14.   April 11, p. 5.
February 29, pp. 5, 9.   April 18, p. 5.
March 7, p. 5.   April 25, p. 5.
March 14, pp. 5, 9.

"The Tragedy of Parris Island." *Dissent,* Fall, 1956, p. 435.

"The Shiny Enemies." *Nation,* January 30, 1960, inside cover.

Letter to the Editor. *Esquire,* January, 1961, p. 15.

"Mailer to Hansberry." *The Village Voice,* June 8, 1961, pp. 11-12.

"Foreword" to *Views of a Nearsighted Cannoneer* by Seymour Krim. New York: Excelsior, 1961, p. 6.

Letter to the Editor. *Playboy,* February, 1963, p. 15.

"The Role of the Right Wing." *Playboy,* February, 1963, pp. 115-16, 119-22.

"Jean Genet and 'The Blacks'—An Impulse to Destroy." *Panorama (Chicago Daily News),* July 13, 1963, p. 3.

"The Fate of the Union: Kennedy and After." *New York Review of Books,* December 26, 1963, p. 6.

"Architects: Blindness is the Fruit of Your Design." *The Village Voice,* June 18, 1964, p. 5.

Letter to the Editor. *New York Review of Books,* April 28, 1966, pp. 26-27.

"A Requiem for the Rube." *The Village Voice,* January 5, 1967, pp. 4, 16.

"A Statement of Aims." *The Village Voice,* January 5, 1967, p. 16.

"Who is to Declare That the Minority Do Not Deserve to Determine the Schools' History?" *New York Times Magazine,* May 4, 1969, pp. 35 plus.

"The Guest Word." *New York Times Book Review,* March 11, 1973, pp. 46, 55.

"A Transit to Narcissus: *Last Tango in Paris.*" *New York Review of Books,* May 17, 1973, pp. 3-10.

Writings on Mailer

Note: Minor reviews of Mailer's work have been omitted.

Aaron, Jonathan. "Existential Sheriff." *The New Journal,* 1 (December 10, 1967), 6-7.

Adams, Laura. "Criticism of Norman Mailer: A Selected Checklist." *Modern Fiction Studies,* 17 (Autumn, 1971), 455-63.

————. "Norman Mailer's Aesthetics of Growth." Diss., McMaster University, 1972.

————. Review of *St. George and the Godfather. Leisure* (*Dayton Daily News*), November 19, 1972, p. 10.

Adelson, Alan M. "Candidate Mailer: Savior or Spoiler?" *New Leader,* June 9, 1969, pp. 14-16.

Aldridge, John W. *In Search of Heresy: American Literature in an Age of Conformity.* New York: McGraw-Hill, 1956.

————. *After the Lost Generation.* New York: Noonday Press, 1958, pp. 133-41, passim.

————. "Victim and Analyst." *Commentary,* October, 1966, pp. 131-33.

————. "From Vietnam to Obscenity." *Harper's,* February, 1968, pp. 91-92, 94-97.

————. *The Devil in the Fire: Essays in American Literature and Culture 1951-1971.* New York: Harper's Magazine Press, 1971, pp. 169-94.

————. "The Perfect Absurd Figure of a Mighty Absurd Crusade." *Saturday Review,* November 13, 1971, pp. 45-46, 48-49, 72.

Allen, Walter. *The Urgent West: The American Dream and Modern Man.* New York: E. P. Dutton, 1969.

Alter, Robert. "The Real and Imaginary Worlds of Norman Mailer." *Midstream,* January, 1969, pp. 24-35.

Alvarez, A. "Norman X." *Spectator,* 7146 (May 7, 1965), 603.

"American Literature Today: Interview with M. L. Rosenthal, Part 1." *Nation,* April 17, 1972, pp. 503-6.

"Americana: Of Time and the Rebel." *Time,* December 5, 1960, pp. 16-17.

Arnavon, Cyrille. "Les Cauchemars de Norman Mailer." *Europe*, 47 (January, 1969), 93-116.

Auchincloss, Eve and Nancy Lynch. "An Interview with Norman Mailer." *Mademoiselle*, February, 1961, pp. 76, 160-63.

Auchincloss, Louis. "The Novel as a Forum." *New York Times Book Review*, October 24, 1965, p. 2.

Balakian, Nona. "The Prophetic Vogue of the Anti-heroine." *Southwest Review*, 47 (Spring, 1962), 134-41.

Baldwin, James. *Nobody Knows My Name*. New York: Dell, 1961, pp. 171-90.

Bannon, B. A., ed. "Authors and Editors." *Publishers Weekly*, January 25, 1971, pp. 177-79.

Barksdale, Richard K. "Alienation and the Anti-Hero in Recent American Fiction." *College Language Association Journal*, 10 (1966), 1-10.

Barnes, A. "Norman Mailer: A Prisoner of Sex." *Massachusetts Review*, 13 (Winter, 1972), 269-74.

Baumbach, Jonathan, ed. *The Landscape of Nightmare: Studies in the Contemporary American Novel*. New York: New York University Press, 1965, pp. 1-15.

Beaver, Harold. "A Figure in the Carpet: Irony and the American Novel." *The English Association Essays and Studies*, 15 (1962), 101-14.

Bell, Pearl K. "The Power and the Vainglory." *New Leader*, February 8, 1971, pp. 16-17.

Bersani, Leo. "The Interpretation of Dreams." *Partisan Review*, 32 (Summer, 1965), 603-8.

Berthoff, Warner. "Witness and Testament: Two Contemporary Classics" in *Fictions and Events*. New York: Dutton, 1971, pp. 288-308. Reprinted in J. Hillis Miller, ed., *Aspects of Narrative*. New York: Columbia University Press, 1971, pp. 173-98.

Bertrand, Suzanne. "Norman Mailer as a Novelist." M.A. Thesis, University of Montreal, 1962.

Bienen, L. B. [*An American Dream*]. *Transition*, 5 (1971), 20-46.

Bissett, Bill. "Review of *An American Dream*." *Canadian Forum*, July, 1967, pp. 92-93.

Bittner, William. "The Literary Underground." *Nation*, September 22, 1956, pp. 247-48.

Blotner, Joseph. *The Modern American Political Novel, 1900-1960*. Austin: University of Texas Press, 1966, pp. 320-22 et passim.

Bondy, François. "Norman Mailer oder Inside von Gut und Böse." *Merkur*, 25 (May, 1971), 449-60.

Bone, Robert A. "Private Mailer Re-enlists." *Dissent*, 7 (Autumn, 1960), 389-94.

Braudy, Leo. "Baldwin and the White Man's Guilt." *The Phoenix*, March 3, 1963, pp. 1-3.

————. "Advertisements for a Dwarf Alter-ego," *The New Journal*, 1, (May 12, 1968), 7-9.

————. *"Maidstone: A Mystery."* *New York Times Book Review*, December 19, 1971, pp. 2-3, 25.

————. "Norman Mailer: The Pride of Vulnerability" in *Norman Mailer*. Englewood Cliffs, New Jersey: Prentice-Hall, 1972, pp. 1-20.

————, ed. *Norman Mailer*. Englewood Cliffs, New Jersey: Prentice-Hall, Twentieth Century Interpretations, 1972.

Breit, Harvey, ed. *The Writer Observed*. New York: World, 1956, pp. 199-201.

Breslow, Paul. "The Hipster and the Radical." *Studies on the Left*, 1, (Spring, 1960), 102-5.

Brookeman, C. E. "Norman Mailer." *Times Literary Supplement*, October 3, 1968, p. 1104.

Brophy, Brigid. *"The Prisoner of Sex* by Norman Mailer." *New York Times Book Review*, May 23, 1971, pp. 1, 14, 16.

Brower, Brock. "Always the Challenger." *Life*, September 24, 1965, pp. 94-96, 98, 100, 102-15, 117.

Brown, C. H. "Rise of the New Journalism." *Current*, June, 1972, pp. 31-38.

Broyard, Anatole. "A Disturbance of the Peace." *New York Times Book Review*, September 17, 1967, pp. 4-5.

————. [*Prisoner of Sex*]. *New York Times*, May 27, 1971, p. 41.

Brustein, Robert. "Who's Killing the Novel?" *New Republic*, October 23, 1965, pp. 22-24.

Bryant, Jerry H. "The Last of the Social Protest Writers." *Arizona Quarterly*, 19 (Winter, 1963), 315-25.

————. *The Open Decision: The Contemporary American Novel and its Intellectual Background.* New York: Free Press, 1970, pp. 369-94 et passim.

Buchanan, Cynthia. "Review of *Existential Errands.*" *New York Times Book Review*, April 16, 1972, pp. 27-28.

Burg, David F. "The Hero of *The Naked and the Dead.*" *Modern Fiction Studies*, 17 (Autumn, 1971), 387-401.

Burgess, Anthony. "The Postwar American Novel: A View from the Periphery." *American Scholar*, 35 (Winter, 1965-66), 150-56.

Byro. *"Beyond the Law." Variety*, October 2, 1968.

Canby, Vincent. "Norman Mailer Offers *Beyond the Law.*" *New York Times*, September 30, 1968.

————. "When Irish Eyes Are Smiling, It's Norman Mailer." *New York Times Drama Section*, October 27, 1968, p. 15.

Carroll, Paul. *"Playboy* Interview: Norman Mailer." *Playboy*, January, 1968, pp. 69-72, 74, 76, 78, 80, 82-84.

Cecil, L. Moffitt. "The Passing of Arthur in Norman Mailer's *Barbary Shore.*" *Renaissance Studies of Washington State University*, 39 (March, 1971), 54-58.

Chase, Richard. "Novelist Going Places." *Commentary*, December, 1955, pp. 581-83.

Christian, Frederick. "The Talent and the Torment." *Cosmopolitan*, August, 1963, pp. 63-67.

Cleaver, Eldridge. "Notes on a Native Son." *Ramparts*, June, 1966, pp. 51-52, 54-56.

Clurman, Harold. "Theatre." *Nation*, February 20, 1967, pp. 252-53.

Cook, Bruce. "Angry Young Rebel with a Cause" [Interview]. *Rogue*, April, 1961, pp. 16-18, 76.

————. "Norman Mailer: The Temptation to Power." *Renascence*, 14 (Summer, 1962), 206-15, 222.

————. "Aquarius Rex." *National Observer*, November 4, 1972, pp. 1, 15.

Cook, William J. "Norman Mailer's American Dream." M. A. Thesis, University of Alberta, 1967.

Coren, Alan. "Portrait of the Artist as a Young Executive." *Atlas*, 10 (August, 1965), 110-12.

Corona, Mario. "Norman Mailer." *Studi Americani,* 11 (1965), 359-407.

Corrington, John William. "An American Dreamer." *Chicago Review,* 18, (1965), 58-66.

Cowan, Michael. "The Americanness of Norman Mailer" in Leo Braudy, ed., *Norman Mailer.* Englewood Cliffs, New Jersey: Prentice-Hall, 1972, pp. 143-51.

Cowley, Malcolm. "Mr. Mailer Tells a Tale of Love, Art, Corruption." *New York Herald Tribune Book Review,* October 23, 1955, p. 5.

————. "The Literary Situation, 1965." *University of Mississippi Quarterly,* 6 (1965), 91-98.

Curley, Dorothy Nyren, et al., eds. *A Library of Literary Criticism: Modern American Literature, Vol. II, 4th Edition.* New York: Frederick Ungar, 1969, 270-78.

Curley, Thomas F. "The Quarrel with Time in American Fiction." *American Scholar,* 39 (Autumn, 1960), 552, 554, 556, 558, 560.

Dabney, Richard Lawson. "Norman Mailer's Hipster." M.A. Thesis, American University, 1969.

Darack, Arthur. "Man Against His Times." *Saturday Review,* September 3, 1966, p. 35.

Davis, Robert Gorham. "Norman Mailer and the Trap of Egotism." *Story,* 33 (Spring, 1960), 117-19.

Decter, Midge. "Mailer's Campaign." *Commentary,* February, 1964, pp. 83-85.

DeMott, Benjamin. "Docket No. 15883." *American Scholar,* 30 (Spring, 1961), 232-37.

————. [*The Prisoner of Sex*]. *Saturday Review,* July 10, 1971, p. 21.

Dickstein, Morris. "A Trip to Inner and Outer Space." *New York Times Book Review,* January 10, 1971, pp. 1, 42-43, 45.

Didion, Joan. "A Social Eye." *National Review,* 17 (April 20, 1965), 329-30.

Dienstfrey, Harris. "The Fiction of Norman Mailer" in Richard Kostelanetz, ed., *On Contemporary Literature.* New York: Hearst, 1964, pp. 422-36.

Dirnberger, Betsy. "The Norman Conquest" [Interview]. *Other Voices* [Elmira College], June, 1969, pp. 36-43.

Dommergues, Pierre. "Norman Mailer: Pourquoi sommes-nous au Vietnam?" *Langues Modernes,* 62 (1968), 123-28.

Donoghue, Denis. "Sweepstakes." *New York Review of Books,* September 28, 1967, pp. 5-6.

Downes, Robin Nelson. *A Bibliography of Norman Mailer.* Tallahassee: Florida State University, 1957 (microcard only).

Duhamel, P. Albert. "Love in the Modern Novel." *Catholic World,* April, 1960, pp. 31-35.

Dupee, F. W. "The American Norman Mailer." *Commentary,* February, 1960, pp. 128-32.

The Editors. "Books by Norman Mailer." *Hollins Critic,* 2 (June, 1965), p. 7.

Eisinger, Chester E. "The American War Novel: An Affirming Flame." *Pacific Spectator,* 9 (Summer, 1955), 272-87.

————. *Fiction of the Forties.* Chicago: University of Chicago Press, 1963, pp. 33-38, 93-94 et passim.

Elliott, George P. "Destroyers, Defilers, and Confusers of Men." *Atlantic,* November, 1968, pp. 74-80.

Enkvist, Nils Erik. "Re-readings: Norman Mailer, *The Naked and the Dead." Moderna Sprak,* 56 (1962), 60-64.

Epstein, Joseph. "Norman X: The Literary Man's Cassius Clay." *New Republic,* April 17, 1965, pp. 22-25.

————. "Mailer Rides Again: Brilliant, Idiosyncratic, Unquotable." *Book World,* September 10, 1967, pp. 1, 34.

"Excerpts from the Boston Trial of *Naked Lunch*" in William Burroughs, *Naked Lunch.* New York: Grove Press, 1959, pp. x-xviii.

Fallaci, Oriana. "Interview with Norman Mailer." *Writer's Digest,* December, 1969, pp. 40-47.

Farrell, James T. "Literary Note." *American Book Collector,* 17 (May, 1967), 6.

Fendelman, Earl B. "Toward a Third Voice: Autobiographical Form in Thoreau, Stein, Adams, and Mailer." Diss.. Yale University, 1971.

Fiedler, Leslie A. "Antic Mailer—Portrait of a Middle-aged Artist." *New Leader,* January 25, 1960, pp. 23-24.

————. "The Breakthrough: The American Jewish Novelist and the Fictional Image of the Jew" in Joseph J. Wald-

meir, ed., *Recent American Fiction*. Boston: Houghton
Mifflin, 1963, pp. 84-109.

———. "Caliban or Hamlet." *Encounter*, April, 1966, pp.
23-27.

———. *Love and Death in the American Novel*, rev. ed.
New York: Dell, 1966, pp. 329, 469.

———. *Waiting for the End*. New York: Dell, 1964, pp.
17-235 passim.

———. *The Return of the Vanishing American*. New York:
Stein and Day, 1968, pp. 14, 157.

Finholt, Richard D. "Otherwise How Explain? Norman
Mailer's New Cosmology." *Modern Fiction Studies,* 17
(Autumn, 1971), 375-86.

Finkelstein, Sidney. "Norman Mailer and Edward Albee."
American Dialog, 2 (February, 1965), 23-28.

———. *Existentialism and Alienation in American Literature*. New York: International Publishers, 1965, pp.
269-76.

Fitch, Robert E. "The Bourgeois and the Bohemian." *An-
tioch Review,* 16 (Summer, 1956), 135-45.

Flaherty, Joe. *Managing Mailer*. New York: Coward-
McCann, 1969.

Fleming, Thomas. "The Novelist as Journalist." *New York
Times Book Review,* July 21, 1968, pp. 2, 4.

Flint, Joyce Marlene. "In Search of Meaning: Bernard Malamud, Norman Mailer, John Updike." Diss., Washington
State University, 1969, pp. 5-146 passim.

Flood, Charles B. *Renascence,* 13 (Autumn, 1960), 47.

Fontaine, Dick, director. *Will the Real Norman Mailer
Please Stand Up?* [Film] British Broadcasting Corp., 1968.

Forsyth, R. A. "'Europe,' 'Africa' and the Problem of Spiritual Authority." *Southern Review,* 3 (1969), 294-323.

Foster, Richard. "Mailer and the Fitzgerald Tradition."
Novel, 1 (Spring, 1968), 219-30.

———. *Norman Mailer*. Minneapolis: University of Minnesota Press, 1968.

Fremont-Smith, Eliot. "A Nobel for Norman?" *New York
Times,* August 22, 1966, p. 31.

———. "Norman Mailer's Cherry Pie." *New York Times,*
September 8, 1967, p. 37.

————. "Family Report." *New York Times,* October 28, 1968, p. 45.

Frohock, W. M. *The Novel of Violence in America.* Boston: Beacon Press, 1957.

Fuller, Edmund. *Man in Modern Fiction: Some Minority Opinions on Contemporary American Writing.* New York: Random House, 1958, pp. 154-62.

Galligan, Edward L. "Hemingway's Staying Power." *Massachusetts Review,* 8 (Summer, 1967), 431-39.

Geismar, Maxwell. *American Moderns: From Rebellion to Conformity.* New York: Hill & Wang, 1958, pp. 171-79.

Gelmis, Joseph. *The Film Director as Superstar.* Garden City, New York: Doubleday, 1970.

Gerstenberger, Donna and George Hendrick. *The American Novel, 1789-1959: A Checklist of Twentieth Century Criticism.* Denver: Alan Swallow, 1961, pp. 177-78.

Gilman, Richard. "Why Mailer Wants to Be President." *New Republic,* February 8, 1964, pp. 17-20, 22-24.

————. "What Mailer Has Done." *New Republic,* June 8, 1968, pp. 27-31.

————. "Norman Mailer: Art as Life, Life as Art" in *The Confusion of Realms.* New York: Random House, 1969, pp. 81-153.

Gilmore, T. B. "Fury of a Hebrew Prophet." *North American Review,* 251 (November, 1966), 43-44.

Gindin, James. "Meglotopia and the WASP Backlash: The Fiction of Mailer and Updike." *Critical Review,* 15 (Winter, 1971), 38-52.

Girson, Rochelle. " '48's Nine." *Saturday Review of Literature,* February 12, 1949, p. 12.

Gittelson, N. "Norman Mailer: Devil in the Fire." *Harper's Bazaar,* July, 1971, p. 14.

Glicksberg, Charles I. "Norman Mailer: The Angry Young Novelist in America." *Wisconsin Studies in Contemporary Literature,* 1 (Winter, 1960), 25-34.

————. "Sex in Contemporary Literature." *Colorado Quarterly,* 9 (Winter, 1961), 277-87.

Goldman, Lawrence. "The Political Vision of Norman Mailer." *Studies on the Left,* 4 (Summer, 1964), 129-41.

Goldstone, Herbert. "The Novels of Norman Mailer." *English Journal,* 45 (March, 1956), 113-21.

Gordon, Andrew. *"The Naked and the Dead:* The Triumph of Impotence." *Literature and Psychology,* 19: 3-13.

Grace, Matthew. "Norman Mailer at the End of the Decade." *Études Anglaises,* 24 (January-March, 1971), 50-58.

Grant, L. "Norman Mailer: Dialogue with the Non-mayor." *Ramparts,* December, 1969, pp. 44-46.

Graves, R. "Norman Mailer at the Typewriter: Writing on the Moon Landing." *Life,* August 29, 1969, p. 1.

Green, Howard. "Reviews." *Hudson Review,* 18 (Summer, 1965), 286-89.

Green, Martin. "Mailer and Amis: *The New Conservatism." Nation,* May 5, 1969, pp. 573-75.

Greenfield, Josh. "Line Between Journalism and Literature Thin, Perhaps, But Distinct." *Commonweal,* June 7, 1968, pp. 362-63.

Greenway, J. "Norman Mailer Meets the Butch Brigade." *National Review,* July 27, 1971, p. 815.

Greer, Germaine. "My Mailer Problem." *Esquire,* September, 1971, pp. 90-93, 214, 216.

Griffiths, David. "TV Violence? It's a Sedative" [Interview]. *TV Times,* November, 1961, p. 18.

Gross, T. L. "Norman Mailer: The Quest for Heroism" in *The Heroic Ideal in American Literature.* New York: Free Press, 1971, pp. 272-95.

Gutman, Stanley T. "Mankind in Barbary: The Individual and Society in the Novels of Norman Mailer." Diss., Duke University, 1971.

Guttmann, Allen. "Jewish Radicals, Jewish Writers." *American Scholar,* 32 (Autumn, 1963), 563-75.

————. "The Conversion of the Jews." *Wisconsin Studies in Contemporary Literature,* 6 (Summer, 1965), 161-76.

————. *The Jewish Writer in America: Assimilation and the Crisis of Identity.* New York: Oxford University Press, 1971.

Halberstam, M. "Norman Mailer as Ethnographer." *Trans-Action,* March, 1969, pp. 71-72.

Hampshire, Stuart. "Mailer United." *New Statesman,* October 13, 1961, pp. 515-16.

Hardwick, Elizabeth. "Bad Boy." *Partisan Review,* 32 (Spring, 1965), 291-94.

Harper, Howard M. "Concepts of Human Destiny in Five American Novelists: Bellow, Salinger, Mailer, Baldwin, Updike." Diss., University of Pennsylvania, 1964.

————. *Desperate Faith: A Study of Bellow, Salinger, Mailer, Baldwin and Updike.* Chapel Hill: University of North Carolina Press, 1967.

Hassan, Ihab. *Radical Innocence: Studies in the Contemporary American Novel.* New York: Harper & Row, 1961, pp. 140-151 et passim.

————. "The Way Down and Out: Spiritual Deflection in Recent American Fiction." *Virginia Quarterly Review,* 39 (Winter, 1963), 81-93.

————. "The Novel of Outrage: A Minority Voice in Postwar American Fiction." *American Scholar,* 35 (1965), 239-53 passim.

————. "Focus on Norman Mailer's *Why Are We in Vietnam?*" in David Madden, ed., *American Dreams, American Nightmares.* Carbondale: Southern Illinois University Press, 1970, pp. 197-203.

Healey, Robert C. "Novelists of the War: A Bunch of Dispossessed" in Harold C. Gardiner, ed., *Fifty Years of the American Novel.* New York: Scribner's, 1951, pp. 257-71.

Hentoff, Nat. "Behold the New Journalism—It's Coming After You!" *Evergreen Review,* July, 1968, pp. 49-51.

Hesla, David. "The Two Roles of Norman Mailer" in Nathan A Scott, ed., *Adversity and Grace.* Chicago: The University of Chicago Press, 1968, pp. 211-38.

Hicks, Granville. "Lark in Race for Presidency." *Saturday Review,* September 16, 1967, pp. 39-40.

Hoffa, W. "Norman Mailer: *Advertisements for Myself*" in Warren G. French, ed., *The Fifties: Fiction, Poetry, Drama.* New York: E. Edwards, 1971, pp. 73-82.

Hoffman, Frederick J. "Norman Mailer and the Revolt of the Ego: Some Observations in Recent American Literature." *Wisconsin Studies in Contemporary Literature,* 1 (Fall, 1960), 5-12.

————. *The Modern Novel in America.* Chicago: Henry Regnery, 1963, pp. xi-xii, 193, 195, 233, 251-52.

————. "Norman Mailer e la Rivolta dell'io." *Il Tempo di Letteratura,* 1 (1963), 201-9.

—————. *The Mortal No: Death and the Modern Imagination.* Princeton: Princeton University Press, 1964, pp. 210-492 passim.

Howe, Irving. "Some Political Novels." *Nation,* June 16, 1951, pp. 568-69.

—————. "Mass Society and Post-Modern Fiction." *Partisan Review* (Summer, 1959), 420-36.

—————. *A World More Attractive.* New York: Horizon Press, 1963, pp. 90-91, 123-29.

"Huntsville Public Library Rocked by Mailer Book." *Library Journal,* January 15, 1968, p. 138.

Hux, Samuel Holland. "American Myth and Existential Vision: The Indigenous Existentialism of Mailer, Bellow, Styron, and Ellison." Diss., University of Connecticut. 1965, pp. 179-211.

—————. "Mailer's Dream of Violence." *Minnesota Review,* 8 (1968), 152-97.

Hyman, Stanley Edgar. "Norman Mailer's Yummy Rump." *New Leader,* March 15, 1965, pp. 16-17.

Iwamoto, Iwao. "Gendai wo Ikiru Messiah." *Eigo Seinen,* 115 (1969), 554-55.

Janeway, William. "Mailer's America." *Cambridge Review,* November 29, 1968, pp. 183-85.

Johnson, Michael L. *The New Journalism: The Underground Press, the Artists of Nonfiction, and Changes in the Established Media.* Lawrence: University Press of Kansas, 1971, pp. 64-84 et passim.

Jones, James. "Small Comment from a Penitent Novelist." *Esquire,* December, 1963, pp. 40, 44.

Kael, Pauline. "The Current Cinema: Celebrities Make Spectacles of Themselves." *New Yorker,* January 20, 1968, pp. 90, 92-95.

Kahn, E. J. "When the Real Norman Mailer Stands Up, Please Don't Lay a Hand on Me." *Holiday,* March, 1968, pp. 36, 37, 43.

Kauffmann, Stanley. "An American Dreamer." *New Republic,* September 16, 1967, p. 18.

—————. "Beatles and Other Creatures." *New Republic,* November 16, 1968, pp. 18, 32.

—————. *Figures of Light.* New York: Harper & Row, 1971, pp. 49-50, 115-17.

Kaufmann, Donald L. "Norman Mailer from 1948 to 1963: The Sixth Mission." Diss., University of Iowa, 1967.

————. *Norman Mailer: The Countdown/The First Twenty Years.* Carbondale: Southern Illinois University Press, 1969.

————. "Catch-23: The Mystery of Fact (Norman Mailer's Final Novel?)." *Twentieth Century Literature,* 17 (1971), 247-56.

————. "The Long Happy Life of Norman Mailer." *Modern Fiction Studies,* 17 (Autumn, 1971), 347-59.

————. "Mailer's Lunar Bits and Pieces." *Modern Fiction Studies,* 17 (Autumn, 1971), 451-54.

Kazin, Alfred. "The Alone Generation: A Comment on the Fiction of the 'Fifties." *Harper's,* October, 1959, pp. 127-31.

————. "How Good is Norman Mailer?" in *Contemporaries,* Boston: Little, Brown, 1962, pp. 246-50.

————. "The Jew as Modern Writer." *Commentary,* April, 1966, pp. 37-41.

————. "Imagination and the Age." *Reporter,* May 5, 1966, pp. 32-35.

————. "The Trouble He's Seen." *New York Times Book Review,* May 5, 1968, pp. 1-2, 26.

————. "The Literary Sixties. When the World Was Too Much With Us." *New York Times Book Review,* December 21, 1969, pp. 1-3, 18.

————. "The World as a Novel: From Capote to Mailer." *New York Review of Books,* April 8, 1971, pp. 26-30.

Kent, Letitia, ed. "Shoot-for-the-moon Mailer." *Vogue,* August 15, 1969, 86-89 plus.

————, ed. "Rape of the Moon" [Interview]. *Vogue,* February 1, 1971, pp. 134-35.

————, ed. "Films vs. Plays." *Vogue,* September 1, 1972, pp. 200 plus.

Kerr, Walter. "Norman Mailer's Wicked 'Deer Park.'" *New York Times,* February 1, 1967, p. 27.

Knickerbocker, Conrad. "A Man Desperate for a New Life." *New York Times Book Review,* March 14, 1965, pp. 1, 36, 38-39.

Krim, Seymour. "A Hungry Mental Lion." *Evergreen Review,* January-February, 1960, pp. 178-85.

————. "An Open Letter to Norman Mailer." *Evergreen Review*, February, 1967, pp. 89-96.

Kroll, Jack. "The Scrambler." *Newsweek*, September 18, 1967, pp. 100-1.

Kunitz, Stanley J. *Twentieth Century Authors*, First Supplement. New York: H. W. Wilson, 1955, pp. 628-29.

Kyria, Pierre. "Regards sur la Littérature Americaine." *Revue de Paris*, March, 1968, pp. 117-22.

Lakin, R. D. "The Displaced Writer in America." *Midwest Quarterly*, 4 (Summer, 1963), 295-303.

Land, Myrick. "Mr. Norman Mailer Challenges All the Talent in the Room" in *The Fine Art of Literary Mayhem*. New York: Holt. Rinehart & Winston, 1963, pp. 216-38.

Langbaum, Robert. "Mailer's New Style." *Novel*, 2 (Fall, 1968), 69-78.

Lasch, Christopher. *The New Radicalism in America [1889-1963]: The Intellectual as a Social Type*. New York: Knopf, 1966, pp. 334-49.

Lawler, Robert W. "Norman Mailer: The Connection of New Circuits." Diss., Claremont Graduate School, 1969.

Leary, Lewis. *Articles on American Literature, 1900-1950*. Durham: Duke University Press, 1954, p. 199.

Lee, John M. "Mailer, in London, Trades Jabs with Audience Over New Film." *New York Times*, October 17, 1970, p. 21.

Lee, Lynn Allen. "The Significant Popular Novel as American Literature, 1920-1930; 1950-1960." Diss., University of Minnesota, 1968, pp. 175-232.

Leeds, Barry H. "An Architecture to Eternity: The Structured Vision of Norman Mailer's Fiction." Diss., Ohio University, 1967.

————. *The Structured Vision of Norman Mailer*. New York: New York University Press, 1969.

Leffelaar, H. L. "Norman Mailer in Chicago." *Litterair Paspoort*, November, 1959, pp. 79-81.

Levine, Paul. "The Intemperate Zone: The Climate of Contemporary American Fiction." *Massachusetts Review*, 8 (Summer, 1967), 505-23.

Levine, Richard M. "When Sam and Sergius Meet." *New Leader*, July 8, 1968, pp. 16-19.

Lewis, R. W. B. "Recent Fiction: Picaro and Pilgrim" in Robert E. Spiller, ed., *A Time of Harvest: American Literature 1910-1960.* New York: Hill & Wang, 1962, pp. 144-53.

Lipton, Lawrence. "Norman Mailer: genius, novelist, critic, playwright, politico, journalist, and general ail-around shit." *Los Angeles Free Press,* May 31, 1968, pp. 27-28.

Lodge, David. "The Novelist at the Crossroads." *Critical Quarterly,* 11 (Summer, 1969), 105-32.

Lowell, Robert. *Notebook 1967-68.* New York: Farrar, Straus and Giroux, 1969, p. 108; 3rd edition, 1970, p. 183.

Lucid, Robert F., ed. *The Long Patrol: Twenty-five Years of Writing From the Work of Norman Mailer.* New York: World, 1971.

————, ed. *Norman Mailer: The Man and his Work.* New York: Little, Brown, 1971.

Ludwig, Jack. *Recent American Novelists.* Minneapolis: University of Minnesota Press, 1962, pp. 24-28.

Lukas, J. Anthony. "Norman Mailer Enlists His Private Army to Act in Film." *New York Times,* July 23, 1968, p. 41.

————. "Mailer Film Party a Real Bash: 1 Broken Jaw, 2 Bloody Heads." *New York Times,* July 31, 1968, p. 29.

Lundkvist, Artur. "Ordspruta och gentlemann agangster: Norman Mailer" in *Utflykter Ned Utlandska Forfattare.* Stockholm: Bonniers, 1969, pp. 155-69.

Macdonald, Dwight. "Our Far-flung Correspondents: Massachusetts vs. Mailer." *New Yorker,* October 8, 1960, pp. 58, 60-66, 154-56.

————. "Art, Life and Violence." *Commentary,* August, 1962, pp. 169-72.

————. "Politics." *Esquire,* May, 1968, pp. 41, 42, 44, 194, 196.

————. "Politics." *Esquire,* June, 1968, pp. 46, 48, 50, 183.

Madden, David, ed. *American Dreams, American Nightmares.* Carbondale: Southern Illinois University Press, 1970, pp. xli-xlii.

Maddison, M. "Prospect of Commitment." *Political Quarterly,* October, 1961, pp. 353-62.

"Mailer for Mayor." *Time,* June 13, 1969, pp. 21-22.

"Mailer Opening." *New Yorker,* October 2, 1971, p. 33.

Malin, Irving. *Jews and Americans.* Carbondale: Southern Illinois University Press, 1965.

Malin, Irving and Irwin Stark, eds. *Breakthrough: A Treasury of Contemporary American-Jewish Literature.* New York: McGraw-Hill, 1964, pp. 1-24.

Maloff, S. "Mailer on the High Wire." *Commonweal,* June 30, 1972, pp. 361-63.

Manso, Peter, ed. *Running Against the Machine.* Garden City: Doubleday, 1969.

Marcus, Steven. "The Art of Fiction XXXII: Norman Mailer: An Interview." *Paris Review,* February, 1964, pp. 28-58. Reprinted in *Cannibals and Christians* and in Leo Braudy, ed., *Norman Mailer.*

Martien, Norman. "Norman Mailer at Graduate School: One Man's Effort." *New American Review,* 1: 233-41. Reprinted in Robert F. Lucid, ed., *Norman Mailer: The Man and His Work.*

Materassi, Mario. "La Rauca Voce di Norman Mailer." *Ponte,* 23 (1967), 630-35.

Matz, C. "Mailer's Opera." *Opera News,* February 21, 1970, pp. 14-16.

Maud, Ralph. "Faulkner, Mailer, and Yogi Bear." *Canadian Review of American Studies,* 2 (Fall, 1971), 69-75.

Maurois, André. "La Guerre, jugée par un romancier Américain." *Nouvelles Litteraires,* August 27, 1950, p. 5.

Maxwell, Robert. "Personal Reactions to a Presidential Candidate." *Minnesota Review,* 5 (August-October, 1965), 244-54.

McCormack, Thomas, ed. *Afterwords: Novelists on Their Novels.* New York: Harper & Row, 1969.

Merideth, Robert. "The 45-Second Piss: A Left Critique of Norman Mailer and *The Armies of the Night.*" *Modern Fiction Studies,* 17 (Autumn, 1971), 347-463.

Millett, Kate. *Sexual Politics.* Garden City: Doubleday, 1970, pp. 314-35.

Modern Ficton Studies. "Studies of Norman Mailer." 17 (Autumn, 1971), 347-463.

Morel, Jean-Pierre. "Pourquoi sommes-nous au Vietnam?" *Études,* 329 (1968), 572-80.

Mudrick, Marvin. "Mailer and Styron: Guests of the Establishment." *Hudson Review*, 17 (Autumn, 1964), 346-66.

Muste, John M. "Nightmarish Mailer." *Progressive*, February, 1965, pp. 49-51.

————. "Norman Mailer and John Dos Passos: The Question of Influence." *Modern Fiction Studies*, 17 (Autumn, 1971), 36-74.

Nadon, Robert J. "Urban Values in Recent American Fiction: A Study of the City in the Fiction of Saul Bellow, John Updike, Philip Roth, Bernard Malamud, and Norman Mailer." Diss., University of Minnesota, 1969.

Newman, Paul B. "Mailer: The Jew as Existentialist." *North American Review*, 2 (1965), 48-55.

Nichols, Dudley. "Secret Places of the Groin." *Nation*, November 5, 1955, pp. 393-95.

Noble, David W. *The Eternal Adam and the New World Garden: The Central Myth in the American Novel Since 1830.* New York: George Braziller, 1968, pp. 197-209.

"Norman Mailer's March." *Times Literary Supplement*, September 19, 1968, p. 1050.

"Norman's Phantasmagoria." *Time*, November 14, 1971, pp. 97-98.

Normand, J. "L'Homme mystifié: Les héros de Bellow, Albee, Styron et Mailer." *Études Anglaises*, 22 (1969), 370-85.

Novak, Michael. *Critic*, 25 (December, 1966/January, 1967), 81.

Oates, Joyce Carol. "Out of the Machine." *Atlantic*, July, 1971, pp. 42-45.

O'Brien, Conor Cruise. "Confessions of the Last American." *New York Review of Books*, June 20, 1968, pp. 16-18.

"Odd Couple." *Newsweek*, May 12, 1969, pp. 37-38.

Ostriker, Dane Proxpeale. "Norman Mailer and the Mystery Woman or, The Rape of the C--k." *Esquire*, November, 1972, pp. 122-25.

"Our Country and Our Culture: A Symposium." *Partisan Review*, 19 (May-June, 1952), 282-326.

Patterson, William. "Bullfight." *Saturday Review*, January 13, 1967, p. 105.

Pearce, Richard. "Norman Mailer's *Why Are We in Vietnam?*: A Radical Critique of Frontier Values." *Modern Fiction Studies*, 17 (Autumn, 1971), 409-14.

Pfeil, Sigmar. "Bemerkungen zu Einigen Bedeutenden Amerikanischen Kriegsromanen über den 2 Weltkrieg." *Zeitschrift für Anglistik und Amerikanistik,* 13 (1965), 61-74.

Phillips, William. "Writing about Sex." *Partisan Review,* 24 (Fall, 1967), 552-63 passim.

Pickrel, Paul. "Things of Darkness." *Harper's,* April, 1965, pp. 116-17.

Pilati, J. "On the Steps of City Hall." *Commonweal,* May 16, 1969, pp. 255-56.

Podhoretz, Norman. "Norman Mailer: The Embattled Vision." *Partisan Review* (Summer, 1959). Reprinted as introduction to Grossett Universal Library's *Barbary Shore* edition; in Joseph J. Waldmeir, ed., *Recent American Fiction*; Norman Podhoretz, *Doings and Undoings* (New York: Farrar, Straus & Giroux, 1959); and in Robert F. Lucid, ed., *Norman Mailer: The Man and His Work.*

—————. *Making It.* New York: Random House, 1967, pp. 352-56.

Poirier, Richard. "Morbid-Mindedness." *Commentary,* June, 1965, pp. 91-94.

—————. "Ups and Downs of Mailer." *New Republic,* January 23, 1971, pp. 23-26. Reprinted in Leo Braudy, ed., *Norman Mailer.*

—————. *The Performing Self.* New York: Oxford University Press, 1971, pp. 5-181 passim.

—————. "Minority Within." *Partisan Review,* 39 (1972), 12-43.

—————. "Mailer: Good Form and Bad." *Saturday Review,* April 22, 1972, pp. 42-46.

—————. "Norman Mailer: A Self-Creation." *Atlantic,* October, 1972, pp. 78-85.

—————. *Norman Mailer.* Modern Masters Series. New York: Viking Press, 1972.

Popescu, Petru. "Norman Mailer: Cei goi si cei morti." *Romania Literara,* February 6, 1968, p. 19.

"PPA Press Conference." *Publishers Weekly,* March 22, 1965, pp. 30-31, 41-45.

Prescott, Orville. *In My Opinion: An Inquiry into the Contemporary Novel.* New York: Bobbs-Merrill, 1952, pp. 146-64.

Prichett, V. S. "With Norman Mailer at the Sex Circus: Into the Cage." *Atlantic,* July, 1971, pp. 40-42.

Pritchard, William H. "Norman Mailer's Extravagances." *Massachusetts Review,* 8 (Summer, 1967), 562-68.

Raes, Hugo. "Nieuw Vooruitstrevend Amerikaans Proza." *De Vlaamse Gids,* 45 (November, 1961), 751-56.

Rahv, Philip. *The Myth and the Powerhouse.* New York: Farrar, Straus and Giroux, 1965, pp. 234-43.

de Rambures, Jean-Louis. "Norman Mailer: l'Enfant Terrible des lettres Americaines." *Realités,* June 1968, pp. 96-105.

Ramsey, Roger. "Current and Recurrent: The Vietnam Novel." *Modern Fiction Studies,* 17 (Autumn, 1971), 415-32.

Reeves, Richard. "Mailer and Breslin Enter Race." *New York Times,* May 2, 1969, p. 24.

————. "See How They Run: A Review of *Managing Mailer.*" *New York Times Book Review,* July 19, 1970, pp. 10, 12, 14.

"Reflections on Hipsterism—An Exchange of Views by Jean Malaquais, Ned Polsky and Norman Mailer." *Dissent,* 5 (Winter, 1958), 73-81. Partially reprinted in *Advertisements for Myself.*

Resnik, Henry S. "Hand on the Pulse of America." *Saturday Review,* May 4, 1968, pp. 25-26.

Richardson, Jack. "The Aesthetics of Norman Mailer." *New York Review of Books,* May 8, 1969, pp. 3-4.

Richler, Mordecai. "Norman Mailer." *Encounter,* July, 1965, pp. 61-64.

Rideout, Walter B. *The Radical Novel in the United States: 1900-1954.* Cambridge: Harvard University Press, 1956, pp. 270-73.

Rijpens, John. "Mailer Weer op Oorlogspad." *De Vlaamse Gids,* 52 (1968) 27-29.

Rodman, Selden. *New York Times Book Review,* July 8, 1962, p. 7.

Rosenthal, Melvyn. "The American Writer and His Society: The Response to Estrangement in the Works of Nathaniel Hawthorne, Randolph Bourne, Edmund Wilson, Norman Mailer, Saul Bellow." Diss., University of Connecticut.

Rosenthal, Raymond. "Mailer's Mafia: The Journalism of a

Writer Who is in Danger of Becoming His Audience."
Book Week, September 4, 1966, pp. 1, 14.

――――. "America's No. 1 Disc Jockey." *New Leader,* September 25, 1967, pp. 16-17.

Rosenthal, T. G. "The Death of Fiction." *New Statesman,* March 22, 1968, p. 389.

Ross, Frank. "The Assailant-Victim in Three War-Protest Novels." *Paunch,* 32 (August, 1968), 46-57.

Ross, Morton L. "Thoreau and Mailer: The Mission of the Rooster." *Western Humanities Review,* 25 (Winter, 1971), 47-56.

Rothe, Anna, ed. *Current Biography,* 1948. New York: H. W. Wilson, 1949, pp. 408-410.

Rubin, Louis D., Jr., "The Curious Death of the Novel: Or, What to Do About Tired Literary Critics." *Kenyon Review,* 28 (1966), 305-25.

"Rugged Times." *New Yorker,* October 23, 1948, p. 25.

Sale, Roger. "Watchman, What of the Night?" *New York Review of Books,* May 6, 1971, pp. 13-17.

Samuels, Charles T. "Mailer vs. the Hilton Hotel." *National Review,* 18 (October 18, 1966), 1059-60, 1062.

――――. "The Novel, USA: Mailerrhea." *Nation,* 205 (October 23, 1967), 405-6.

Sarris, Andrew. *Confessions of a Cultist: On the Cinema, 1955-1969.* New York: Simon & Schuster, 1970, pp. 396-400.

Schickel, R. "Stars and Celebrities." *Commentary,* August, 1971, pp. 61-65.

Schrader, George A. "Norman Mailer and the Despair of Defiance." *Yale Review,* 51 (December, 1961), 267-80.

Schroth, Raymond A. "Between the Lines: Norman Mailer." *America,* November 30, 1968, p. 558.

――――. "Mailer and His Gods." *Commonweal,* 90 (May 9, 1969), 226-29.

――――. "Mailer on the Moon." *Commonweal,* 94 (May 7, 1971), 216-18.

Schulz, Max F. *Radical Sophistication: Studies in Contemporary Jewish-American Novelists.* Athens: Ohio University Press, 1969, pp. 69-109.

————. "Norman Mailer." *Contemporary Literature*, 13 (Spring, 1972), 243-48.

Scott, James B. "The Individual and Society: Norman Mailer Versus William Styron." Diss., Syracuse University, 1964.

Shaw, Peter. "The Tough Guy Intellectual." *Critical Quarterly*, 8 (Spring, 1966), 13-28.

————. "The Conventions, 1968." *Commentary*, December, 1968, pp. 93-96.

Sheed, Wilfred. "One-man Dance Marathon." *New York Times Book Review*, August 21, 1968, pp. 1, 38.

————. *"Miami and the Siege of Chicago:* A Review." *New York Times Book Review*, December 8, 1968, pp. 3, 56.

————. "Norman Mailer: Genius or Nothing" in *The Morning After*. New York: Farrar, Straus & Giroux, 1971, pp. 9-17.

Sisk, John P. "Aquarius Rising." *Commentary*, May, 1971, pp. 83-84.

Smith, Marcus A. J. "The Art and Influence of Nathanael West." Dissertation Abstracts, 25 (1965), 4155-56.

Smith, William James. "The Stage." *Commonweal*, 85 (March 10, 1967), 657-58.

Sokoloff, B. A. *A Bibliography of Norman Mailer*. Folcroft, Pennsylvania: Folcroft Press, 1969.

Sokolov, Raymond A. "Flying High with Mailer." *Newsweek*, December 9, 1968, pp. 84, 86-88.

Solotaroff, Robert. "Down Mailer's Way." *Chicago Review*, 19 (June, 1967), 11-25.

Spatz, Jonas. *Hollywood in Fiction: Some Versions of the American Myth*. The Hague: Mouton, 1969.

Spender, Stephen. "Literature." *The Great Ideas Today*, 1965, pp. 166-211.

Spicehandler, Daniel. "The American War Novel." Diss., Columbia University, 1960, pp. 200-3.

Stark, John Olsen. "Norman Mailer's Work from 1963 to 1968." Diss., University of Wisconsin, 1970.

————. *Barbary Shore:* The Basis of Mailer's Best Work." *Modern Fiction Studies*, 17 (Autumn, 1971), 403-8.

Stern, Richard G. "Hip, Hell and the Navigator: An Interview with Norman Mailer." *Western Review*, 23 (Winter, 1959), 101-9. Reprinted in *Advertisements for Myself*.

Stevenson, David L. "Styron and the Fiction of the Fifties." *Critique,* 3 (Summer, 1960), 47-58.

Swados, Harvey. "Must Writers be Characters?" *Saturday Review,* October 1, 1960, pp. 12-14, 50.

Swenson, May. *Poetry,* 102 (May, 1963), 118.

Tanner, Tony. "The Great American Nightmare." *Spectator,* 7192 (April 29, 1966), 530-31.

―――. "In the Lion's Den." *Partisan Review,* 34 (Summer, 1967), 465-71.

―――. "On the Parapet" in *City of Words: American Fiction 1950-1970.* New York: Harper & Row, 1971, pp. 348-71.

Thorp, Willard. *American Writing in the Twentieth Century.* Cambridge: Harvard University Press, 1960, pp. 136-47. passim.

"Three Confessions: Norman Mailer." *Times Literary Supplement,* 7: 76-81.

"Tilting at Politics." *Economist,* June 14, 1969, p. 48.

Toback, James. "Norman Mailer Today." *Commentary,* October, 1967, pp. 68-76.

―――. "At Play in the Fields of the Bored." *Esquire,* December, 1968, pp. 22, 24, 26, 28, 30, 32, 34, 36, 150-55.

Trachtenberg, Alan. "Mailer on the Steps of the Pentagon." *Nation,* 206 (May 27, 1968), 701-2.

―――. "Repeat Performance." *Nation,* 207 (December 9, 1968), 631-32.

Tracy, R. "Review of *Cannibals and Christians." Southern Review* (Summer, 1970), 890.

Trilling, Diana. "Norman Mailer." *Encounter,* November, 1962, pp. 45-56. Reprinted in *Claremont Essays* (New York: Harcourt, Brace Jovanovitch, 1962, pp. 175–202); Nona Balakian and Charles Simmons, eds., *The Creative Present* (Garden City. Doubleday); Robert F. Lucid, ed., *Norman Mailer: The Man and His Work*; Leo Braudy, ed., *Norman Mailer.*

"Two Bucks—20 Dances." *Newsweek,* March 12, 1962, p. 104.

Velde, Paul. "Hemingway Who Stayed Home." *Nation,* 198 (January 20, 1964), 76-77.

Vidal, Gore. "The Norman Mailer Syndrome." *Nation,* 190 (January 2, 1960), 13-16.

————. "Norman Mailer: The Angels Are White" in *Rocking the Boat*. Boston: Little, Brown, 1962.

Volpe, Edmund L. "James Jones—Norman Mailer" in Harry T. Moore, ed., *Contemporary American Novelists*. Carbondale: Southern Illinois University Press, 1964, pp. 106-19.

Wagenheim, Allan J. "Square's Progress: *An American Dream. Critique,* 10: 45-68.

————. "Is It Time for an Epitaph? Notes on Modern Essay." *Denver Quarterly,* 3 (Winter, 1969), 85-90.

Wain, John. "Mailer's America." *New Republic,* October 1, 1966, pp. 19-20.

Waldmeir, Joseph J. "Accommodation in the New Novel." *University College Quarterly,* 11 (November, 1965), 26-32.

————. *American Novels of the Second World War.* The Hague: Mouton, 1969, pp. 15-152 passim.

Waldron, Randall H. "The Naked, the Dead, and the Machine: A New Look at Norman Mailer's First Novel." *PMLA,* March, 1972, pp. 271-77.

Walker, Joe. "A Candid Talk with Norman Mailer." *Muhammad Speaks,* June 20, 1969, pp. 11-12.

Wallace, Mike. "Norman Mailer" [Interview] in *Mike Wallace Asks,* Charles Preston and Edward A. Hamilton, eds. New York: Simon & Schuster, 1958, pp. 26-27.

Weales, Gerald. "The Park in the Playhouse." *Reporter,* April 6, 1967, pp. 47-48.

————. *The Jumping-Off Place: American Drama in the 1960's.* New York: Macmillan, 1969, pp. 218-21.

Weatherby, W. J. "Talking of Violence" [Interview]. *Twentieth Century,* 168 (Winter, 1964-65), 109-14.

Weber, Brom. "A Fear of Dying: Norman Mailer's *An American Dream." Hollins Critic,* 2 (June, 1965), 1-6, 8-11.

Weinberg, Helen. *The New Novel in America: The Kafkan Mode in Contemporary Fiction.* Ithaca: Cornell University Press, 1970, pp. 108-40 et passim.

————. *Midstream.* November, 1971, pp. 66-78.

Weinraub, Bernard. "Mailer the Author Will Donate Prize to Mailer the Politician." *New York Times,* May 6, 1969, p. 35.

Widmar, Kingsley. *The Literary Rebel.* Carbondale: Southern Illinois University Press, 1965, pp. 18-243 passim.

Wiener, David Morris. "The Politics of Love: Norman Mailer's Existential Vision." Diss., Syracuse University, 1972.

Willingham, Calder. "The Way It Isn't Done: Notes on the Distress of Norman Mailer." *Esquire,* December, 1963, pp. 306-08.

Wills, Garry. "The Art of Not Writing Novels." *National Review,* January 14, 1964, pp. 31-33.

————. [Review of *The Prisoner of Sex*]. *Book World,* July 11, 1971, p. 1.

————. [Review of *St. George and the Godfather*]. *New York Times Book Review,* October 15, 1972, pp. 1, 22.

Winegarten, Renee. "Norman Mailer—Genuine or Counterfeit?" *Midstream,* 11 (September, 1965), 91-95.

Winn, Janet. "Capote, Mailer and Miss Parker." *New Republic,* February 9, 1959, pp. 27-28.

Witt, Grace. "The Bad Man as Hipster: Norman Mailer's Use of the Frontier Metaphor." *Western American Literature,* 4 (Fall, 1969), 203-17.

Wolfe, Tom. "Son of Crime and Punishment; Or, How to Go Eight Fast Rounds with the Heavyweight Champ—and Lose." *Book Week,* March 14, 1965, pp. 1, 10, 12-13.

"Women's Lib: Mailer vs. Millett." *Time,* February 22, 1971, p. 71.

Wood, Margery. "Norman Mailer and Nathalie Sarraute: A Comparison of Existential Novels." *Minnesota Review,* 6 (1966), 67-72.

Woodley, R. "Literary Ticket for the 51st State." *Life,* May 30, 1969, pp. 71-72.

Woodress, James. "The Anatomy of Recent Fiction Reviewing." *Midwest Quarterly,* 2 (Autumn, 1960), 67-81.

Wüstenhagen, Heinz. "Instinkt kontra Vernunft: Norman Mailer's ideologische und aesthetische Konfusion." *Zeitschrift Für Anglistik und Amerikanistik,* 16, (1968), 362-89.

CONTRIBUTORS

Laura Adams, the editor of this volume, is Assistant Professor of English at Wright State University, Dayton, Ohio. She is the author of a Ph.D. dissertation and several shorter pieces on Mailer.

Matthew Grace is Assistant Professor of English at Bernard M. Baruch College of the City University of New York.

Richard M. Levine is a free-lance writer residing in New York. He is a former associate editor of both *Newsweek* and *The New Leader.*

Raymond A. Schroth, S.J., writes a column for *America* and has been a regular contributor to *Commonweal.*

Max F. Schulz is Professor of English at the University of Southern California, Los Angeles, and the author of *Radical Sophistication: Studies in Contemporary Jewish-American Novelists.*

Richard D. Finholt is at work on a Ph.D. dissertation on Mailer at Northern Illinois University, DeKalb.

Michael Cowan is Associate Professor of English and American Literature at the University of California, Santa Cruz.

Tony Tanner, currently a lecturer at Cambridge University, is the author of, among other works, *Conrad's Lord Jim, Saul Bellow,* and most recently *City of Words: American Fiction 1950-1970.*

Barry H. Leeds is Assistant Professor of English at Central Connecticut State College and the author of one of the first full-length studies of Mailer, *The Structured Vision of Norman Mailer.*

Gerald Weales is Professor of English at the University of Pennsylvania. He is a specialist in modern American drama and the author of *The Jumping-Off Place: American Drama in the 1960's.*

Leo Braudy is Associate Professor of English at Columbia University. His books include *Narrative Form in History and Fiction: Hume, Fielding, and Gibbon; Jean Renoir: The World of His Films.* Recently he has edited *Norman Mailer: A Collection of Critical Essays.*

Michael L. Johnson is Assistant Professor of English at the University of Kansas and the author of *The New Journalism.*

Jane O'Reilly is, like Mr. Levine, a free-lance writer living in New York. She is a frequent contributor to such magazines as *Holiday* and *New York.*

Joyce Carol Oates is Associate Professor of English at the University of Windsor and the distinguished author of novels, volumes of short stories, poems, and literary criticism too numerous to list.

Bruce Cook, author of *Beat Generation,* has published previous articles on Mailer in *Rogue* and *Renascence.*

Richard Poirier is Professor of English at Rutgers University and a renowned interpreter of American literature. His most recent contribution to Mailer criticism is *Norman Mailer* in the Viking Modern Masters series.

INDEX